Schriftenreihe Politische Kommunikation und demokratische Öffentlichkeit

Edited by
Prof. Dr. Frank Marcinkowski
Prof. Dr. Barbara Pfetsch
Prof. Dr. Gerhard Vowe

Volume 17

Kim Murphy

Government Communications in a Digital Age

A Comparative Study of Online Government Communications in Germany and Great Britain

Nomos

This publication was produced as part of the research group „Political Communication in the Online World" (1381) funded by the German Research Foundation (die Deutsche Forschungsgemeinschaft), subproject 6.
Diese Publikation entstand im Rahmen der von der Deutschen Forschungsgemeinschaft (DFG) geförderten Forschergruppe „Politische Kommunikation in der OnlineWelt" (1381), Teilprojekt 6.

The Deutsche Nationalbibliothek lists this publication in the Deutsche Nationalbibliografie; detailed bibliographic data are available on the Internet at http://dnb.d-nb.de

a.t.: Berlin, Univ., Diss., 2018
original titel: Comparing Online Government Communications from an Organisational & Network Perspective: A Comparative Study of Great Britain and Germany

ISBN 978-3-8487-5658-2 (Print)
978-3-8452-9803-0 (ePDF)

British Library Cataloguing-in-Publication Data
A catalogue record for this book is available from the British Library.
ISBN 978-3-8487-5658-2 (Print)
978-3-8452-9803-0 (ePDF)

Library of Congress Cataloging-in-Publication Data
Murphy, Kim
Government Communications in a Digital Age
A Comparative Study of Online Government Communications in Germany and Great Britain
Kim Murphy
276 p.
Includes bibliographic references.
ISBN 978-3-8487-5658-2 (Print)
978-3-8452-9803-0 (ePDF)

D188

1st Edition 2019

Acknowledgements

This thesis is the result of just over three years of research into online government communications in a number of different countries as part of the DFG-funded research project "Networked Media Government Relations" (2014-2017), a subproject of the research group "Political Communications in the Online World" (DFG Forschergruppe 1381).

First, I would like to thank my first supervisor Prof. Dr. Juliana Raupp of Freie Universität Berlin for her supervision, support and advice over the last four years and I would also like to thank Prof. Dr. Patrick Donges of Leipzig Universität for his feedback and critique within the research group and for acting as my second supervisor. In addition, I would like to thank a number of other members of the research group who generously provided advice and feedback over the years at various workshops, colloquiums and conferences, in particular, Prof. Dr. Gerhard Vowe, PD Dr. Marco Dohle, Prof. Dr. Barbara Pfetsch, Dr. Paula Nitschke, Dr. Thomas Häussler, and in particular, my colleagues within the project, Dr. Jan Niklas Kocks and our former student assistant, Tina Stalf. Outside the research group, I would also like to thank Dr. Isabelle Borucki, who very kindly gave me valuable feedback on my PhD.

At Freie Universität Berlin I was extremely lucky to have the advice, support, kindness and friendship of a number of special colleagues and friends over the years, including, Dr. Viorela Dan, Dr. Daniel Maier, Marlene Kunst, Angela Osterheider and Dr. Julia Drews.

Finally, and most importantly, I would never have reached this final point without the encouragement, support and patience of my husband Gabriele Greco and my wonderful parents, Marie and Paul Murphy.

Table of Contents

List of Figures

List of Tables

List of Abbreviations

AA	Auswärtiges Amt
AG's Office	Attorney General's Office
BIS	Department for Business, Innovation and Skills
BMAS	Bundesministerium für Arbeit und Soziales
BMBF	Bundesministerium für Bildung und Forschung
BMEL	Bundesministerium für Ernährung und Landwirtschaft
BMF	Bundesministerium der Finanzen
BMFSFJ	Bundesministerium für Familie, Senioren, Frauen und Jugend
BMG	Bundesministerium für Gesundheit
BMI	Bundesministerium des Innern
BMJV	Bundesministerium für Justiz und für Verbraucherschutz
BMUB	Bundesministerium für Umwelt, Naturschutz, Bau und Reaktorsicherheit
BMVg	Bundesministerium der Verteidigung
BMVI	Bundesministerium für Verkehr und digital Infrastruktur
BMWi	Bundesministerium für Wirtschaft und Energie
BMZ	Bundesministerium für wirtschaftliche Zusammenarbeit und Entwicklung
BPA	Bundespresseamt
BPB	Bundeszentrale für politische Bildung
BPK	Bundespressekonferenz
BR	Bundesregierung
CDU	Christian Democratic Union
CO	Cabinet Office
COI	Central Office for Information

DCLG	Department for Communities and Local Government
DCMS	Department for Culture, Media and Sport
DE	Germany
DECC	Department of Energy and Climate Change
DEFRA	Department for Environment, Food and Rural Affairs
DEG	Digital Era Governance
DfE	Department for Education
DFG	German Research Foundation
DFID	Department for International Development
DfT	Department for Transport
DH	Department of Health
DWP	Department for Work and Pensions
FB	Facebook
FCO	British Foreign & Commonwealth Office
GB	Great Britain
GCN	Government Communication Network
GCS	Government Communication Service
GICS	Government Information and Communication Service
ICTs	Information and Communication Technologies
KA	Kanzleramt
MoD	Ministry of Defence
MoJ	Ministry of Justice
NIO	Northern Ireland Office
NPM	New Public Management
PM	Prime Minister
PM's Office	Prime Minister's Office (Number 10 Downing Street)
RGA(s)	Research Guiding Assumption(s)
RQ(s)	Research Question(s)
RT(s)	Retweet(s)

SD	Standard Deviation
SNA	Social Network Analysis
SPD	Sozialdemokratische Partei Deutschlands
TW	Twitter
U.S.	United States
YT	YouTube

1. Introduction

For almost two decades now, the field of political communications has been preoccupied by how political parties and politicians are using the Internet and social media platforms for election campaigning. New digital technologies were initially trumpeted as possessing transformational qualities for politics and democracy, qualities that could potentially erode representative democracy and replace it with a deliberative democracy (Gibson & Ward, 2009). However, the results of numerous studies have revealed a more sober picture of its effects on politics and democracy. Political parties, individual politicians and governments mostly use online platforms for top-down communication, often as a way of gaining attention in the traditional media and rarely for engaging directly with citizens (Chadwick, 2013; Davis, 2010a; Gurevitch, Coleman, & Blumler, 2009; Jackson & Lilleker, 2011).

On the other hand, new digital technologies have led to transformations in how citizens engage in politics (Bennett, 2012; Chadwick, 2013; Papacharissi, 2010; Wright, 2012). These technologies are supporting new forms of political participation and engagement, but this participation is often taking place outside the boundaries of traditional political organisations and formal institutions (Bennett, 2012; Bennett & Segerberg, 2012; Castells, 2008) and increasingly in a private sphere (Papacharissi, 2010). Digital technologies are also supporting new types of political organisation (Bennett & Segerberg, 2012; Bimber, Stohl, & Flanagin, 2009; Chadwick, 2007), and in some cases (e.g., in the area of contentious politics), formal organisations are being replaced by individuals engaging in digital networks (Bennett & Segerberg, 2012, p. 748). In this sphere, online interaction is characterised by individuals engaging in personalised communications with other networked individuals (Bennett, 2012; Castells, 2010; Klinger & Svensson, 2015; Van Dijk, 2012). This increasing individualisation of communications and participation outside of formal organisations poses significant challenges to political organisations and organisational communications (Gibson & Ward, 2009) and also to the legitimacy of political institutions.

This raises serious challenges for formal organisations like political parties and government organisations in trying to reach and engage with citizens. This thesis argues, that the study of online political communications, has for too long, been dominated by a focus on how political parties and politicians are adapting online communications for electoral campaigning purposes (Klinger, Roesli, & Jarren, 2015; Sanders, Canel Crespo, & Holtz-Bacha, 2011). Despite the increasing professionalisation (Sanders & Canel, 2013), mediatisation (Borucki, 2014 b; Garland, Tambini, & Couldry, 2017) and personalisation of government communications (Figenschou, Karlsen, et al., 2017), political communications as a field has largely neglected how governments are adapting to the new media environment and the normative consequences of these changes (Canel & Sanders, 2012; Graber, 2003). Like political parties, government organisations must also find ways of adapting to the communications environment. For government organisations, their democratic legitimacy is dependent on their ability to be able to communicate political decisions to the public (Borucki & Jun, 2018; Sarcinelli, 2011). In today's hybrid media environment (Chadwick, 2013), this means that governments must increasingly employ those communication channels that citizens are using in order to reach them. There is also an expectation on the part of citizens, that politicians should adopt more participatory and personalised communications practices (Loader, Vromen, & Xenos, 2015). However, so far governments have not proven to be very good listeners or interactive in this regard (Chadwick, 2013; Gurevitch et al., 2009; Meijer, Koops, Pieterson, Overman, & ten Tije, 2012). This study argues that there is an urgent need to better understand how government organisations are using new digital technologies in their day-to-day communications to interact with citizens and media, and to consider the normative consequences of the adaptation, or non-adaptation, of digital technologies.

Another weakness of online political communications research until now has been its failure to understand technology use "within current political and social contexts" (Gibson & Ward, 2009, p. 37). Comparative studies of online political communications are still the exception rather than the norm (De Vreese, 2017; Foot, Xenos, Schneider, Kluver, & Jankowski, 2009). As a consequence, little is known about how different political systems and cultures are shaping how political or governmental actors use digital technologies and how they interact online. While previous comparative studies have enriched our understanding of how different political systems influence the types of media systems, political communications and journalism cultures that emerge (e.g., Hallin & Mancini, 2004; Hanitzsch, 2012; Pfetsch, 2001, 2003; Pfetsch & Esser, 2012), very few studies have examined how different political systems are shaping the new media environment. This study, therefore, fills an important theoretical gap in the field, by identifying and examining the various macro-level factors in Germany and Great Britain, that are possibly shaping government organisational communications in the new media environment. This study also fills an important empirical gap by analysing how government organisations in two different countries are using online technologies to communicate with citizens and media and the macro-level factors that are shaping their online communications.

In addition, this study argues that the macro level alone cannot explain how government organisations or individual government actors use online technologies. Within the field of political communications, the organisational perspective has often been overlooked (Donges, 2008). According to Nitschke, Donges and Schade there is "a tendency to disregard the influence of the organisational form or institutional environments in the online communication of political organisations" (2014, p. 2). The consequence of this has been a lack of understanding within political communications around how the organisational environment of political, or government, organisations determines how they adapt and use digital technologies. There is also a tendency in political communications research to treat government organisations in the same category of analysis as political parties, when comparing their online communications. However, this study argues, that government organisations are a unique organisational form facing different constraints to other types of organisations (Horsley, Liu, & Levenshus, 2010; Liu & Horsley, 2007; Liu, Horsley, & Levenshus, 2010). Government organisations face numerous tensions and constraints in using online technologies (Mergel, 2012) due to their public service function, politicised organisational environment, bureaucratic and hierarchical organisational structure, and various legal constraints regulating what governments can communicate (Graber, 2003; Kocks & Raupp, 2014; Liu et al., 2010; Meijer & Torenvlied, 2014). The theoretical part of this research adopts an organisational and network theoretical perspective in order to better understand how the organisational environment shapes the use of online technologies in a networked media environment. In doing so, this research hopes to contribute to a better understanding of how the macro and meso level shape the online communications of government organisations.

The network perspective complements the organisational perspective and provides an overarching theoretical lens through which this thesis views the changes in the new media environment and the particular challenges faced by government organisations. Like the organisational perspective, the network perspective argues that online communications cannot be explained by the macro level alone (Reese & Shoemaker, 2016; Van Dijk, 2012). In the networked media environment, a number of scholars argue it is necessary to take a multi-level perspective and examine how the relationship *between*, and *within*, different levels of analysis are changing (Monge & Contractor, 2003; Van Dijk, 2012). A central characteristic of the networked media environment is the dissolving boundary between different levels of analysis, but in particular, between the meso and micro level as organisational communications becomes increasingly individualised (Monge & Contractor, 2003; Van Dijk, 2012). Both the organisational and network perspectives play a central role in formulating the research guiding assumptions of this dissertation. The network perspective also influences the empirical design of this study in terms of the categories of analysis and the empirical methods chosen.

While a number of studies on government communications have examined specific features of government communications in different countries, for example, the professionalisation of government communications (Sanders et al., 2011; Sanders & Canel, 2013), centralised organisational structures (Canel & Sanders, 2014; Gregory, 2006, 2012; Vogel, 2010), or legislation affecting government communications (Holtz-Bacha, 2013; Kocks & Raupp, 2014), very few have empirically investigated how these macro structures or unique organisational features are influencing actual online communications. This study has, therefore, been designed as a comparative study and the empirical analysis involves an examination of government organisational websites and social media pages in Germany and Great Britain. This thesis examines how government organisational actors are using online platforms to interact and network with citizens and media and analyses important differences and similarities between the countries at the macro level and between government organisations at the meso level. The research and methodological design of this dissertation will be elaborated on in the next section of this chapter.

In summary, this thesis seeks to fill a number of theoretical and empirical gaps in the field of government communications, comparative government communications and online political communications. It contributes much-needed insight into how government organisations in different countries are using online technologies, the macro-level factors that are shaping their communications in the online sphere and how the unique organisational environment also determines their use of websites and social media. It examines whether government organisations, like political organisations, are also engaging in more individualised communications in the online sphere and the democratic consequences of these new online communications practices.

1.1 Research Design

This dissertation is designed as a comparative study to compare and examine online government organisational communications in Germany and Great Britain. There are a number of reasons why these countries are a suitable comparison and why they were selected. First, this dissertation was conducted within a three-year research project funded by the German Research Foundation (DFG)[1], a project that examined networked media government relations in three different countries, Germany, Great Britain and Italy. This author decided to narrow the focus to Germany and Great Britain to make the dissertation more manageable. By limiting it to two countries, it enabled the author to carry out a more extensive empirical analysis of their online government communications.

While there have been many comparative studies of political communications in Germany and Great Britain (e.g., Esser, 2008; Hallin & Mancini, 2004; Holtz-Bacha, Langer, & Merkle, 2014; Vaccari, 2016), there have been few comparative studies of government communications in these countries (some examples include Sanders et al., 2011; Vogel, 2010), and even fewer studies empirically examining how their different macro structures shape government communications practices (either offline or online). In fact, there continues to be very few studies outside the United States (U.S.) examining how executive government institutions such as government ministries are using social media. Germany and Great Britain have many important similarities at the structural level, for example, they have strong centralised organisational structures for government communications, but they also have structural differences related to their political systems that make them a compelling and worthwhile comparison.

---

1 This PhD dissertation was written as part of the project "Networked Media Government Relations" (2014-2017), a subproject of the research group "Political Communications in the Online World" (DFG Forschergruppe 1381). Data collected as part of the online content analysis of websites and social media pages stems from this project. This author was responsible for writing, designing and carrying out the online content analysis within the project. Additional categories of analysis that were of interest for this dissertation were incorporated into the content analysis. The additional social network analysis (SNA) was designed by this author for this dissertation.

The methodological approach of this thesis involves a quantitative online content analysis of the organisational websites and organisational and individual social media pages – Facebook, Twitter and YouTube – of 27 executive government organisations in Great Britain and 17 executive government organisations in Germany. This resulted in a total sample of 44 government websites and 120 social media pages. The online content analysis examines the extent to which government actors engage in top-down communications, encourage active participation on social media, respond directly to users, share information, connect with others and the transparency of their day-to-day online communications. The online content analysis is based on online content saved between March and July, 2015. The second methodological approach involves a social network analysis (SNA) of government Twitter networks using retweet data collected as part of the online content analysis. The purpose of the SNA is to further incorporate the network theoretical perspective into the empirical analysis and to facilitate a more in-depth analysis of government interaction online. Within the wider field of political communications an increasing number of studies are combining quantitative online content analysis with SNA (e.g., Adi, Erickson, & Lilleker, 2014; Anstead & Chadwick, 2017; Kleinnijenhuis, van den Hooff, Utz, Vermeulen, & Huysman, 2011; Maier, Waldherr, Miltner, Jähnichen, & Pfetsch, 2017; Nuernbergk, 2016; Nuernbergk & Conrad, 2016) to examine online interaction and political participation from different perspectives, including a network perspective. Employing these two empirical methods, this dissertation seeks to answer the following overarching research question:

> How are government organisations and individuals in Germany and Great Britain using websites and social media to communicate with citizens and media in their day-to-day communications?

Connected to this are two further sub-questions,

> To what extent are they using websites and social media to interact with media and citizens? and, to what extent are they using websites and social media to network with media and citizens?[2]

As mentioned above and in the previous section, interaction and political participation are emerging in new and different forms in the online sphere. Interaction online operates according to a network logic (Klinger

2 The full list of research questions will be presented at the outset of Chapter 5, the methodology chapter.

& Svensson, 2015, 2016). Yet political communication researchers have been unduly influenced by theories of the public sphere and deliberative democratic theory leading to a narrow interpretation of interaction, one focused on rational discourse and deliberation (e.g., Coleman & Blumler, 2009). A number of scholars criticise this normative approach to interaction, as it limits our understanding of the kinds of interaction that may be taking place online (Chadwick, 2009; Dahlgren, 2005; Davis, 2010 b; Papacharissi, 2009 b; Wright, 2012) and overlooks new forms of interaction emerging (Klinger & Svensson, 2015; Vaccari, Chadwick, & O'Loughlin, 2015; Vaccari, Valeriani, et al., 2015). For example, interaction and participation takes place at different levels (e.g., low and high-threshold interaction), it has networking as well as discursive characteristics and it can have hybrid features related to how users combine different platforms (e.g., dual screening) (Jenkins, Ford, & Green, 2013; Vaccari, Chadwick, et al., 2015; Vaccari, Valeriani, et al., 2015). According to these authors, we should not dismiss certain forms of interaction or participation as "passive" as they may lead to higher forms of interaction (Jenkins et al., 2013, pp. 154-155). This dissertation incorporates these perspectives into the methodological approach of this study in a number of ways. They contribute to the definition of interaction in the online content analysis which defines interaction as taking place at a number of different levels and having networking features. Networking is viewed as a form of interaction. Therefore, networking is a category of analysis (along with a number of other categories) within the online content analysis and it is the central focus of the SNA.

According to the organisational and network theoretical perspectives adopted in this dissertation, another feature of the new media environment is the increasing personalisation and individualisation of organisational communications, facilitated by social media and digital networks (Bennett, 2012; Bennett & Segerberg, 2012; Gibson & Ward, 2009; Monge & Contractor, 2003; Svensson, 2015; Van Dijk, 2012). In the networked media environment, there is no longer a clear boundary between organisational and individual communications as individuals increasingly employ more personalised communications. This dissertation explores the extent to which this phenomena is also affecting government organisational communications, that is, the extent to which the boundary between official government communications is becoming blurred with the personalised communications of individual government actors. In order to examine this, within the methodological design, online government communications is defined as both the organisational and individual social media pages of executive government actors. This study considers the individual social media pages to be part of their organisational communications, as these actors are the public face of their organisations (Nitschke & Murphy, 2016; Taylor & Cooren, 1997). Therefore, the individual social media pages of government ministers are analysed along with the organisational pages of government ministries.

1.2 Outline of the Study

In Chapter 2, the literature review presents an overview of theoretical, empirical and comparative studies examining how different governments are using new digital technologies and adapting to the new media environment. It highlights numerous theoretical, empirical and comparative research gaps in the study of government communications. Government communications is an under-researched field within political communications and comparative studies are rare (Canel & Sanders, 2012). This has led to a limited understanding of how governments (outside the U.S.) are adapting online technologies and how this is affecting or changing the relationship between government, citizens and media. This chapter also draws attention to the lack of comparative research in the wider field of online political communications (De Vreese, 2017), and how little is known about how different macro structures affect the use of online technologies by political actors. At the end of the literature review, a number of conclusions are made, which will eventually contribute to some of the research guiding assumptions later on in this dissertation.

Chapter 3 provides an in-depth analysis of the specific macro-level structures affecting government communications in Germany and Great Britain. It examines the most important similarities and differences between the countries in terms of their political systems, media systems, the organisation of political media relations, the regulation of government communications, and the development of centralised structures of government communications in both countries. It provides a comprehensive overview of the key macro-level factors that are relevant for the study of government communications in an online age. This chapter also provides an important theoretical contribution to the study of comparative government communication by bringing together all these structural factors into one study and by considering which factors possibly shape their technology usage. A number of these macro-level features will also play a role in formulating the research guiding assumptions of this dissertation.

Following the examination of the macro-level characteristics shaping government communications, Chapter 4 moves on to an examination of the meso level and seeks to understand how the organisational environment and which organisational factors shape the use of digital technologies within government organisations. This chapter begins by examining how the wider political organisational environment is changing as a result of digital technologies and the possible implications of these broader changes for government organisational communications. It then analyses the unique organisational environment of government communications and the internal organisational factors that shape the adaptation of these technologies. Consideration is given to the consequences of these changes in the organisational environment for the comparative analysis of government communications. The author then presents the overarching theoretical perspective of this thesis, the network perspective, and outlines the central features that are relevant for examining organisational communications in an online age. Finally, this chapter presents the research guiding assumptions of this dissertation based on the theoretical reflections in Chapters 2, 3 and 4.

Chapter 5 presents the overarching research questions and related subquestions to be investigated in the empirical part of this dissertation. In order to answer these questions, this study carries out a quantitative online content analysis of the websites and social media pages of executive government actors, combined with a SNA of government retweets. One of the most important challenges in comparative research is the establishment of equivalence throughout the methodological design (Rössler, 2012; Wirth & Kolb, 2004). Chapter 5 explains the various steps taken to ensure equivalence throughout, both in the sampling and the development of the codebook for the content analysis. This chapter also makes an important empirical contribution to the field by establishing an equivalent definition of online executive government communications for the two countries. Online government organisational communications is defined as including the individual social media pages of the main representatives of these organisations (e.g., government ministers). Finally, this chapter provides a full overview and definition of all categories of analysis within the online content analysis and the SNA.

Chapter 6 presents the results of the online content analysis of government organisational websites and organisational and individual social media pages and the results of the SNA of government retweet networks in Germany and Great Britain. It presents the various similarities and differences found at the macro level, the differences found at the meso level between government organisations, and the results of the analysis of individual social media pages and whether there has been a blurring of the boundary between government organisational and individual communications. The results reveal a number of macro-level factors that are shaping their online interactions and networking, although not always in the way that had been assumed. The results also reveal large differences between government organisations in both countries, confirming that there are also internal organisational factors that determine how organisations adapt and use social media.

Chapter 7 is devoted to the discussion and interpretation of the empirical results. In this chapter, the research guiding assumptions and corresponding research questions are each addressed, discussed and interpreted one by one. Finally, a number of conclusions are drawn about the democratic implications of these findings, the limitations of the empirical design, and the implications for future research.

Chapter 8 summarises and reflects on the overall theoretical and empirical contribution of this study to the field of government communications and comparative political communications. It also considers in more detail the various limitations of this study, presents a number of suggestions for future research in online government communications, and reflects on the normative and democratic consequences of the findings.

In summary this dissertation sets out to fill a number of theoretical and empirical gaps in the study of government communications, comparative government communications and the wider field of online political communications. This author believes that this study progresses the field of government communications by drawing attention to the various levels of analysis shaping government communications in this networked communications sphere, and identifying specific macro-level structures shaping government interaction online. It helps to better understand why government organisations are adapting, or not adapting, digital technologies in the same way as other political actors. It also illuminates potential tensions that may arise in the future as governments potentially move beyond a top-down communicative approach to become more interactive online. Finally, this author hopes that this study will encourage and assist others to carry out further comparative research in this important, but neglected, field.

2. Online Political & Government Communication Research

One of the challenges of studying government communications is that it doesn't fit neatly into any one field or discipline. It crosses the fields and subfields of political science, comparative politics, public administration and governance, political communications, public relations, organisational communications and legal studies. It can be analysed from many perspectives including from a communications, political science, legal or a historical perspective (Raupp, Kocks, & Murphy, 2018). Government communications does not have a clear research home and this is reflected in the inter-disciplinary nature of the literature review presented in this study. It also helps to explain why government communications tends to be an under-researched subfield of political communications (Canel & Sanders, 2012).

Depending on which disciplinary approach is taken, the focus of the research differs and the answer to fundamental questions such as "what is government communications?" alters depending on the perspective (Raupp & Kocks, 2018, p.7). Political science perspectives tend to examine how media is shaping political systems and the institutional structures of government (e.g., Heffernan, 2006; Korte, 2002), the normative role of communications in serving democratic legitimacy (e.g., Borucki, 2014b; Borucki & Jun, 2018; Sarcinelli, 2011) and the improvement of public services through e-government and e-democracy (e.g., Dunleavy & Margetts, 2015). In contrast to this, public relations perspectives tend to focus on strategic communications and the professionalisation of government communications (e.g., Canel & Sanders, 2014; Gregory, 2006; Liu & Horsley, 2007; Sanders & Canel, 2013; Sanders et al., 2011; Young & Pieterson, 2015). Political communications often focus on political media relations with a particular focus on micro-level actors such as the relationship between press spokespersons, so-called "spin doctors" and journalists (e.g., Davis, 2009; Marx, 2008; Pfetsch, 2001, 2003).

The main focus of this literature review is the analysis of theoretical, empirical and comparative studies examining how different governments, individual government actors and organisations are using new digital technologies and how they are adapting to the demands of a changing media environment. To date, there has been very little theoretical, empirical or comparative research into how governments are using websites and social media to engage with media and citizens. Instead, political communications has focused mostly on how political parties and social movements are using online technologies for election campaigns (Klinger et al., 2015). Therefore, this literature review will also present relevant studies from the subfields of comparative political communications and online political communications in order to understand how the relationship between politics, media and citizens is changing in the new media environment.

While this literature review specifically focuses on studies relevant for comparing government communications in an online age, Chapter 3 will explore in greater detail the political structures, centralised institutions of government communications and the unique macro characteristics of government communications in Germany and Great Britain[3]. Chapter 3 will examine and consider the macro-level factors that possibly shape the use of digital technologies in both countries. Chapter 4 will examine the unique organisational environment of government organisations and the organisational constraints that this places on the use of digital technologies by government actors.

2.1 Political Communications in an Online Age: Theoretical Perspectives

In order to better understand how governments are using online technologies and the challenges they face, it is useful and relevant to begin by examining how digital technologies are changing the wider field of political communications, including media systems, political media relations and how citizens interact and engage with politics. In particular, this section looks at how digital technologies are leading to fundamental changes in perceptions of what it means to participate in politics. The online sphere is supporting new forms of participation characterised by personalised and networked communications in social networks (Bennett, 2012; Chadwick, 2009). In this section, an overview of some of the most important theoretical perspectives from the field of online political communications will be presented. Government communications takes place within the broader

3 The following studies (among others) of government communications will be drawn on in Chapter 3 as they address particular aspects of the macro structures in Germany and Great Britain that are highly relevant for this study: Borucki (2014 a, 2014 b); Kocks & Raupp (2014); Kocks (2016); Holtz-Bacha (2013); Young (2007); Marx (2008); McNair (2004); Vogel (2010); Gregory (2006, 2012); Nuernbergk (2016).

field of political communications and so it can be assumed that government communications has not been left untouched by changes in the wider environment.

Papacharissi (2009 b, 2010) made a number of important contributions to understanding the unique features of the online public sphere and political participation within this sphere. She puts forward three arguments why the online sphere cannot be viewed as a deliberative public sphere in the habermasian sense. She argues that digital technologies have enabled the emergence of a public space rather than a deliberative democratic public sphere (2009 b, p. 239). Her three arguments why this is a public space include:

> the self-centred nature of online expression lends a narcissistic element to political deliberation online, which is distinct from the objectives of the public sphere. Second, patterns of civic engagement online suggest selective uses of online media to supplement the representative model of democracy and mobilise subversive movements. Finally, the proliferation of online public spaces that are part commercial and part private suggests a new hybrid model of public spaces, where consumerist and civic rhetoric coexist. (2009 b, p. 230)

However, this does not mean that this online space lacks a democratic character or that citizens are not politically engaged. To say that digital technologies have failed to support the emergence of a deliberative public sphere, is to underestimate and misunderstand the potential and characteristics of these technologies (Papacharissi, 2009 b). Online technologies are transforming participation in other ways, for example, through a convergence of the public and private sphere (Papacharissi, 2010). In late modern democracies, the distinction between the public and private is challenged as public life is relegated to the private sphere (Papacharissi, 2010, p. 48). The boundary between the public and private has become increasingly blurred. In Papacharissi's (2010) view, convergence means not only a convergence of public and private spheres, but also a convergence of media platforms and of the economic, political and social spheres. The consequence of this, however, is that it is becomingly increasingly difficult to identify political behaviour as it increasingly takes place in a private sphere alongside social and economic activity. She says that "humans rarely convene to discuss matters that are solely political, then neatly dispersing into social or other activities when political affairs are taken care of. Individuals discuss politics among and together with other things, and this practice helps them connect politics to essential parts of their everyday routines"

(2010, p. 78). It is the view of this dissertation, that this retreat to the private sphere raises significant normative challenges for political institutions and governments in trying to reach citizens and engage with them in the spaces where they communicate. The changes that Papacharissi describes also raise empirical challenges for researchers as they need to find new ways of examining and identifying political behaviour within these private spheres.

Similar to Papacharissi's description of the blurring of the private and public sphere, Bennett (2012) describes the personalisation of politics as a central characteristic of political participation in the age of digital networks. Bennett describes a new type of personalisation facilitated by digital networks. He sees increasing online personalisation as being connected to our increasingly fragmented and individualistic society. Online technologies enable individuals to politically engage and organise using digital networks. They are supporting hybrid forms of political participation that are both individualistic and collective (citizens participate as individuals but always connected to others) and this type of political participation and engagement is taking place "outside of conventional institutional structures" (Bennett, 2012, p. 27). In another study, Bennett and Segerberg (2012) also describe how individuals are engaging less with traditional political organisations and institutions. They explain how political organisations are in some cases taking a more background role in order to facilitate individualised and personalised participation. However, as citizens increasingly engage in contentious politics outside the realm of traditional political structures, this poses significant challenges and consequences for political organisations and governments in maintaining democratic legitimacy[4].

Like Papacharissi, Wright (2012) criticises habermasian and normative approaches to understanding political communication in an online age. These approaches result in a narrow understanding of politics and cause researchers to set unrealistic standards for assessing online political discussion and participation (Wright, 2012, p. 245). He rejects both the cyber-optimist perspective (e.g., Coleman & Blumler, 2009; Rheingold, 1993) that a revolution has taken place, but he also rejects the cyber-realist "politics as usual" perspective of Margolis and Resnick (2000), who say that the same power structures will dominate online as offline. Instead, he proposes a more balanced perspective called a "normalised revolution" and suggests

4 Chapter 4 will provide a detailed analysis of political organisational and network perspectives on these changes and also what this means for government organisations communicating in this online environment.

three ways in which researchers should consider change as a result of technology:

> 1. Scale: revolutions can occur on myriad scales from the local to the global; 2. Speed: time is less important than the significance of change; 3. Invention and innovation: revolutions can take time, and involve a variety of technologies and applications. Thus, we should not look to the latest technology in isolation. (Wright, 2012, p. 252)

According to Wright's perspective, technologies are having a significant effect on political institutions, but they are not leading to an overthrow of established political institutions or a new form of deliberative democracy. As Wright says, the changes may be slow and incremental, but they may still be having a transformative effect on politics. It is something that will only become apparent over time. This is a valuable perspective for this dissertation for viewing the changes taking place within government and how they use online platforms to engage with citizens. Most importantly, Wright warns against technological determinism saying that it is not just technologies that shape politics and institutions, but they are also shaped and exploited by their social and political contexts (Wright, 2012, p. 246), a viewpoint that is central to this comparative study.

While the online communications environment may be characterised by increasingly personalised communications in spheres that are both public and private, another characteristic of this new media environment is hybridity. Chadwick (2013) presented a theoretical paradigm called the "hybrid media system" for understanding the changes in the political communications environment as a result of digital technologies. The hybrid media system is characterised by the interaction and interdependence of old and new media logics. According to this perspective, online media cannot be understood in isolation from offline media, but the two logics must be understood in terms of how they interact, shape, influence and depend on one another. It is this interaction that defines the new media environment and differentiates it from previous eras of political communication. In support of this theoretical paradigm, Chadwick presents empirical research involving interviews with political party and government spokespersons in Great Britain. He found that parties and government (in Great Britain) mostly use the internet to gain exposure in older media and they continue to apply older media logics to their use of new media (2013, p. 196). The internet is not used to support online engagement, but it is typically used to gain exposure in offline media (Chadwick, 2013, p. 197).

Klinger and Svensson (2015, 2016) provide a different theoretical perspective for understanding political communications in an online age, but one which has many overlaps with Chadwick's (2013) hybrid media concept. Klinger and Svensson (2015, 2016) argue that the online environment operates according to a distinct new logic called the "network logic". This logic overlaps with the mass media logic, but it has distinct characteristics that differentiates it from the mass media (or old media logic as Chadwick calls it). However, similar to Chadwick's hybrid media perspective, the network logic is not replacing the mass media logic, but they intertwine with each other (Klinger & Svensson, 2015, p. 1251). In contrast to Chadwick they focus on the specific characteristics of this new logic that sets it apart from other logics. Klinger and Svensson's core argument is that social media platforms follow other "rules of the game" than traditional mass media. This perspective draws heavily from the network society perspectives conceptualised by Manuel Castells (2000 b) and Van Dijk (2006). Klinger and Svensson emphasise three distinct ways in which social media differs to mass media, that is, how content is produced, distributed and used. Social media has changed the way information is distributed, the rationale is to encourage others in the network to share, comment and recommend content to other users (Klinger & Svensson, 2015, p. 1248). Unlike mass media, information is no longer delivered to a clear audience, instead it is distributed through networks (Klinger & Svensson, 2015, p. 1248). Social media has also transformed media use, for example, media users are not necessarily connected geographically, but are connected through networks based on interests and issues (Klinger & Svensson, 2015, p. 1250). Papacharissi previously wrote about the emergence of new forms of interaction and the network logic encapsulates these new forms of interaction. The network logic, and the network society perspectives that it draws from, are valuable perspectives for the theoretical analysis of political communications in an online age. Finally, Klinger and Svensson point out that, it is also necessary to consider how political institutions and media systems shape the use of social media platforms as they "can resonate only within the bounds of institutional design and contexts" (Klinger & Svensson, 2016, pp. 34-35).

Both Klinger and Svensson (2016) and Wright (2012) emphasise the need to understand not only how social media is changing politics and government, but equally, how different political contexts, cultures, institutional structures and media systems shape the adoption of online technologies. Svensson (2015) and Van Dijk (2006) highlighted the non-neutrality of social media saying that media use cannot be understood in isolation from the society we live in (Svensson, 2015, p. 348). In a similar vein, Gurevitch et al. said "technologies are culturally shaped as well as shaping" (2009, p. 176). These are issues that must be addressed through further comparative research and also an organisational perspective of how different organisational contexts shape technology usage. Anstead and Chadwick (2009), called for more institutional and organisational perspectives within the field of online political communications. According to them, a comparative approach to analysing the relationship between technology and political institutions has the potential to offer renewed understanding of the development of the Internet in political communications. It is necessary to look at the characteristics of different political institutions and how these shape technology use as "institutions will mediate eventual outcomes" (Anstead & Chadwick, 2009, p. 56).

While most of the theoretical studies above described how interaction and political participation is changing and how different types of media are interacting and shaping one another in this hybrid and networked media environment, very few studies examine or consider how governments or political institutions are adapting to this environment. Nor do they consider the specific challenges, constraints and normative consequences that governments face in this environment. In relation to how governments have responded so far, Gurevitch et al. (2009) concluded that "in the interactive era, government has not proved to be a particularly good conversationalist. Politicians speak with increasing frequency about the need for government to listen to and converse with the public, but there are very few examples of good practice" (p.174). They describe how governments must respond, "politicians, parties, and governments cannot expect to attract public attention simply because of the legitimacy of their positions; authority within the new media ecology has to be earned by demonstrating commitments to interactive and networked communication that do not come easily to elite political actors" (2009, p.175). They warn that there is a risk that governments could become further disconnected and risk a loss of legitimacy if they fail to effectively respond and adapt to these changes in how citizens, media and social movements communicate.

2.2 Government Communications in an Online Age

This next section focuses on what is known so far about how governments are adapting to the changed media environment. Three categories of studies have been identified which specifically examine governments and the use of online technologies. The first category examines a number of studies on the emergence of e-government and e-democracy, which includes studies from the fields of political science (public administration and government studies) and political communications. The second category of studies examine the motivations of government actors around their use of online tools and online initiatives at the local government level. These studies provide a rare and important insight into the organisational constraints that government actors face and their reasons for using online tools within local government. The final category of studies are those that specifically examine how governments are using social media to date.

2.2.1. E-government & e-democracy research paradigms

Government communications takes place within organisations that are both public sector and government organisations making them unique compared to other types of organisations (Graber, 2003). For this reason, government communications is often examined from a public administration perspective. Public administration studies on how governments are using the Internet typically focus on e-government policies and the potential of e-government for improving and transforming public service delivery and public bureaucracies (Dunleavy & Margetts, 2015; Dunleavy, Margetts, Bastow, & Tinkler, 2006). As a result, online government communications is often closely associated with e-government and concepts like *Digital Era Governance* (DEG) (Dunleavy et al., 2006). In a study by Dunleavy et al. (2006), they argue that the Internet and email has the potential to bring about organisational and cultural change within government agencies making these organisations more efficient and responsive. The e-government paradigm views digital technologies as having the potential to bring about a new form of public management replacing or building upon previous management forms like *New Public Management* (NPM).

E-government studies focus on the role of information and communication technologies (ICTs), not just in service delivery, but also on their potential for reshaping governance and renewing democracy (Chadwick & May, 2003). For example, Chadwick and May (2003) examined and compared different models of government citizen interaction underpinning e-government in the U.S., Great Britain and the European Union. They theorised that there are three models of interaction underpinning e-government: a managerial, participative or consultative model. They concluded that "the democratic possibilities of the Internet are likely to be marginalised as a 'managerial' model of interaction becomes dominant" (Chadwick & May, 2003, p. 272). They found that the managerial approach, which focused on the efficient delivery of services and information to citizens, dominated in the U.S., Great Britain and the European Union (Chadwick & May, 2003). When governments speak of efficiency, what they mean is quicker, less costly and less bureaucratic access to public information. In the managerial model of e-governance, described by Chadwick and May, government strives to resemble the private sector and treats citizens as passive consumers of government services.

In light of the managerial approach, they predicted that "even if a 'digital state' emerges, there are likely to be significant problems with incorporating citizen participation into policy making" (Chadwick & May, 2003, p. 293). These earlier e-government models that Chadwick and May described are important to understanding the development of ICTs in government, the values that underpinned their use and explain the approaches to digital technologies that followed. Chadwick was highly sceptical that a more consultative or participatory approach would emerge. He agreed with Margolis and Resnick's (2000) cyber pessimist outlook that the internet would not lead to fundamental structural changes in government and democracy, but they would instead be incorporated into existing power structures.

In another study, Chadwick (2003) criticises the narrow focus of political science on the concept of e-government which led to a concentration on administrative reforms rather than considering the larger democratic questions around how ICTs could contribute to creating an e-democracy. He highlighted the different approaches between political science and political communications towards digital technologies "Public administration scholars, public policy analysts and public management specialists focus on e-government, whereas political communication specialists, social movement scholars, and democratic theorists sharpen their analytical tools on e-democracy" (Chadwick, 2003, p. 444). Political scientists tend to consider e-government developments in isolation from e-democracy. In contrast to e-government, the concept of e-democracy "is associated with efforts to broaden political participation by enabling citizens to connect with one another and with their representatives via new information and communication technologies" (Chadwick, 2003, p. 448). The e-democracy paradigm regards consultation and deliberation as central to democracy. Chadwick called for e-government policies to combine the norms and practices of e-democracy.

As political communication scholars increasingly turned their attention to examining the emergence of e-democracy online, Habermas's public sphere became the dominant theoretical framework for understanding political communications in the online sphere (Chadwick, 2009). Chadwick (2009) says that this led to a narrow focus on citizen deliberation and the emergence of rational discourse within government-created online consultation forums. An example of this approach was Coleman and Blumler's (2009) study on democratic citizenship in an internet age in which they compared two different online consultations set up by the British government. They examined why certain online consultations are a success or failure and describe the conditions needed for supporting rational discourse such as "access to balanced information, an open agenda, time to consider issues, freedom from manipulation or coercion, a rule-based framework for discussion, participation by an inclusive sample of citizens, scope for free interaction between participants, and finally recognition of differences between participants." (Coleman & Blumler, 2009, pp. 40-41). While this study provides a valuable insight into how rational discourse and interaction can be supported by government, this study overlooks a key characteristic of online participation, that is, that most political discussion is taking place outside of institutional forums (Dahlgren, 2005).

A number of scholars have criticised this public sphere framework in the study of e-democracy, deliberation and online participation (e.g., Dahlgren, 2005; Davis, 2010 b; Papacharissi, 2009 b; Van Dijk, 2012; Wright, 2012). The public sphere perspective resulted in "an often-romanticised 'Athenian' or 'public sphere' model as a yardstick to both judge and empirically measure outcomes" (Chadwick, 2009, p. 9). Although the reality of e-democracy fell far short of the normative habermasian ideal, this does not mean that e-democracy has failed (Chadwick, 2009; Papacharissi, 2010). While online government consultations may have attracted small numbers of citizens, there have been other initiatives that have attracted large numbers of participants, for example, the British Prime Minister's e-petitions initiative (Chadwick, 2009). As highlighted previously in Section 2.1, the Internet and in particular the Web 2.0, are supporting new forms of political behaviour and civic engagement, but these are not limited to dialogue within online consultations or discussion forums (Chadwick 2009; Papacharissi, 2010).

These studies show that the examination of government communications in an online age has often been understood through the narrow lens of e-government (e.g., delivery of public services and policy-making) and e-democracy (e.g., greater citizen consultation in policy making). These studies are relevant for this dissertation as they help to understand the approach to ICTs within government to date, that is, ICTs were viewed as capable of improving citizen government interaction through the efficient delivery of services and information. However, this thesis argues that both the fields of political science and political communications need to widen their understanding of government communications in an online age. The dominant and restrictive focus on e-government and e-democracy concepts to date has led to little examination of how government organisations are using social media to interact or network with citizens in an online age. Only then can a conclusion be drawn about whether governments are successfully engaging with citizens and media online.

2.2.2. Motivations behind online initiatives within local government

While there have been a number of studies examining government communications from an e-government and e-democracy perspective, there have been very few studies examining how governments are using social media, or more general use of e-participation initiatives, to engage with citizens. To date there have been very few studies at the national level examining government online initiatives, but there have been some insightful studies at the local government level. These studies provide an important insight into the motivations behind the implementation of online participatory initiatives within government. They also provide a unique insight into the institutional constraints (or perceived constraints) that government organisations face in implementing online participatory initiatives.

In Klinger et al.'s (2015) study of online engagement initiatives by local Swiss city administrations, they believe that political communications research needs to better understand the motivations and challenges behind the implementation, or non-implementation, of online participatory initiatives (Klinger et al., 2015, p. 1927). Political communications has failed to answer the question why governments mostly use one-way push strategies online. Klinger et al. reference Mergel and Bretschneider (2013) who said that "social media adoption in government organisations is more complicated" due to the unique organisational environment (2015, pp. 1927-1928). In order to explore the institutional and organisational factors that shape online tools and initiatives, they examined the perceptions of local government city administrators with regards to the implementation of online initiatives including social media. Their findings show that those local administrations who did not implement online participation tools adopted a *strategic rationality* based on a cost-benefit approach, while those that adopted online platforms did it based on a *normative rationality*, that is, they worried about the normative costs of not doing so (2015, p. 1940). City administrators are generally not motivated by a desire to foster citizen participation (in fact, they are highly sceptical of it). Those who implement online initiatives want to be perceived as modern and see it as their duty to inform (Klinger et al., 2015). Decisions around non-implementation are often based on a lack of financial resources and a perception that formal decision-making processes are incompatible with informal bottom-up participation (2015, p. 1937-1938).

Coleman and Firmstone (2014) examine the motivations behind online and offline citizen engagement in a local city council (local government) in Great Britain. The authors argue that in today's society there is an obligation on government to not just represent, but to provide opportunities for citizens to speak up and to be heard by government. However, they found that local politicians mostly understood political engagement to mean informing citizens about the work that the city council does. Citizen engagement was understood solely "in terms of linear knowledge dissemination" (Coleman & Firmstone, 2014, pp. 829-830). The interviewees admitted that much of their public engagement initiatives were simply "tokenistic exercises intended to give an appearance of consulting citizens" (2014, p. 831). Overall there was a lack of understanding of what public engagement should look like and how to evaluate, or measure, engagement efforts. Social media was generally used, or seen, as a tool for publicity and reputation management. Overall, the findings indicate a general lack of understanding among government officials and politicians around what public engagement is, what it should look like, and what the outcome should be (both in the context of offline and online engagement initiatives).

Chadwick (2011 a) also examined the motives of local government actors, but this time within a local government authority in the U.S. Similar to Klinger et al. (2015), the purpose of this study is to draw attention to "the fragile and uncertain adoption of online engagement by public organisations" (2011 a, p. 22) and to understand the "institutional impediments to e-democracy in government settings" (2011 a, p. 23). He sought to examine how a complex array of different actors and interests can shape whether an online initiative is a success or failure within a government setting (2011 a, p. 23). Chadwick identifies five sets of variables that account for the failure of this particular online initiative, "budget constraints and organisational instability; policy shifts inside the social services agency; political ambivalence among elected representatives; the perception of legal risks that led to a cautious, depoliticised approach; and problems generated by the outsourcing of part of the initiative" (2011 a, p. 27). His findings demonstrate the importance of understanding the relationship between structure and agency and how a range of organisational factors can determine the outcome of online engagement efforts within government settings (2011 a, p. 35).

In summary, these studies demonstrate the importance of understanding the unique organisational environment of government organisations and how this shapes and determines the use, or non-use, and also the success, or failure, of online initiatives and tools. These studies reveal that governments still have a lot to learn about the potential of social media and other online tools for improving citizen engagement. Government administrators and politicians do not yet see, or understand, or in some cases, are simply sceptical of the benefits of social media and regard citizen engagement as simply the dissemination of information. These studies not only highlight that governments mostly use one-way push strategies online, but they help to understand why this is the case. These studies also demonstrate important similarities across the U.S, Great Britain, and Switzerland despite differences in their politics, culture and media systems.

2.2.3. Governments & social media

Studies on social media use by governments generally examine the potential of social media for changing the relationship between government and citizens. This section summarises what is known so far about how social media emerges within government organisations and how they use social media. The studies highlight the increased expectation for bidirectional interaction that accompanies social media use. This contrasts with Section 2.2.2 which specifically examined the motives behind the use of online initiatives at the local government level. It also contrasts with the e-government and e-democracy paradigms outlined in Section 2.2.1 which predominantly focused on the delivery of public services rather than fostering a new relationship between government and citizens.

In an examination of social media use by government organisations in the U.S., Mergel and Bretschneider (2013) presented a three-stage model for explaining how social media diffuses (or emerges) across government and public sector organisations. Unlike previous studies in this literature review, their study, or model "does not attempt to explain the adoption decision or stages of technical implementation; rather, it looks at the organisational dynamics of the process" (2013, pp. 390-391). The three stages of social media adoption include:

> agencies experiment informally with social media outside of accepted technology use policies. Next, order evolves from the first chaotic stage as government organisations recognise the need to draft norms and regulations. Finally, organisational institutions evolve that clearly outline appropriate behavior, types of interactions, and new modes of communication that subsequently are formalised in social media strategies and policies. (2013, p. 390)

This three-stage theoretical model describes social media use as a process of institutionalisation. When social media use enters the final stage it can be described as institutionalised within the organisation. Their theoretical model suggests that the more institutionalised social media becomes within public sector organisations, the more formalised and controlled the organisational structures become for managing these technologies. In the first stage, social media emerges from the bottom up by individuals experimenting within organisations, but once social media becomes a formal part of organisational communications, it is increasingly controlled from the top down as regulations, policies and codes of practices are introduced. They also suggest that government organisations go through these three stages at different speeds and that some organisations do not move beyond certain stages.

According to Mergel (2012) "the acceptance and broader adoption of sophisticated tactics that go beyond information and education paradigm such as true engagement or networking strategies are still in its infancy" (p. 281). Despite large numbers of U.S. citizens receiving political information from their Facebook and Twitter feeds, governments are "slow in adopting the tools to connect to their audiences where they prefer to receive information and news" (Mergel, 2012, p. 282). Innovation in government is constrained by top-down decision-making processes and communications practices and processes that were designed for a pre-social media era. Social media triggers tensions within these organisations, that is, the tension between the demands for innovation, interaction and transparency, but also the requirement to use them responsibly (Mergel, 2012). Yet government is expected to adapt and use social media in the same interactive way and at the same pace as other actors in society (Mergel, 2012, p. 283). These tensions are essential to understanding how social media is used in government. Social media leaves "little room for research, deliberation, and a formal vetting process" (Mergel, 2012, p. 283). As a result, governments are using social media in a hyper reactive mode "social media tactics are changing as a response to changes in citizen behaviour and expectations, but not necessarily as a direct result of a clear strategic move to support the existing mission" (Mergel, 2012, p. 290).

According to Mossberger, Wu and Crawford (2013) "the rapid diffusion of social network use among local governments, and the emergence of open data portals present new possibilities for transforming relationships between government and citizens through more open government and citizen participation" (p. 354). In an empirical study they examine and compare the use of social media and other online tools across 75 U.S city governments between 2009 and 2011. Using Mergel's (2013) typology of social network strategies for civic engagement, they carry out a content analysis assessing the extent to which social media is used for 1) representation of the agency/organisation (push strategies) 2) engagement of citizens (pull strategies) and 3) networking with the public (Mossberger et al., 2013, p. 355). Similar to Mergel's (2012) findings, one-way push strategies again dominate. However, in additional interviews carried out by Mossberger et al. (2013) in three of the cities, the interviewees indicated that pull and networking strategies are also a goal of online communications. The authors found some examples of this, but not among all organisations. This suggests a gap between the goals of online communication and their actual use.

According to Meijer et al., "the promise of Government 2.0 is impressive but its potential has not or hardly been realised yet in practice" (2012, p. 59). This claim seems accurate when one considers the results of those studies above examining social media use within government. Meijer et al. (2012) also describe how the use of social media is constrained by the bureaucratic institutional environment and the tensions that social media causes within these organisations "open learning is needed for innovation but open learning conflicts with the nature of bureaucracy in which formalisation and a hierarchical chain of command lines are core principles" (p. 62). Like Mergel (2012), they also say that "regulations and reporting structures hamper the collaboration, creating and sharing between governments and citizens" (Meijer et al., 2012, p. 64).

Much of the studies to date on government use of social media highlight the extent to which government has failed to use its full potential (Meijer et al., 2012). Governments are in reactive mode and there seems to be little strategy behind their use of social media (Mergel, 2012). They continue to use it predominantly as an informational tool for pushing out information. They have not yet understood its potential for interaction and networking, or if they do, it is hindered by top-down communications practices and processes which limit their ability to respond in real time. These studies also draw attention to important tensions that social media triggers within government organisations. These tensions are essential to understanding how government organisations adapt social media. However, what this section also demonstrates is that research to date on how governments use social media stems predominantly from the U.S. There continues to be a general lack of research looking at how governments are adopting social media outside of the U.S. and those studies that exist are limited and often at the local government level.

2.3 Comparative Government & Political Communications Studies

The next section, Section 2.3.1, considers a number of comparative studies of government communications, however, general comparative studies of government communications are still rare (Canel & Sanders, 2012). There are even fewer studies comparing how different governments are using new digital technologies. The studies presented below provide an insight into important differences in the centralised structures for government communications across countries and the different macro structures that shape government communications[5]. However, due to the lack of comparative studies examining how governments use new digital technologies, Section 2.3.2 will also consider comparative studies in the wider field of political communications, in particular, studies examining the use of websites and social media by political actors across different countries. These studies give an important insight into whether, and how, different political systems or cultures shape the use of digital technologies.

2.3.1. Comparative government communications

In a study by Sanders et al. (2011) they criticise the field of political communications saying "systematic research on how successful governments are adapting to the new challenges and the way they communicate with

5 As mentioned previously, Chapter 3 will elaborate on the specific macro and centralised structures shaping government communications in Germany and Great Britain.

the media and the citizens is sparse" (p. 2). There is too much theoretical and empirical focus on election communications within the field of political communications rather than a focus on day-to-day communications outside of election periods (Sanders et al., 2011, p. 2). Sanders et al. (2011) carried out one of the few comparative studies of government communications within the field of political communications. Their three-country study compares the professionalisation of centralised government communications structures in Germany, the United Kingdom and Spain. Applying a strategic planning and management perspective they view professionalisation as expressed through the emergence of formal rules and guidelines, legislation, organisational structures and financial resources. They regard professionalisation as a positive development in which professionalised processes such as formal rules and codes of practice ensure government fulfils its function as a provider of impartial information rather than engaging in partisan communications.

This study represents a significant theoretical contribution to the field of comparative government communications. They provide a framework for comparing the professionalisation of centralised government communications by identifying a range of organisational indices that shape communications, such as, financial resources, regulations, professional training, codes of practice and so forth. Their study also provides important institutional knowledge of the centralised communications structures in the three countries, how these structures have developed and the various macro factors that shape these organisational structures. Their study highlights the importance of considering these centralised structures in any comparison of government communications. However, their study has a number of weaknesses and limitations. They assume that professionalisation is a positive development for government communications, however, they do not empirically examine how professionalisation shapes actual communications practices. They briefly consider the possible negative consequences of such formalised and centralised government communications structures and processes. While they question whether "professionalism is compatible with government communication that is manipulative or more colloquially described as 'spin'" (2011, p. 2), however, they do not delve any further into the possible negative consequences of these professionalised, centralised and managed communications structures. There is a need to carry out further comparative research and empirically examine whether more professionalised communications potentially results in more controlled and managed government communications in an online age.

In a subsequent and similar comparative study, Sanders and Canel (2013) widen their comparative research and examine the professionalisation of centralised government communications structures across fifteen different countries. This study takes a comparative case study approach rather than a traditional comparative research design. In this study, they build on their previous research by expanding their framework for comparing centralised government communications. Based on the case studies presented, they identify the following categories for comparing centralised government communications: structure, technical infrastructure – such as the development of e-government, process, non-partisanship, transparency, and citizen participation. Like their previous study, it represents an important step forward for understanding the centralised institutional structures that influence and shape government communications and identifying categories of analysis for examining these structures. However, their research again lacks empirical analysis of how these structures shape communication processes and practices in different countries. They also fail to discuss or address how these centralised structures are changing in a new media environment and the impact of new digital technologies on centralised organisational structures.

Another comparative study that provides an insight into different institutional structures of government communications is Vogel's (2010) doctoral dissertation, a three-country comparison of the changing structures of government communications in Great Britain, Germany and Switzerland. In her dissertation, Vogel examines how the structures have changed using a document analysis and expert interviews. The central contribution of this thesis to the field of comparative government communications is its theoretical work in defining government and government communications. Vogel says that until now neither the fields of communication studies, political science, legal studies or public administration have adequately defined government, and this has resulted in a lack of clarity around what constitutes government communications (2010, p. 33). She provides a critical overview of the many ways in which government can be defined and viewed, this includes, as an agency/administration, an institution, an organisation, a network or a core executive (2010, pp. 35-43)[6]. She argues that an organisational perspective is the most suitable perspective for analysing the changing structures of government communications. This is one of the

6 Definitions of government and government communications in the context of this study will be addressed and discussed in detail in Chapter 5 which presents the methodological approach of this study.

few comparative studies that addresses the unique challenges of defining government and government communications for comparing different governments. It is also one of the few studies that takes an explicit organisational perspective of government and in this way provides an important theoretical contribution to this field.

In her habilitation's dissertation, Pfetsch (2003) compares political communication cultures in the U.S. and Germany. In this study, she seeks to connect the macro and micro levels by examining the perceptions, orientations and norms of individual journalists and political (including government) spokespeople in the two countries. According to Pfetsch, the political communication system cannot be explained by indicators related only to the institutional structure of the political and media system, but it must also incorporate the subjective orientations of the actors in this system (2003, p. 34). This comparative approach allows her to understand how different political and media systems shape the orientations and perceptions of actors within those systems. In doing so, she is able to identify two different types of political communication cultures, one in which a media logic dominates (in the U.S.) and the other characterised by a political logic (in Germany). Her study is a significant contribution to the field of both comparative political and government communications as it moved comparative research beyond a focus solely on institutional structures by connecting the macro and micro levels through the political communications cultures perspective. Her study also highlights that comparative empirical research should not seek to draw causal explanations, but its purpose is to understand the structural environment in which communication takes place and to understand how this context enables or restrains communication at lower levels (2003, p. 66).

Sievert and Nelke (2014) criticise the lack of comparative analysis of how governments use social media within the field of political communications. Their study attempts to fill this gap by comparing social media use by governments in a number of European countries. In relation to Germany, they state that although government communicators recognise the increasing use and importance of the Internet by citizens, the government has not yet begun to implement online initiatives aimed at creating dialogue (2014, p. 13). In a contribution from Borucki (2014 a) in Sievert and Nelke's (2014) study, she examines and compares government websites in Germany, Austria, Switzerland and Great Britain in order to establish if their websites feature links to social media platforms, and if so, which platforms. She specifically analyses the organisational websites of the office of the head of government and three ministries in each country. In Great

Britain, she found that government organisations use a variety of social media platforms (e.g., Facebook, LinkedIn, Twitter and YouTube) with each social media page embedded and linked from the government websites. Whereas in Germany, she found limited use of social media, for example, the website of the federal government and the website of the German Chancellor's Office featured the Twitter account of Steffen Seibert (the head of government communications) and a link to the Chancellor's YouTube page. The other ministries mostly featured either a Twitter account or a YouTube account. Borucki concludes that government organisations still have a significant amount of catching up to do with other political actors and there are not only differences between the countries in how they use social media, but also between the various government organisations within the countries (2014 a, p. 43). Despite the highly descriptive nature of this comparative empirical analysis, the findings still shed light on the different ways in which governments are adopting social media both across countries and within countries. However, the results of this content analysis are based on a content analysis of websites and social media from 2011, at a time when governments were only beginning to adopt social media. She does not examine how governments actually use social media, but simply looked at whether they are present on social media or not. There is a clear need for comparative empirical studies that go further than this and examine how governments use these channels for interaction and networking.

The comparative studies outlined in this section demonstrate the importance of understanding not only the different macro-level structures (e.g., different political systems) that shape government communications, but also the institutional structures that shape government communications. Therefore, this thesis will consider how the increasing professionalisation of centralised structures for government communications possibly affects actual communication practices, in particular online communications. This section highlighted that there are very few comparative studies examining government communications and there are even less examining how different governments are adapting to the new media environment and using new digital technologies (e.g., Sievert & Nelke, 2014; Borucki, 2014 a). Due to the lack of comparative government communications studies, the next section will look to the wider field of comparative political communications. Although this field is also described as an understudied field (Foot et al., 2009; Holtz-Bacha et al., 2014), it has begun to examine and compare how different political organisations are using websites and social media in political election campaigns.

2.3.2. Comparative online political communications

In one of the first comparative studies examining the websites of political actors, Gibson and Ward (2000) propose a methodology (a coding scheme) for examining and comparing the effectiveness of political party and electoral candidates' websites. Their methodology seeks to answer the questions "why these political actors are using the new media and whether some are using it more effectively than others?" (p. 302). According to them, their approach "is designed to have broader applicability to sites of other political actors such as interest groups, municipal governments, and civic or community-based pro-democracy advocates" (p. 302). They identify five functions of political party websites which are used as categories of analysis: 1) information provision 2) campaigning 3) resource generation 4) networking and organisation strengthening and 5) promoting participation (p. 305). One of the weaknesses of their methodological approach is the categorisation of government and party political actors as the same. This results in the same categories of analysis being applied to both government and political party websites. Functions such as campaigning and resource generation are very clearly functions of political parties and electoral candidates, but not governments. This lack of understanding around the organisational differences between political and government actors, is a typical feature of some of the earlier studies in the field of online political comparative communications.

In a later study, Gibson, Margolis, Resnick and Ward (2003) applied this coding scheme to a comparative content analysis of the websites of political parties in the U.S. and the UK. They sought to investigate whether there has been a convergence of online election campaign practices across the two countries. They concluded that there has been a convergence and that "information provision and resource generation are consistently emphasised while promoting participation and establishing electronic networks, both within and outside of the party, are less of a priority. Web-based communication is largely a party-led and top-down phenomenon rather than two-way dialogue" (Gibson et al., 2003, p. 66). Based on these findings, they conclude that differences in national contexts are not shaping online electoral practices. However, it is necessary to widen comparative research beyond the U.S. and the UK, two very similar countries (Hallin & Mancini, 2004), before concluding that national contexts are not shaping online electoral practices. This study, and the previous study, highlight the strong focus on political parties and election websites within the field of comparative political communications.

According to Foot et al. (2009) "cross-national similarities and differences in the adoption and adaptation of information and communication technologies by political actors in the context of democratic politics remain understudied" (p. 40). Foot et al. argue that comparative research is necessary in order to examine whether "national political cultures contextualise technology adoption and adaptation" (2009, p. 41), or whether there has been a transnational diffusion of political web practices regardless of structural differences between countries. In their large-scale cross-national study, they examine the political websites produced during 19 election campaigns in 2004 across Europe, North America and Australasia. They analyse four web functions: informing, involving, connecting and mobilising. Their definition of political actors includes election candidates, political parties, government agencies, news media and civic groups. Despite this weakness in their definition of political actors, their study is important in that it seeks to test whether there is a connection between different political cultures and web practices. Unlike Gibson et al. (2003), their results support the hypothesis that there is a significant connection between political cultures and web practices.

In another comparative empirical study, Russmann (2011) takes a slightly different focus to the previous comparative studies and examines the extent to which political parties use their websites to target different voter groups. In order to do this, she undertook a comparative structural analysis of political party websites during the 2008 Austrian and the 2009 German national elections. She describes both the Austrian and German political systems as being dominated by catch-all parties that tend to form grand coalitions without any strong ideological differences between the parties. It was hypothesised that catch-all parties would try to target a broader electorate in their web tactics, whereas smaller parties would have distinctive policy stances and clear target groups. However, both hypotheses were found to be false and suggest that parties in both countries do not yet engage in strategic web targeting practices. While its hypotheses were found to be false, this study was a significant development for the field of comparative research as it sought to draw connections between specific macro-level features of the political system and the specific usage of online tools. Previous comparative studies did not seek to carry out such explanatory analyses.

Although online technologies have been used in political communications for almost twenty years, comparative research on online political communications continues to be rare. The studies that exist, and some of which were presented above, mostly examine political party websites during elections. In a recent review of the state of research in comparative political communications, De Vreese (2017) criticised the lack of online comparative research. He stated that "many studies so far offer descriptive comparative accounts of the availability, contents, and uses of political communication online, but systematic comparative and explanatory analyses are rare" (2017, p. 10). Comparative political communications predominantly focuses on comparing media systems, mainstream news coverage, political media relations and political journalism rather than online political communications (De Vreese, 2017). This section highlights the progress made, but also the significant theoretical and empirical progress that still needs to be made in identifying which macro-level factors influence the use of digital technologies by governments and political organisations. Future research needs to move beyond a narrow focus on election websites and examine a range of online platforms, in particular social media. Future studies also need to apply categories of analysis that are relevant for government and which better reflect the new ways governments and citizens are engaging online (e.g., through more personalised communications on social media). This study seeks to address these weaknesses found in previous studies.

2.4 Summary

While this review of research drew attention to a range of findings that are relevant for understanding how government organisations are adopting social media and other online platforms, it also drew attention to a number of large research gaps in the field of government communications, and more broadly, in political communications. Based on the studies presented here, it is clear that government communications continues to be an under-researched subfield of political communications (Canel & Sanders, 2012). The literature review revealed just how little is known about how governments (outside of the U.S.) are using websites and social media. Little is also known about how different political systems and cultures shape the use of online technologies, and vice versa, how these technologies are influencing how governments communicate with citizens. There is a clear need for more comparative research within the field of online political communications. There are still only a handful of comparative studies examining how political parties use websites for election campaigning. But there is a scarcity of comparative studies examining how political parties or governments are using websites and social media for interaction and networking outside of election periods.

Therefore, this study fills an important empirical gap by conducting a comparative analysis of how government organisations use websites and social media in two different countries, Germany and Great Britain. It also fills a theoretical gap by examining the macro-level and organisational factors that possibly shape and constrain government communications in an online age. Despite the many research gaps in the field of government communications, the literature review revealed some important findings which will be considered and examined in the theoretical and empirical parts of this dissertation. The findings of this chapter will also play a role in the formulation of research guiding assumptions presented at the end of Chapter 4. Here is a summary of the most important conclusions from the review of literature in the field:

- Political participation in the new media environment is taking place outside of institutional politics (Bennett, 2012) posing significant challenges for political organisations and governments in maintaining democratic legitimacy in this sphere.
- The online sphere has changed what it means to interact and participate in politics (Bennett, 2012; Chadwick, 2013; Klinger & Svensson, 2015, 2016; Papacharissi, 2009 b, 2010); political participation is increasingly defined by individuals engaging in personalised communications across social networks (Bennett, 2012).
- However, online technologies are not neutral, they must still be understood within the political system and society in which they are used (Klinger & Svensson, 2016; Wright, 2012).
- They must also be understood within their organisational context. The use of online engagement initiatives and social media within government organisations is shaped and constrained by a range of internal organisational factors and tensions triggered by social media (Chadwick, 2011 a; Klinger et al., 2015; Meijer et al., 2012; Mergel, 2012; Mergel & Bretschneider, 2013).
- Government organisations use social media predominantly for one-way information provision (Meijer et al., 2012; Mossberger et al., 2013); engagement, interaction and networking is still in its infancy within government (Mergel, 2012).
- The more institutionalised that social media becomes within government organisations, the more these organisations try to control, or manage, how these technologies are used, for example, through the implementation of codes of practice and guidelines (Mergel & Bretschneider, 2013).

- Centralised government communications structures are becoming increasingly professionalised across different countries (Sanders & Canel, 2013); however, little is known about how these structures influence communication practices in the new media environment.

The next chapter, Chapter 3, will examine and identify the most important macro-level factors shaping government communications in Great Britain and Germany. In particular, it will examine in detail the organisation and development of the centralised structures for government communications in the two countries. Following this, Chapter 4 will take an organisational and network theoretical perspective of the changing media environment and examine the theoretical challenges in comparing government organisational communications in a networked media environment.

3. Background: Political, Media & Government Communication Structures

The literature review in Chapter 2 highlighted the limited amount of comparative research of government communications and also a continuing scarcity of comparative studies of online political communications. As Gibson and Ward (2009) said, one of the weaknesses of online political communications is the failure to "place it within current political and social contexts" (p. 37). An essential aspect of comparative empirical research is the attempt to understand the structural environment or the context in which communication takes place (Pfetsch, 2003). It seeks to understand how these macro structures enable or restrain communications behaviour at lower levels (Pfetsch, 2003). Therefore, this chapter provides a detailed analysis of the key institutional (macro) differences between Germany and Great Britain in terms of their political systems, media systems, the centralised structures and organisation of government communications, the regulation of government communications, and also, differences in the development of online government communications in both countries. This chapter includes a number of important variables related to their political systems that were overlooked in previous comparative political communications studies of Germany and Great Britain. For example, this study examines the extent to which their political systems are centralised or decentralised (Humphreys, 2012) and considers the extent to which power and media resources are centralised in the offices of the head of government, particularly the Prime Minister's Office (PM's Office) in Great Britain. Other considerations include important differences in their legal systems, how this shapes the regulation of government communications, and ultimately how this potentially influences online communications by government.

In doing so, this chapter provides a comprehensive overview of the most important macro-level factors shaping government organisational communications in the two countries. This chapter argues that these macro-level factors must be considered as possible influencing variables in any comparative study of government organisational communications in Germany and Great Britain. The macro factors outlined in this chapter will play a role in forming some of the research guiding assumptions of this thesis (which will be presented in full at the end of Chapter 4). Based on the large number of differences outlined in this chapter, particularly in relation to their political systems and the centralised organisational structures for government communications, it is clear that in comparing government communications, these countries should continue to be treated as *most different systems* (Przeworski & Teune, 1970).

3.1 Decentralised, Regulated & Formalised: German Institutional Structures

Germany, like Great Britain, is a parliamentary democracy. Due to Germany's proportional voting system, however, most governments in Germany are coalition governments rather than single party governments like in Great Britain (Sanders et al., 2011, p. 6). The most recent German government (2013-2017) was made up of the Christian Democratic Union (CDU), the Christian Social Union of Bavaria (CSU) and the Social Democratic Party (SPD). Political parties play a particularly strong role in Germany's representative system of government which are assigned a special role in the constitution[7] (Holtz-Bacha, 2013; Pfetsch, 2003). In comparing the political communications culture of Germany with the U.S., Pfetsch explained that "in a representative system of government such as that of Germany, support for a coalition government depends both on the parliamentary party fractions and on the power constellation in the second chamber, the Bundesrat" (2001, p. 50). This means that policy formation is strongly influenced by party and coalition motives (Pfetsch, 2001, p. 50). The political system is dependent on consensus among the parties in order to function and as a result, these structural conditions strongly shape the political communications culture in Germany (Pfetsch, 2001, 2003).

Germany is a federal state and this also strongly influences both the structures of the media system and the political communications environment (Humphreys, 2012). Humphreys (2012) says that federalism is a defining feature of Germany's political system and it should be considered when comparing Germany with other countries. He criticises that this feature was for the most part overlooked in Hallin and Mancini's (2004) seminal study *Three Models of Media and Politics*. Federalism supports a decentralised political system and a consensus approach to politics. Sanders et al.

7 According to Article 21 of German Basic Law (das Grundgesetz) political parties play a central role in the formation of the political will of citizens; they are what connects the state and citizens (Pötzsch, 2009).

(2011) also point out how federalism shapes approaches to government communications in Germany, for example, "the communication management of the government always has to take into account the concerns of the coalition partners in the government and the interests of the sixteen states' governments, particularly if there is a state election on the horizon" (p. 8). There are sixteen federal states (Bundesländer) and this means that there is always an election on the horizon. Germany also has strict laws demarcating what governments can and can't communicate both during and in the run up to election periods (Holtz-Bacha, 2013; Kocks & Raupp, 2014). Consequently, government communicators must regularly pay heed to a range of rulings by the constitutional court around what can and can't be communicated during election periods (Holtz-Bacha, 2013; Kocks & Raupp, 2014).

While the German Federal Constitutional Court (Bundesverfassungsgericht) has issued a number of rulings affecting government communications since the mid-1960 s, the most influential ruling was issued on March 2, 1977 in relation to communications during election periods (Holtz-Bacha, 2013; Kocks & Raupp, 2014). On the one hand this ruling reaffirmed that government public relations (Öffentlichkeitsarbeit) is an essential activity of government in helping to form the will of the people, but it also ruled that state organs should "abstain from advertising in favour of any of the competing parties" (Holtz-Bacha, 2013, pp. 48-49). The ruling states that government communications "reaches its limits where electoral advertising begins" (Holtz-Bacha, 2013, pp. 48-49). This landmark ruling continues to shape government communications today and is one of the reasons why government communications in Germany is regarded as having a strict public relations or informational function (Holtz-Bacha, 2013, p. 50).

Government communications in Germany can, therefore, be described as being highly formalised and regulated in comparison to Great Britain and other countries (Kocks & Raupp, 2014, p. 277). In an online media age, these rulings could be a source of uncertainty and tension around how and to what extent, government communicators should interact with citizens online (Kocks & Raupp, 2014). Social media has brought about new and heightened expectations of how governments should communicate and interact with citizens (Block & Feldgen, 2018; Coleman & Firmstone, 2014). The government is no longer expected to simply inform citizens of government activities, but they are also expected to encourage participation and engage in dialogue (Kocks & Raupp, 2014, p.279). This raises new challenges and tensions for government organisations around how they should communicate with citizens in this formal and regulated, but rapidly changing, communications environment. According to Holtz-Bacha (2013), the rulings of the German constitutional court restrict how strategic governments can be in adapting their communications to the new media environment. It is unclear whether activities such as engaging in dialogue with citizens and media, potentially goes beyond the public relations and informational function of government communications in Germany.

The German Federal Press and Information Office (BPA) is the central institution for coordinating government communications in Germany (Holtz-Bacha, 2013). Established in 1949, it has the status of a supreme federal authority and is directly subordinate to the Chancellor (Holtz-Bacha, 2013, p.48). According to the German Federal Centre for Political Education (BPB), there are 460 employees in the BPA, which is a continuous reduction of staff numbers from 750 employees in 1990 (Bundeszentrale für politische Bildung, n.d.). According to the most recent figures from 2015, the BPA has an annual budget of €57,606 million (Deutscher Bundestag, 2015). The head of the BPA has the status of state secretary[8] and is typically a former journalist (Holtz-Bacha, 2013). The current head of government communications, Steffen Seibert, was previously a journalist with Germany's second public service broadcaster (ZDF). While the head of the BPA works for the whole of government, they are usually appointed by the Chancellor and the Chancellor also determines how much power they are assigned (Holtz-Bacha, 2013; Vogel, 2010). Generally, senior government communicators such as the head of government communications, could be described as being political appointees in Germany (Sanders et al., 2011, p. 15). Vogel (2010) also refers to this personal relationship between the head of the BPA and the Chancellor. She says that due to this close relationship the BPA and the Chancellor's Office (KA) have come to be viewed as leadership instruments of the Chancellor (2010, pp. 115-116).

While the BPA has the function of coordinating communication activities across government, each ministry also has its own communication department and resources (Holtz-Bacha, 2013). According to Article 65 (das Ressortprinzip) of the German Basic Law (das Grundgesetz), each minister is responsible for the independent management of its own ministry (Heinze, 2012, p.77). Based on these rights of ministers, comes the entitlement to their own budget and communication resources (Heinze, 2012, p.77). Ministries are expected to communicate on policy issues that fall within

8 The position of State Secretary (Staatssekretär) in Germany is one level below ministerial level. This position should not be confused with the position of "Secretary of State", which in Great Britain is the title given to government ministers.

their remit (Holtz-Bacha, 2013). However, the amount of resources allocated to each ministry varies, with some ministries allocated more than others for communication activities, including, for example, the amount of personnel for social media activities (Deutscher Bundestag, 2015). While the BPA plays an important role in coordinating government communications, there can also be a tension in this relationship. One particular reason for this is that the ministers come from different coalition parties and as a consequence there is often a blurring of the line between the public relations efforts of the ministries and the personal and political ambitions of the ministers (Holtz-Bacha, 2013). In this regard, the BPA has little influence over individual ministries (Holtz Bacha, 2013) and it is assumed to take a back seat to the communications of the ministries (Heinze, 2012, p.77). Alongside federal ministries and ministers, there are a range of other actors who play a prominent role in government communications in Germany. These include not only the head of government communications at the BPA, the Chancellor, the ministers at the federal level, but also ministers at the state level, state secretaries within federal ministries and government spokespersons at the level of state secretary (Heinze, 2012, p.77). All of these characteristics would indicate that federalism in Germany shapes a more decentralised approach to government communications.

The German Federal Press Conference (BPK) is a membership association that was founded in 1949 by political correspondents in Germany. The BPK organises press conferences with government ministers and their spokespersons a number of times a week. This forum gives over 900 German and foreign political journalists, who are registered members of the organisation, the opportunity to directly question government ministers and their spokespersons in an open and transparent forum (Bundespressekonferenz, n.d.). The BPK is a unique feature of political communications in Germany and demonstrates a formal and transparent approach to political media relations. It allows a large number of political journalists regular and equal access to government ministers and spokespersons. However, while on the one hand, the BPA and the BPK suggest a formalised, regulated and transparent relationship between government and media, on the other hand, there is also evidence that there are strong informal ties between politicians and media in Germany (Reinemann & Baugut, 2014). The relationship between politicians and leading traditional media outlets can also be described as elitist and exclusive (Kocks, 2016; Kocks & Raupp, 2015).

Despite processes of digitalisation in Germany, political actors communicate almost exclusively with political journalists from established mainstream media outlets (Kocks, 2016; Kocks & Raupp, 2015). Government media networks rarely feature new online media actors and when online media outlets do feature in their networks, they are usually the online versions of established mainstream offline outlets (Kocks, Raupp, & Murphy, 2016). The online Twitter networks of political journalists in Germany have also been described as being a closed elite network (Nuernbergk, 2016). Nuernbergk examined the Twitter networks of political journalists in Germany and found they operate in a journalism-centred bubble (2016, p. 877). The close relationship between media and politics can also be seen from the fact that the head of the BPA is typically a leading political journalist. In the case of Steffen Seibert, he previously worked for the public state broadcaster ZDF and has the option of returning to his position at the public broadcaster when he finishes working for the government (Brauck & Schult, 2016).

In relation to government communications online, there have been a number of important online and offline government campaigns in recent years which have encouraged direct dialogue with citizens and participation in government decision and policy making. In 2014, the German Federal Government launched the "Digitale Agenda" for 2014-2017 (Bundesregierung, 2014). This policy centres on the question of how new digital opportunities can be used to support society as a whole. The campaign resulted in a national public consultation with citizens using a mixture of online tools and offline events. In 2015, the government also initiated a citizen dialogue called "Gut Leben in Deutschland – was uns wichtig ist [good life in Germany – what is important to us]" in which the government asked citizens about their perceptions of the quality of life in Germany. This was a large government initiative using online tools and offline events to communicate directly with citizens. The findings of the citizen dialogue were eventually published in spring 2016 (Bundesregierung, 2016).

A number of government organisations in Germany have had a presence on Facebook, Twitter and YouTube since 2009-2011[9]. Since October 2011, the German Chancellor Angela Merkel has answered questions submitted by members of the public on her YouTube channel called "Die Kanzlerin Direkt" (Sievert & Nelke, 2014). The public are asked to send questions and the ten most popular are selected (Sievert & Nelke, 2014, p. 21). However, this citizen interaction takes place in a very controlled environment (e.g., it is unclear who submits and selects the questions for the Chancel-

9 The German Chancellor is also on Instagram since 2015.

lor). However, the launch of the Facebook page of the German Federal Government in February, 2015 represented a new active and professional approach to engaging with citizens on social media. Social media content is managed by a dedicated team of eight staff members within the BPA (Deutscher Bundestag, 2015) and they are responsible for regularly posting content and responding directly to individual comments on Facebook. According to Block and Feldgen, Facebook is not a broadcasting channel, the conception is based on dialogue, and that means that the user rightly expects that the Government engages with citizens, answers their questions and criticisms (2018, p. 253). These online developments in Germany, particularly over the last three years, indicate an attempt by the government, in particular the German Federal Government through the BPA, to encourage an active, regular and direct dialogue between citizens and government in relation to government decision making.

In their study *Three Models of Media and Politics*, Hallin and Mancini (2004) categorised the media system in Germany as belonging to the North Central European/ Democratic Corporatist Model along with the Netherlands, Switzerland, Austria, Belgium and the Scandinavian countries. In their typology of eighteen western media systems, they categorised the media systems of these countries as belonging to one of three different models. They traced common characteristics and historical developments in their media systems and connected these to shared characteristics in their political systems. One of the main characteristics of the Democratic Corporatist Model is a high degree of political parallelism in the media with newspapers typically affiliated (historically, but less so today) to a political party or a social/civil society organisation (e.g., trade unions). However, in the Democratic Corporatist Model, a high level of political parallelism exists alongside a strong commercial media market, strong mass circulation press and high levels of journalistic professionalisation (Hallin & Mancini, 2004, pp. 144-145)[10].

According to Hallin and Mancini, while the commercial press (rather than a party political press) dominates today in the countries of the Democratic Corporatist Model, the media systems of these countries are still shaped by the history of a strong political press (2004, p. 160). They tend to have stronger political leanings compared to newspapers in the countries of the Liberal Model, in particular, in comparison to the U.S. These countries also have a strong welfare state and as a result, media is regarded as a

10 However, a more partisan character emerged in the press in Germany after World War II (Hallin & Mancini, 2004, p. 155).

social institution rather than simply something to be used for pure business interest (Hallin & Mancini, 2004, p. 163). This can be seen in the strong support and investment in public service broadcasting in these countries. Compared to Great Britain and the BBC model of public service broadcasting, civil society organisations and political parties play a role in governing public service broadcasting (Hallin & Mancini, 2004, pp. 165-167). The strong role of the State also influences approaches to media regulation in these countries. Compared to the Liberal Model, the State plays a strong role in regulating the media through, for example, hate speech laws[11] and ensuring balanced programming during election periods. The State also ensures a strong and free press through press subsidies and strong press councils (although this is not the case in Germany or Switzerland) (Hallin & Mancini, 2004). In Germany, the constitutional court also plays an important role in regulating the media and there is a federal system of regulation with each federal state responsible for their own media regulation. However, Hallin and Mancini (2004) acknowledge that due to the history of totalitarianismin in Germany, this has resulted in a relatively liberal system of regulation compared to the other Democratic Corporatist countries (p.161).

German media is also characterised by "the strong position of the regional press and by a system of public service broadcasting that also has a strong regional component" (Reinemann & Baugut, 2014, p. 76). The most important source of political information for German citizens continues to be traditional regional broadcasters and newspapers of which there are 340 regional newspapers and nine regional public service broadcasters (Reinemann & Baugut, 2014). Political journalism in Germany, like in many other countries, is facing a range of pressures including increasing commercialisation, audience fragmentation, digitalisation and the rise of online media (Reinemann & Baugut, 2014, p. 90). Despite the pressures exerted on traditional news media,

> digital versions of traditional offline media dominate online news. Pure online journalistic media hardly play a role for the general public as a source of political information, which can also be traced back to

---

11 Germany was one of the first countries in Europe to introduce legislation tackling hate speech on social media platforms. In January 2018, the German government enacted legislation called the Network Enforcement Act (NetzDG) which introduced fines for social media platforms who fail to remove hate speech from their platforms (Oltermann, 2018).

> the quite diverse media landscape and the strong position of public service broadcasters also on the web. (Reinemann & Baugut, 2014, p. 90)

Overall, traditional media outlets still dominate in Germany and social media plays a more limited role in the political information habits of Germans compared to other countries (Reinemann & Baugut, 2014).

In summary, there are a number of structural factors at the macro level that differentiate the political system, the media system, the centralised structures of government communications, and government media relations in Germany from Great Britain. Overall, the centralised institutional structures of government communications in Germany could be described as being highly formalised and regulated. However, while there are well-resourced and professionalised centralised communication structures, the ministries and ministers have significant autonomy with regards to government communications (federalism supports strong decentralised structures). The institutional structures for managing political media relations in Germany (e.g., the BPK) could also be described, like the BPA, as being highly professionalised, formalised and regulated. Compared to the system for regulating political media relations in Great Britain (which will be explained in the next section), the BPK provides a uniquely transparent and regulated institutional structure for government media interactions. The BPA is also long established and well-resourced and the German constitutional court plays a central role in regulating government communications and media. However, as outlined in this chapter, this regulated and formal communications environment may constrain the government's ability to be able to adapt to changes in the new media environment and engage with citizens and new media actors online. In addition, the media system in Germany continues to be dominated by the major traditional offline news outlets despite increasing digitalisation. The next section in this chapter will outline in detail the very different path that government communications has taken in Great Britain and a variety of differences in the media, political and legal systems in Great Britain.

3.2 Centralised & Professionalised: British Institutional Structures

The political system in Great Britain is a majoritarian parliamentary democracy (Hallin & Mancini, 2004). While Great Britain has a multi-party system, the majority voting system has effectively supported a two-party system (Holtz-Bacha et al., 2014). This has for the most part resulted in majority governments made up of one of the two major parties, either the

Labour Party or the Conservative Party. However, in recent years the political landscape has changed considerably, something that has been evident following the 2014 Scottish referendum and the 2016 referendum on Great Britain's membership of the European Union (i.e., Brexit) (Applebaum, 2017). The strengthening of support for the Scottish Nationalist Party (SNP) and the UK Independence Party (UKIP) has made it increasingly difficult for the two larger parties to achieve an overall majority and establish a one-party majority government (Applebaum, 2017). Two of the last three general elections have resulted in a coalition or special agreement[12] between one of the major parties and a smaller party, for example, the Conservative Party/Liberal Democrat coalition (2010-2015) and the current Conservative minority government supported by a special agreement with the Democratic Unionist Party (DUP) following the 2017 election (Prime Minister's Office, 2017).

While there is devolved government in Scotland, Wales and Northern Ireland, Great Britain has a centralised political system with power located in Westminster (Sanders et al., 2011), and power increasingly centralised in the PM's Office (Dowding, 2013; Vogel, 2010). Great Britain has a highly centralised political system compared to Germany (Humphreys, 2012). Müller (2011) describes how "cabinet government has given way to prime ministerial government" (p. 135) in Great Britain. The Prime Minister (PM) has sweeping powers, which unlike the Chancellor in Germany, are not constricted or balanced by federalism, coalitions, or consensus politics (Korte, 2002). Dowding (2013) wrote about what he described as the "prime ministerialisation" of British politics characterised by the centralisation of power in the PM's Office. This can be seen in terms of increased media attention and demands on the PM and also increased institutional resources within the PM's Office, for example, through increased staff numbers such as special advisors and a concentration of media resources (Dowding, 2013, p. 623; Heffernan, 2006). The office has been strengthened with a larger personal office, centralisation of the government's press machine, the increasing importance of cabinet committees, and continued decline in the coordinating role of cabinet meetings (Dowding, 2013, p. 627).

12 The Conservative Party agreed to a special arrangement with the DUP called the "Confidence and Supply Agreement" on December 14, 2017. As part of this agreement the DUP agreed to support the Conservative Party on key votes in parliament. However, it is not a coalition government as there is no joint programme for government or any DUP members within the cabinet.

Vogel (2010) describes how the political system and its institutions shape the structures of government communications differently in Great Britain compared to Germany. In particular, she refers to the absence of federalism, the majoritarian political system which supports mostly one-party governments and the strong concentration of power in the PM's Office. She argues that these system-level differences make it easier for the British government to adapt the structures of government communications according to their own political demands and interests as there is no onus on the government to consult with other parties or coalition partners (Vogel, 2010, p. 75). The following sections in this chapter will outline the many and extensive changes that have occurred in the centralised structures of government communications in Great Britain, a trait that is in stark contrast to the more stable institutional structures found in Germany.

In both countries, executive government organisations such as ministries have their own press offices and resources for carrying out press relations and communications. At the same time, both Germany and Great Britain have centralised organisational structures that coordinate and oversee government communications across all of government. Both countries have centralised structures that were first established after World War II. For example, the BPA was established in 1949 in Germany[13] and the Central Office for Information (COI) was established in Great Britain in 1946 (Cabinet Office, 2011). However, there are large differences in how these centralised structures have developed, in particular, how they have developed over the past twenty years and how they are currently organised.

The main centralised organisation for government communications in Great Britain is the Government Communication Service (GCS) which launched on January 1, 2014, replacing the Government Communication Network (GCN)[14]. In comparison to the BPA in Germany, GCS isn't an executive government organisation with its own direct employees. Instead, it is organised as a professional membership body for all government communicators with the aim of professionalising the communication sector across government. It is, in effect, a professional network. Its remit includes improving the skills and abilities of government communicators through professional training and networking (Government Communica-

13 Information taken from www.bundesregierung.de.

14 Prior to GCN the centralised organisation for government communications was known as the Government Information and Communication Service (GICS). GICS was set up under former Prime Minister Tony Blair which replaced the previous Government Information Service (GIS) (Gregory, 2012).

tion Service, 2015). Table 1 below highlights the different functions and remit of GCS compared to the BPA in Germany. The table shows that the BPA has a strong informational function, while GCS is predominantly a professional body. GCS is located in the Cabinet Office (CO) and is led by Alex Aiken, who is Executive Director of GCS[15].

Table 1. Main Functions of the BPA in Germany Compared to GCS in Great Britain

Federal Press and Information Office	Government Communication Service
Internal communication: – Provide information about the work of government and national and international media coverage (of the government) to government employees, ministers and ministries **External communication:** – Provide information on government policies and decisions on central government websites (e.g., www.bundeskanzlerin.de) – Conduct media relations – Communicate directly with citizens through media and government social media channels	– Providing leadership for communicators – Setting membership criteria and assessing professional skills – Providing support for continuing professional development through learning and development opportunities – Establishing talent management programmes – Setting out career pathways for members – Publishing professional reports and Best Practice – Providing networks for government communication professionals to collaborate – Guiding professional behaviour – Enabling fairer access to the profession – Providing career support and opportunities – Coordinate government communications, support departments and executive agencies

Source: Own Table; information taken from the BPA homepage at www.bundesregierung.de and the Government Communication Service (GCS) Handbook (2015).

15 This was previously a higher ranking position called "Permanent Secretary". The background to the demotion of this position will be explained in more detail further on in this chapter.

In Great Britain, it is not just GCS that plays a centralised role in government communications, the PM's Office and the CO also play a central role in overseeing and coordinating government communications. The centralised organisational structures for government communications are divided across the PM's Office, the CO and GCS. In Great Britain the centralised responsibility for government communications was, until 2011, divided across three government organisations: the PM's Office, the CO and the Central Office of Information (COI) (Vogel, 2010). The COI, which was responsible for government advertising and marketing campaigns, was closed in 2011 in order to reduce the government deficit (Cabinet Office, 2011, 2013). Centralised government communications structures are now located across the PM's Office and the CO, with GCS and its executive director located within the CO. Operating within the PM's Office, is the PM's official spokesman (a civil servant) and also a director of communications who is a special advisor (a political appointee) (Gregory, 2012). According to Gregory "No 10[16] has a communication function including a significant press office which supports departments, the Nations (Northern Ireland, Scotland, Wales), the English regions and the specialist media" (2012, p. 368). Canel and Sanders (2014) highlight that government communications in Great Britain follows the U.S. model where communications is divided between a strategy unit (Office of Communications) and an implementation unit dealing with day-to-day communications (the Press Office), whereas in Germany, communications functions are divided differently. They are divided according to geography (national and international press units) and the type of media (press and social media units) (Canel & Sanders, 2014, p. 108).

In order to understand the current structure of government communications in Great Britain and GCS's function as a professional body, it is necessary to look back to the period when the Labour Party was in government (1997-2004) with Tony Blair as PM. It is important to understand the consequences of this period for government communications, in particular, government actions and communications in the lead up to, and during, the Iraq war (Sanders et al., 2011). The election of a Labour Party government in 1997 under Tony Blair, the appointment of Alistair Campbell as Blair's director of communications and strategy and the government's decision to go to war in Iraq, could be described as a defining period in the history of government communications in Great Britain (Sanders et al.,

16 "No 10" means "Number 10" which is another name commonly used to refer to the PM's Office located at Number 10 Downing Street.

2011). It is a period which has shaped the structures and regulation of government communications to this day. Following Blair's election, there were concerns that government communications was being politicised due to increasing numbers of politically appointed special advisors within government (Gregory, 2012). During this period the number of special advisors increased from 31 to 70 between 1997-1998 and reached a peak of 84 in 2004 (Gregory, 2012, p. 369). This increased the role and influence of political appointees within government ministries. Alongside the increasing influence of political special advisors, the Director of Communications Alistair Campbell, was given the authority to direct civil servants (Gregory, 2012). These developments led to a highly blurred boundary between the work of political advisors and impartial civil servants/government communicators working for GICS[17] (Gregory, 2012). This made it difficult for government communicators, who were meant to be impartial civil servants, to carry out their work free from political influence. This measure was later criticised in a number of reviews of government communications (e.g., House of Lords Select Committee on Communications, 2009; Phillis, 2004). Another example of the politicisation of government communications during this period was the accusation that Alistair Campbell had "sexed up" a government dossier containing false information arguing for the war in Iraq, a dossier which Blair presented in parliament (Gregory, 2012). Gregory describes how the Independent Review of Government Communications, chaired by Bob Phillis, was set up "amid mounting clamour about the politicisation of the civil service, spin, inappropriate use of government services and an increasingly adversarial relationship between the press and the government" (2012, p. 371). The review, which became known as the Phillis Review (2004), led to a significant reorganisation and professionalisation of government communications in Great Britain (Sanders et al., 2011)[18].

17 GICS went on to become GCN and has since become GCS.

18 While this era of government under the Labour Party was a defining period for government communications in Great Britain, however, a study by Garland et al. (2017) examining the mediatisation of the UK Government, found that many of these trends were already emerging following Margaret Thatcher's election as Prime Minister for the Conservative Party in 1979. According to the authors, this included, for example, "the coordination of government presentation, the strategic drive for positive coverage, the demand from ministers for more persuasive communication, and the role of special advisors in providing more politically inspired narratives" (2017, p. 503).

Among the many recommendations of the Phillis Review (2004) were that: GICS be reorganised as the Government Communication Network (GCN) and it should be open to all civil servant communicators; politically appointed special advisors should no longer have the authority to direct civil servants; and the new GCN should be led by a permanent secretary who should be a civil servant of the highest rank rather than a political appointee (Gregory, 2012, p. 371). The report, whose recommendations were accepted in full by the government, was a significant effort to depoliticise government communications as it sought to draw a clear boundary between the role and duties of civil service government communicators and those of politically appointed special advisors (Gregory, 2012). It was also significant that the head of the new GCN would be led by a civil servant of the most senior rank, which was another important part of the effort to depoliticise government communications[19].

The context of the Blair years is critical to understanding why the centralised organisation for government communications was set up as a professional body for civil servants. According to Sanders et al. (2011) "the civil servant head of the Government Communication Network is responsible for establishing standards of excellence and training for the civil service corps engaged in communication" (p. 14). As outlined in Table 1, some of the key tasks of this organisation included the implementation of training programmes for government communicators. According to Gregory "substantial effort was put into developing a strategic planning model which was more marketing-based and aimed at achieving behaviour change" (2012, p. 371).

The focus on professionalisation, training and the demarcation of the roles and responsibilities of government communicators from those of political appointees is an important difference with Germany. However, other striking differences include the amount of money spent on government communications, in particular the amount spent on government advertising and marketing, and the number of people employed in the sector which increased significantly as part of the government's professionalisati-

19 This recommendation by the Phillis Review was implemented. Howell James occupied the position from 2004 to 2008 and Matt Tee from 2008 to 2011. However, the post has since been abolished and replaced by the position of Executive Director, a position that is at a lower grade than the position of Permanent Secretary (Gregory, 2012). Alex Aiken is the current Executive Director of GCS. This post was also supposed to be located in the CO, but it has been moved to the PM's office raising questions about GCS's ability to remain impartial and depoliticised (Gregory, 2012).

on efforts (Gregory, 2012). According to a report by the House of Lords Select Committee on Communications (2009) on the implementation of the recommendations of the Phillis Review "the number of communications staff employed by government departments had risen from 795 in December 1998 to 1376 in September 2008 and that the press officer corps in central Whitehall departments had risen from 216 in December 1998 to 373 in September 2008" (Gregory, 2012, p. 372). In 2009/10 the total cost of communications was £1.01 billion, with £540 million spent on direct communications (advertising and marketing) and £329 million for staffing costs (Cabinet Office, 2011). While the spend on advertising and marketing has been reduced with the abolishment of the Office for Direct Communication (COI) in 2012, there continues to be a considerable focus on government advertising and marketing within government communications in Great Britain. Gregory questions this approach saying,

> While this is laudable in many ways and replicates professional communication in the private sector, the question has to be asked about whether a campaigning approach designed to deliver efficient and effective communications allows enough latitude for the public to be simply informed about policies and processes so that they can hold the government to democratic account. (2012, p. 374)

The focus on professionalisation and strategic communications, in particular large spending on advertising and marketing, appears to be a very different approach to that of government communications in Germany.

In order to further understand the differences in government communications between the two countries, it is also necessary to compare how Great Britain regulates government communications. Unlike Germany's constitution (das Grundgesetz) which outlines the fundamental rights of citizens and the separation of executive powers, Great Britain doesn't have a written coded constitution (Vogel, 2010). This creates an uncertainty in identifying and understanding the institutional structures of government and where the centre of power lies in the British government "not only does the UK lack a written constitution, but also the collection of legal texts and selected laws serving as placeholders can only narrowly set the centre's location" (Döhler, Fleischer, & Hustedt, 2007, p. 11). While the German federal constitutional court plays an important role in regulating communications by the German government, Great Britain takes a non-statutory approach to the regulation of government communications. Regulation is characterised by "enshrining principles of good practice in codes and guidelines" (Sanders et al., 2011, p. 15). The predominant emphasis in these reports and guidelines is on depoliticising government communications through the implementation of codes of ethics and standards of conduct for ministers, civil servants, political advisors and government communicators. This focus can be traced back to the politicisation of government communications under Tony Blair. Table 2 below outlines a number of reports, reviews and codes of practices published since 1997 and demonstrates the difference in approach to the regulation of government communications in Great Britain compared to Germany.

Table 2. Key Regulations Affecting Government Communications in Great Britain

Codes/Guidance/Reports/ Legislation	Purpose/Focus
The Mountfield Report (1997)	Guidance for civil servants and special advisors about their respective roles
Communication Act (2003)	Ensures that government information campaigns remain non-political
Independent Review of Government Communications (2004) (the Phillis Review)	Outlines key principles of government communications and proposes overhaul of structures
Freedom of Information Act (2005)	Disclosure of government information
Propriety Guidance (2006)	Expected standards, practices and behaviour for government communicators
Civil Service Code (1996; updated 2006)	Outlines core values and standards for all civil servants
1st Report of Session 2008-09: Government Communications Report with Evidence (2009) (House of Lords Select Committee on Communications)	Assessment of the implementation of the recommendations of the Phillis Review (2004)
Code of Conduct for Special Advisors (Updated 2010)	Established that advisors cannot instruct civil servant government communicators

Codes/Guidance/Reports/ Legislation	Purpose/Focus
Constitutional Reform & Governance Act (2010)	Put the Civil Service Code on a statutory footing
Ministerial Code (2010; updated 2018)	Standards of conduct for ministers/ requires them to uphold the impartiality of the civil service
Review of Government Direct Communication and the Role of the COI (2011)	Called for the closure of COI / reorganisation of government communications
Government Communication Service Propriety Guidance (2014)	Defines how government communicators can present government policies without political bias

Source: own table; information taken from www.gov.uk; Vogel, 2010; Gregory, 2006, 2012.

Similar to Germany, Great Britain has an institutionalised structure for managing and conducting government media relations. In Germany, government media relations takes place through the BPK. This has ensured a formal, regulated and transparent approach to government media relations by allowing all 900 accredited political journalists regular and equal access to government ministers and their respective spokespersons[20]. However, the Westminster lobby system (more commonly referred to as "the Lobby") operates in a more exclusive and secretive manner. Chadwick describes the Lobby as being "infamous for being one of the most secretive and restrictive systems in the liberal democratic world for managing interactions between senior politicians and journalists" (2017, p. 186). The Lobby, which is in existence for over 200 years (Press Gallery, 2015), refers to an exclusive group of around 200 parliamentary journalists (Chadwick, 2017) that have privileged access to the twice daily Lobby briefings by the PM's spokesperson along with the right to enter the members' lobby in the Palace of Westminster, where they can have informal conversations, or interview MPs, on so-called "lobby terms" (House of Lords Select Committee on Communi-

20 Although as Reinemann and Baugut (2014) point out, there are also examples in Germany of journalists and media organisations having too close relationships with politicians. The authors cite the examples of the Christian Wulff and Karl-Theodor zu Guttenberg affairs which revealed an unhealthy close relationship between the *Bild* newspaper and these politicians.

cations, 2009). On "lobby terms" means that journalists must not attribute their information for a story to any source (BBC, 2015). The Phillis Review (2004) strongly criticised the Lobby system for creating an "inner circle" among journalists with privileged access and described "their credibility damaged by the impression that they are involved in a closed, secretive and opaque insider process" (House of Lords Select Committee on Communications, 2009, p. 12).

One of the defining features of the Lobby is the principle of source confidentiality. The principle of "don't name your source" (i.e., lobby terms) has further contributed to the Lobby's secretive reputation (Press Gallery, 2015). For much of its existence, lobby journalists have been required to use non-attributable sources in their news reports (Chadwick, 2017). However, Alistair Campbell introduced some changes in 2002, which included allowing journalists to attribute information they received during the daily press briefings to "the Prime Minister's official spokesman", and he widened the daily press briefings to include specialist and foreign journalists (Press Gallery, 2015). McNair (2004) outlines some other positive reforms of the Lobby system during the Blair years. For example, Blair introduced a weekly live televised media conference to answer journalists questions and appeared regularly on live political programmes to answer difficult questions (McNair, 2004). In addition, the morning press briefings by the PM's spokesperson have been opened up to all accredited parliamentary journalists, however, the afternoon briefing remains confined to those journalists with exclusive lobby passes (House of Lords Select Committee on Communications, 2009).

Chadwick (2017) says that the Lobby continues to be very much a secretive world and source confidentiality remains a weapon used by all actors involved. The Report of the House of Lords Committee on Communications (2009) examining the implementation of the recommendations of the Phillis Review (2004) found that insufficient reforms have been made to the Lobby. Government ministers continue to politicise information by leaking government announcements to a select group of journalists in order to secure positive news coverage (House of Lords Select Committee on Communications, 2009). The report also described how there was little appetite among journalists (in particular those in the inner circle) for challenging the status quo and making the Lobby more transparent and open to all journalists. Davis (2009) also describes journalists in Great Britain as being very much political actors with the Lobby system enabling journalists to take part in the political process and influence political policy agendas. In order to maintain this close relationship, journalists allow themselves to be instrumentalised by politicians as this ensures continued access to political sources and exclusives (Davis, 2009). According to McNair, during the Blair years this close relationship between politics and media had a highly corrosive effect on political journalism "the journalism of political process betrayed the normative ideals of the fourth estate in a liberal democracy, colluding with the spin doctors and media minders in a cosy insiders' conspiracy against public understanding" (2004, p. 332). However, Davis (2009) also describes political journalist relations in Great Britain as being a two-way relationship; it is intense and close, but it is also antagonistic. Although this relationship is more secretive in Great Britain, it is also more antagonistic than in Germany.

Hallin and Mancini (2004) categorise Great Britain's media system as belonging to the Liberal Model alongside Ireland, the U.S. and Canada. The key characteristics of the Liberal Model include the limited role played by the State in the media system, early development of a mass circulation commercial press, low political parallelism and the strong professionalisation of journalism which is characterised by a neutral style of news reporting (Hallin & Mancini, 2004). Hallin and Mancini acknowledge that Great Britain is an outlier within the Liberal Model and has numerous differences with the U.S. media system. A number of scholars dispute Hallin and Mancini's categorisation of Great Britain within this model and argue that Germany and Great Britain's media systems are in fact more similar (e.g., Brüggemann, Engesser, Büchel, Humprecht, & Castro, 2014; Esser, 2008; Norris, 2011). Brüggemann et al. argue that Great Britain does not belong to the Liberal Model due to its strong public service broadcasting sector and politically polarised tabloid press (2014, p. 1043). They also argue that Germany does not belong to the Democratic Corporatist Model and that the two countries should be categorised together in a new category (Brüggemann et al., 2014). Norris (2011) also criticises Hallin and Mancini's classification of Great Britain and says that it has more in common with the Democratic Corporatist North European Model.

While Great Britain and Germany's media systems have much in common such as highly professionalised journalism, strong public service broadcasting, a strong welfare state (although stronger in Germany) alongside high political parallelism, however, the British media market, in particular the press, could be described as much more competitive, partisan and adversarial (Garland et al., 2017). In this respect, it has more in common with the U.S. media system. Holtz Bacha et al. (2014) describe a much more competitive media market in Great Britain saying that the press market "in the UK is more highly competitive, with a strong tabloid culture and openly partisan; and the more fluid boundaries of privacy, both in terms of legislation and journalistic norms" (p. 168)[21]. Davis (2014) says that due to its majoritarian political system, extreme market forces in the media system, in particular its "free market press business model", that Great Britain is closer to the U.S. model (p. 111). Chadwick (2013) also describes a highly competitive media system in the digital age for which he developed the concept of the hybrid media system. Chadwick describes how "the old media environment, dominated by media and political elites working in traditional television, radio, and newspapers, remains highly significant for British politics, but politics is increasingly mediated online" (2011 b, p. 5). Within Britain's hybrid media environment, news is taking place in real time and social media is affording non-elite actors the opportunity to intervene in "the political information cycle" which has replaced the old 24/7 news cycle (Chadwick, 2011 b, pp. 6-8).

However, despite some scholars suggesting that Germany and Great Britain are most similar media systems, this chapter demonstrated that there continue to be significant differences between the countries across a number of macro-level categories (not just the media system). Section 3.2 outlined the key characteristics of the institutional structures of government communications in Great Britain, a number of significant differences in the political system of Great Britain (e.g., majoritarian, highly centralised political system and prime ministerialisation), and described a more secretive, exclusive and informal approach to political media relations, and finally, a more competitive and adversarial media system (despite some mentioned similarities). The centralised structures for government communications in Great Britain could be described as highly complex (Gregory, 2012), unstable (i.e., constantly changing) and lacking transparency, particularly in relation to the distribution of responsibilities across GCS, the

21 One recent example which signals how the press market in Great Britain differs to other press markets is the example of the Leveson Inquiry. In 2011, former Prime Minister David Cameron established an official inquiry headed by Lord Justice Brian Leveson to investigate the cultures, practices and ethics of the press following the News International phone hacking scandals which had revealed illegal and improper behaviour by the press. The Leveson Report, published in 2012, criticised the too close relationship between politicians and the press, a relationship that lacked transparency, did not serve the public interest, and affected important public policy issues, such as, press regulation (Leveson, 2012, p.1429-1439). One of the recommendations of the report was that Great Britain needed a stronger system of press regulation and a new press authority with legal status.

PM's Office, and the CO. There is little information available as to how communications responsibilities are divided across and within these organisations. While GCS is responsible for the professionalisation of the sector, the real power appears to lie with the PM's Office who has an increasingly centralised role in government and increased media resources. Finally, the need to demarcate partisan from non-partisan communications has come to define the overall approach to the organisation and regulation of government communications in a post-Blair era in Great Britain, a characteristic that has been absent in Germany.

3.3 Summary & Research Guiding Assumptions I

When the overall differences – particularly in relation to the political system and the structures and organisation of centralised government communications – are assessed, it appears appropriate to categorise these countries as being more different than similar (see Chapter 5 for more on the comparative research design of this study). The strong regulation of government communications through the federal constitutional court in Germany compared with a non-statutory approach in Great Britain is a key difference between the two countries. There are also notable differences in how government communications is organised. For example, there is a highly regulated and formalised approach to government media relations in Germany, typified by the BPK. This is in stark contrast with the closed and secretive lobby system in Great Britain. In addition, GCS in Great Britain has been established as a professional body with very different organisational functions to the BPA in Germany.

According to Blumler and Gurevitch "a central ingredient in any framework for comparative political communication analysis must be a set of dimensions specifying how the linkages between the political and mass media organisations may vary in different societies" (1995, p. 61). While it is important to consider how different political systems, media systems and political communication cultures shape political communications in an online age, this chapter has also argued that the centralised institutional structures of government communications is another important structural category that should be considered when examining and comparing communications at lower levels (meso or micro levels), and whether that be offline or online communications.

Table 3 below outlines the key structural categories identified in this chapter. These are the categories most relevant for the comparison of government communications in Germany and Great Britain. While there are many other notable differences between the two countries that could be listed in this table, such as differences in media policy, media concentration and media market size (Humphreys, 2012), however, this table focuses on the differences that this author believes are most influential in shaping government organisational communications.

Table 3. Key Structural (Macro) Differences Between Germany and Great Britain

Key structural variables	Germany	Great Britain
Political System	– Federal State – Decentralised system – Coalition government/cabinet government/consensus politics – Multi-party system/ strong role of parties/ parliamentary factions	– Majoritarian democracy – Centralised system/ Westminster Model – One-party government (typically)/ cabinet government/increasing prime ministerialisation – Multi-party system/two parties dominate
Media System	– Democratic Corporatist Model – Strong regional media (press & broadcasting) – Federal system of media regulation; federal constitutional court plays strong regulatory role; liberal press regulation	– Liberal Model – Media centred around Westminster – National system of media regulation; liberal press regulation – More competitive media market/ highly partisan national press/more influential tabloid press

Key structural variables	Germany	Great Britain
Government Media Relations	– Federal Press Conference (BPK) (membership association) – Formal, regulated and open to all accredited political journalists – Elitist relationship	– The Lobby System (membership association) – Exclusive group of journalists/secretive/non-attributable sources – Elitist/intensely close/highly antagonistic /lack of transparency
Legal System & Regulation of Government Communications	Written codified federal constitution known as Basic law – Federal constitutional court plays important role – 1977 constitutional court ruling; most important ruling related to electoral advertising and public relations as an essential government activity	Unwritten constitution/common law system – Non-statutory approach to the regulation of government communications – Numerous reports, codes of practice, guidance (see Table 2 in this chapter)/ focus on demarcating partisan from non-partisan communications – Phillis Review (2004)

Key structural variables	Germany	Great Britain
Centralised Structures of Government Communications	– Federal Press and Information Office (BPA) – Strong informational function; media relations; direct communications with citizens	– Government Communication Service (GCS) – GCS organised as a professional body; focus on professionalisation of the sector – Complex and unstable centralised structures; GCS, PM's & CO – Demarcation between government communicators and political special advisors – Increasing resources in the PM's Office

Source: Own table; information taken from Chadwick, 2013; Davis, 2009; Dowding, 2013; Gregory, 2012; Hallin & Mancini, 2004; Holtz-Bacha, 2013; Humphreys, 2012; Kocks & Raupp, 2014; Kocks, 2016; Korte, 2002; Müller, 2011; Pfetsch, 2001; Reinemann & Baugut, 2014; Sanders et al, 2011.

Based on the key macro factors identified in this chapter, this study assumes that the centralised organisations for government communications – the BPA and GCS – will both play a prominent role in online government communications in the two countries. However, this study assumes that the PM's office will also play a central and active role in online government communications in Great Britain due to the increasing centralisation of media resources and power in the PM's office. It is also assumed that there will be a stronger personalisation of online government communications around the Prime Minister in Great Britain due to the prime ministerialisation of politics in Great Britain (Dowding, 2013). Due to the consensus and decentralised form of politics and government in Germany, this study assumes that no one organisation will dominate government communications in the online sphere in Germany (although the BPA will play a prominent role). In addition, due to a more regulated and formal organisation of government communications in Germany, this study assumes that government organisations will be more reserved in how they use online technologies for interacting with citizens and media, and that they will use social media primarily as an informational tool. The macro-level factors identified in this chapter will form an important part of the research guiding assumptions of this dissertation. These will be presented in full at the end of Chapter 4 following an examination of organisational and network theoretical perspectives on the changing media environment and the theoretical challenges in comparing organisational government communications in a networked media environment.

4. Theoretical Analysis: An Organisational & Network Perspective

While Chapter 3 presented the key characteristics of the political systems and centralised structures of government communications in Germany and Great Britain, this chapter examines the meso level and seeks to understand the organisational factors that possibly influence how governments use digital technologies. This chapter also examines how the organisational communications environment is changing in a digital age and the consequences of this for the comparative analysis of government communications in a networked media environment. Within the field of political and comparative communications, an organisational perspective of the changes in the new media environment is too often missing (Donges, 2008). There has been a general lack of theoretical reflection within political communications on how the meso level is changing under the conditions of digitalisation and the consequences for the relationship between the macro and meso levels. Instead, the focus within comparative political communications until now, has mostly been on how the macro level shapes communications at the micro level, usually among individual politicians.

There are many theoretical strands of research relevant for this thesis and which are rarely considered together in the field of political communications, that is, organisational, comparative and network perspectives. Section 4.1 will examine how the broader political organisational environment is changing as a result of digital technologies, the new forms of political organisation that are emerging and the consequences for government organisations. Section 4.2 will then look at another overlooked topic within the field of political communications, that is, the government organisational environment. This section will examine how these organisations, as bureaucratic public sector organisations, differ to other types of organisations; how their unique organisational environment is changing as a result of digitalisation and how this environment shapes and constrains the adoption of digital technologies. Section 4.3 will analyse the theoretical development of comparative political communications and consider how this subfield not only overlooks the meso level, but it has yet to reflect on the significant changes in how individuals and organisations interact with politics and the changing relationship between levels of analysis in the new media environment. Finally, Section 4.4 proposes a network perspective as the most suitable perspective for understanding communications in the new media environment and for understanding the changing nature and relationship between macro, meso and micro levels of analysis. The network perspective provides the overarching perspective, or lens, through which this dissertation views government organisational communications and the challenges for government organisations communicating in this networked sphere.

At the end of this chapter, I will bring together the most important findings from this theoretical chapter along with the key findings of the literature review in Chapter 2 and the macro-level factors in Chapter 3, and present a number of theoretically grounded research guiding assumptions around how I expect government organisations in Germany and Great Britain to use online digital technologies such as websites and social media. In summary, the overarching aim of this theoretical section is to better understand the changing organisational communications environment, how this shapes the use of new communications technologies, and more specifically, the challenges for comparing government organisations in the new media environment.

4.1 Political Communications in an Online Age: The Missing Meso Perspective

New digital technologies and the emergence of new types of organisational forms such as large protest, social and political movements (e.g., Occupy movement, Black Lives Matter, the Alt-right, Pegida in Germany, Italy's Five-Star Movement and Bernie Sanders among many others), have called into question previous understandings of organising and what an organisation is. It has triggered a reassessment of fundamental understandings of what constitutes an organisation, what an organisation looks like when one emerges, what should be considered organisational communication in today's online environment and produced new organisational theories such as the communications constitutes organisation (CCO) theory. In this new media environment, traditional political organisations are also undergoing dramatic changes and facing new challenges. As described in Chapter 2, more and more citizens are engaging with politics outside of traditional political institutions and organisations (Bennett, 2012; Castells, 2008). In the face of this crisis of legitimacy, political parties are looking to new political and social movements and adapting some of their organisational practices (Chadwick, 2007; Chadwick & Stromer-Galley, 2016; Penney,

2017). While this thesis does not suggest that government organisations are undergoing the same changes, it argues however, that the wider political organisational environment is still relevant for understanding the challenges that traditional political and government organisations face in the new communications environment.

Political organisations are often overlooked within the study of political communications and digitalisation. Instead, individual actors and organisations are typically labelled as "political actors" and they are rarely differentiated within the field (Donges, 2008; Donges & Jarren, 2014). This results in the micro and meso level both being treated the same, with the consequence that important aspects of the organisational perspective are ignored (Nitschke et al., 2014). According to Nitschke et al. (2014) there is "a tendency to disregard the influence of the organisational form or institutional environments in the online communication of political organisations" (p. 2).

There is a need for greater theoretical reflection on how organisational structures react to changes in the media environment (Donges, 2008), how certain organisational structures constrain the use of online platforms, or how these structures may change and how this differs across countries. For example, within the subfield of government communications, many scholars have highlighted the numerous structural constraints that government organisations face in how they communicate, in particular, legal and political constraints from the macro environment (Chadwick, 2011 a; Graber, 2003; Kocks & Raupp, 2014; Liu et al., 2010). According to Donges (2008), it is important to consider both the macro and meso environment and how these interact with each other. On the one hand, organisations are structures in which individual actors act, while on the other side, organisations are corporate actors that act within society (Donges, 2008, p. 16). In effect, this means that researchers need to examine not only the macro environment and how this shapes communications in organisations, but also how different organisational structures shape the use of digital technologies. Therefore, this study takes a much needed organisational perspective in the examination of online government organisational communications.

There are a number of new theoretical concepts in the field of organisational communications that are relevant for this study. The following section presents a number of theoretical perspectives and new concepts examining the effect of new digital technologies on political organisations, including new concepts of organisation and individual participation in organisations in a digital age. It examines the role of digital technologies in facilitating new forms of political organisation and how some traditional political organisations (e.g., political parties) are responding to changes in the wider organisational environment. It addresses a range of theoretical themes that emerge in the literature, including the increasing prominence of personalised communications and the blurring or hybridisation of organisational boundaries and forms.

4.1.1. Political organisations and digital technologies

According to Gibson and Ward (2009) there are three different perspectives within the field of political communications about how technology is reshaping political organisations. They present three theories of organisational change in an online age: erosion, equalisation and normalisation theory. Erosion theory assumes that the structures of representative democracy are being replaced by a more direct form of democracy. Equalisation theory predicts that new technologies are leading to a levelling of the playing field, that more marginalised actors are entering the political arena and communicating alongside established actors. Thirdly, the normalisation theory assumes that those actors with the most financial resources offline will also dominate online, that the same power structures offline will be replicated online (Gibson & Ward, 2009, pp. 32-34; see also Margolis & Resnick, 2000). However, they say that new technologies are having less of a revolutionary effect on traditional political organisations than newer organisational forms such as protest movements (Gibson & Ward, 2009, p. 34; see also Wright, 2012). While digital technologies may not be radically transforming traditional political organisations, they do highlight an important trend that is affecting organisational communications in a digital age, that is, "the notion of the mass organisational model has been challenged by the individualisation of participation within organisations" (Gibson & Ward, 2009, p.27).

While technologies may not be having the predicted revolutionary effect on traditional political organisations, they are, however, having transformational effects within the field of protest politics. Using the example of the G20 protests from 2008 and protest groups like *Occupy* and *Los Indignados*, Bennett and Segerberg (2012) identified a new organisational logic called "connective action" that has emerged. This new logic is different to collective action efforts which typically involved organisations taking on a clear role within protests and individuals identifying with those organisations leading the collective action (e.g., trade unions, political parties). Instead, connective action involves something different. It is characterised by individuals engaging in personalised message sharing across digital networks. Bennett and Segerberg (2012) identified not only a clear change in how individuals involved in this connective action perceive their relationship with other organisations, but also a change in the role of organisations within such protests or collective action efforts. Unlike previous collective action efforts, connective action involved very little coordination by organisations (or if it did, those organisations took a decidedly background role) and most participants in the protests did not identify with any organisation nor were they members of an organisation (Bennett & Segerberg, 2012, p. 741). Individuals employed personalised action frames to spread the word across their personal digital networks (Bennett & Segerberg, 2012, p. 742). Within this new organisational logic, communication and technologies not only become "a prominent part of the organisational structure" (Bennett & Segerberg, 2012, p. 739), but digital networks become the actual organisation itself. In reference to Castells (2000 a) they describe how "formal organisations are losing their grip on individuals, and group ties are being replaced by large-scale, fluid social networks" (Bennett & Segerberg, 2012, p. 748).

Alongside the increasing prominence of personalised communications in digital networks (as a new form of organising), another emerging characteristic of organisational communications in a digital age, is the intentional blurring of organisational boundaries or the hybridisation of different organisational forms (Bennett & Segerberg, 2012; Chadwick, 2007; Chadwick & Stromer-Galley, 2016). Digital technologies are enabling organisations to take a more flexible approach to their organisational form. Depending on the context or setting, organisations may present themselves as being one of many different forms, for example, an interest group, a social movement or a grassroots political movement. Other times they decide to take a more background role. Organisations are "learning to shift among different organisational repertoires, morphing from being hierarchical, mission-driven NGOs in some settings to being facilitators in loosely linked public engagement networks in others" (Bennett & Segerberg, 2012, p. 758). Chadwick also writes that in the online environment, distinctions are becoming less clear, "rapid institutional adaptation and experimentation" is becoming routine, and organisations look at what other organisations are doing and borrow from others (2007, p. 284).

While Bennett and Segerberg (2012) concentrated on protest politics and movements, Chadwick asks a question that is particularly pertinent for the study of traditional political and government organisations, that is, "is the internet enabling organisational change among traditional interest groups and political parties, such that they are starting to resemble the looser network forms characteristic of social movements?" (2007, p. 284). He says that traditional political organisations, like interests groups, are also adapting digital network repertoires like those described by Bennett and Segerberg (2012). For example, they are borrowing some of the practices of social movements. He refers to "the convergence of previously distinct organisational repertoires" (2007, p. 295). While political parties may not be transforming their organisational form to the same extent as political or social movements, some political parties are however, demonstrating organisational hybridity through the adaption of digital network repertoires (Chadwick, 2007; Chadwick & Stromer-Galley, 2016). Chadwick and Stromer-Galley say that in the U.S. "digitally enabled activist networks are reshaping parties" and encouraging a "party-as-movement mentality" (2016, p. 287). While political parties have often been portrayed as having strong and definite organisational structures, they say that "in reality, their organisational boundaries are porous" (2016, p. 285). However, in their study they focus predominantly on parties and political movements in the U.S. and Great Britain. In particular, they focus on Bernie Sanders's 2016 campaign for the Democratic presidential nomination and Jeremy Corbyn's 2015 election for the Labour Party leadership in Great Britain. It is unclear whether such characteristics would be found among political organisations in other countries with different political systems and media systems such as Germany (Hallin & Mancini, 2004) and in political parties with "establishment" candidates rather than "outsider" candidates like Bernie Sanders and Jeremy Corbyn.

Similar to Chadwick and Stromer-Galley, Penney (2017) also focuses on the Bernie Sanders 2016 campaign to become the presidential nominee of the U.S. Democratic Party and describes the emergence of both formal and informal organisational campaign practices[22]. Penney (2017) describes how the Sanders campaign employed a mix of centralised top-down networks (what the author calls "controlled interactivity"), while also supporting decentralised bottom-up digital networks involving grassroots citizen supporters outside of the formal organisational campaign structures. In reference to Bennett and Segerberg (2012), the author says that "these organisational types combine the personalisation of crowdsourced communication with at least some of the structural hierarchy of more traditional organisations" (2017, p. 421). Penney states that the Sanders campaign demon-

22 For more on how organisations mix formal and informal organisational practices, see also Bimber, Flanagin, & Stohl (2005).

strates that political organisations are starting to integrate both formal and informal communication practices into their campaigns. The Sanders campaign also challenges "the common assumption that organisational capacity stems only from clearly bounded entities" (Penney, 2017, p. 421). There can be formal and informal organisational communication practices carried out by individuals both inside and outside of organisational structures. The author acknowledges that these informal practices (i.e., the use of bottom-up digital networks) also present risks for parties during election campaigns in terms of being able to control what others communicate outside of the formal organisational structure.

Some of the changes outlined by Chadwick and Stromer-Galley (2016) and Penney (2017) in relation to the integration of formal and informal organisational practices within political parties, have also been the result of political parties loosening the criteria for organisational membership and introducing opportunities for citizens to become party supporters or registered supporters rather than fully-fledged members (Chadwick & Stromer-Galley, 2016). This has had a significant effect on organisational boundaries and brought about a more flexible relationship between individuals and formal political organisations, such as in political parties and political interest groups. According to Nitschke and Murphy "membership loses its status as one of the primary concepts for drawing the distinctive line between an organisation and its environment" (2016, p. 264). Online technologies, such as social media, have also contributed to weakening this boundary between an organisation and its environment as individuals can increasingly "participate in organisational activities and benefit from organisational resources without being a formal member of the organisation" (Nitschke & Murphy, 2016, p. 264). One of the consequences of this is that it is becoming increasingly difficult to differentiate between the communications of an individual and a political organisation (Nitschke & Murphy, 2016).

Bimber et al. (2005; 2009) state that new forms of technologically-enabled organisation, demonstrate that collective action is no longer dependent on formal organisation. Instead "informational, communication and coordination functions are requisite for the production of public goods" (Bimber et al., 2005, p. 377). While traditional collective action theory viewed formal organisation as necessary for the production of public goods, they argue that public goods can now be produced without traditional organisations and resources, simply using new communication technologies. The authors reframe collective action theory and describe this new process of collective action as a form of "boundary crossing" between public and private interests. They define it as the following,

> individuals maintain a realm of private interests and actions. When they make these interests or actions known to others in some way, they cross a boundary between private and public realms. When that boundary is crossed by two or more people in conjunction with a public good, a collective action has occurred. (Bimber et al., 2005, p. 377)

While their concept of boundary-crossing is a useful concept for identifying when a collective action takes place in a digital age, it is also useful for understanding how individuals engage in politics in a digital age and the very subtle difference between private and public interests. As mentioned above, it is increasingly difficult to differentiate between individual and organisational communications. However, the concept of boundary crossing suggests that when an individual makes a private interest public, that is the point when the communications of an individual becomes collective and can be considered organisational communication (Nitschke & Murphy, 2016).

However, most of the perspectives on organisation and organisational change described above, view a digital network as being an organisational structure in itself. Within the organisational logic of connective action for example, the network becomes the organisation (Bennett & Segerberg, 2012). However, there are differing viewpoints on what constitutes an organisation, when does an organisation exist and whether networks should be considered organisations. For example, Ahrne and Brunsson (2011) put forward the concept of formal and partial organisations in which they define "organisation as a decided order, including one or more of the elements of membership, hierarchy, rules, monitoring and sanctions" (p. 84). In their view, an organisation is always a decided order, whereas networks are "qualitatively different from organisation" (2011, p. 88). Unlike organisations, networks are emergent social orders rather than decided orders. They believe that an organisation always "constitutes attempts to create a specific order" (2011, p. 90). Organisations can also decide to become a partial organisation incorporating just some of the elements that typically define an organisation. However, their definition of organisation contradicts understandings of organisation as espoused by authors in the field of collective action and contentious politics.

An important process, that was described in some of the studies above, by Chadwick and Stromer-Galley (2016) and Penney (2017), was that organisations look to other organisations in their environment to assess how other organisations are using digital technologies. Although the studies did not explicitly refer to institutional theory, the changes and behaviour that they describe have many commonalities with institutionalism. The concept of environment scanning is known as isomorphism within institutionalist theory, whereby organisations mimic other organisations in their environment (DiMaggio & Powell, 1991; Donges & Jarren, 2014; Donges & Nitschke, 2016; Meyer & Rowan, 1991). Some scholars adopt an institutionalist perspective and argue that this perspective best describes how political organisations are adapting to the mediatisation of politics in a digital age. Adopting this perspective, Donges and Nitschke write that organisations follow the rules and requirements of their organisational environment in order to achieve legitimacy rather than efficiency (2016, p. 128). Donges and Jarren describe the mediatisation of political organisations as being "neither a strategic option nor an enforcement of adaptation...this reaction is the consequence of perceiving the media and mediated communication as gaining in importance in their environment" (2014, pp. 188-189). In response, organisations introduce new rules and resources for communication and changes in communications output. This concept of political organisations as being neither strategic nor rational is an important theoretical contribution in the debate on how organisations adopt digital technologies. In contrast, many of the previous studies outlined in this section (e.g., Bennett & Segerberg, 2012; Chadwick, 2007), presented organisations as being rational actors who make strategic decisions around the use of digital technologies. However, Donges and Jarren present a different perspective and argue that political organisations should rather be considered "as loosely coupled and open systems of action" (2014, p. 187).

4.1.2. Summary: political organisational perspectives

Conventional political organisations are adopting practices that were once the domain of social or political movements in order to shift between different organisational identities (Chadwick, 2007; Chadwick & Stromer-Galley, 2016; Penney, 2017). They are using communication practices that are both top-down and bottom-up, combining elements of top-down controlled interactivity with bottom-up grassroots activities (Penney, 2017). Digital networks allow a loose, flexible identity and a more porous organisational boundary. It allows organisations and individual actors to employ both formal communication practices and informal practices (inside and outside their organisational boundary). It describes how organisational communications and bottom-up interactivity are initiated by individuals active in social networks. Organisational communications can emerge outside of an organisation's boundaries (i.e., grassroots networks) and become integrated into formal communications practices, or such practices co-exist alongside formal organisational practices (Penney, 2017). Based on these new theoretical perspectives, this study assumes that government organisations will also take advantage of online platforms to present a looser, more blurred organisational identity, employing both formal and informal communication practices in their online communications, most notably through increased personalised communications on social media. This study assumes, however, that government organisations will face more constraints than political organisations in adapting to this new organisational environment and using digital technologies due to stronger organisational boundaries, less flexible organisational structures and greater macro constraints.

Until now, organisations have been theoretically conceptualised as structures in which individual actors communicate and those individuals are constrained by the structures in which they communicate (Donges, 2008). However, new theoretical conceptualisations of organisation and organising (e.g., Bennett & Segerberg, 2012; Bimber et al., 2005) suggest that digital technologies are supporting flexible organisational structures in which individuals are able to act both within and outside of these formal organisational structures. The actions of individual actors are less constrained by structures than previously conceptualised by Giddens (1984). Individual relationships to organisations are also becoming more flexible. These theoretical reflections reveal the changing nature and dynamic of organisations and organising and also the changing relationship between individual actors and organisations. Many of these theoretical contributions reveal how organisations can be considered as "structures in which individuals communicate or as outcomes of processes of communication" (Nitschke & Murphy, 2016, p. 272). Communication, information and digital networks are becoming the organisation self, without the need for a formal organisation or a "decided order", as Ahrne and Brunsson (2011) suggested is necessary.

However, while these studies presented interesting examples of organisational change, enabled by digital technologies, it could be argued that many of the cases presented in these studies are quite unique due to the flexible and decentralised nature of new social and protest movements (Gibson & Ward, 2009). The reality is that political parties are most likely adopting digital technologies at a slower pace, in different ways and in a non-rational and non-strategic manner as Donges and Jarren (2014) pointed out. It could also be argued that some of the examples in this section (e.g., Bernie Sanders) are also unique to the media and political system of the U.S. In reference to Burt and Taylor (2001, p. 72), Gibson and Ward (2009) say that the adaption of technologies are "shaped by the social conditions, philosophies and value systems within which the technologies are immersed" (p. 35). In order to understand how different types of organisations adopt technologies, it is necessary to also consider the organisational form and their institutional environments (Mergel, 2016; Nitschke et al., 2014).

Finally, it is necessary to reflect on what the consequences or implications of these changes are for government organisations. These studies revealed that digital technologies are bringing about a transformation in how citizens engage with formal political organisations such as political parties. Individuals are identifying and engaging less with political institutions as alternative avenues emerge for citizens to participate in collective action efforts and affect change outside of formal political organisations (Bennett, 2012; Bimber et al., 2005; Bimber et al., 2009). This raises challenges for formal institutions, such as political parties and governments, in trying to reach and engage with citizens. Government organisations, much like political organisations, must find ways of adapting and maintaining legitimacy (Borucki, 2014 b; Sarcinelli, 2011) in this new organisational and communications environment. If they fail to adapt, they risk becoming irrelevant and creating a larger gap between citizens and their political and governing institutions (Mergel, 2012). The next section in this chapter will consider the unique organisational form of government organisations and the structural limitations that these organisations face in using online technologies[23].

4.2 Government Organisations: An Overlooked Organisational Form

Despite the fundamental importance of government organisations to our system of governance and democracy, they are for the most part, overlooked within political communications research (Graber, 2003; Horsley et al., 2010; Klinger et al., 2015; Sanders et al., 2011). According to Graber,

23 See Table 4 at the end of Section 4.2.2 for an overview of the key theoretical concepts on political organisations in an online age. This table identifies the key differences and similarities between political and government organisations.

the lack of theoretical examination of this organisational form "is puzzling, as well as unfortunate, because the communication problems of public bodies differ from those in the private sector in many important ways" (2003, p. 7). Within the field of political communications, most studies tend to focus on political parties and overlook the many important differences between government/public sector organisations and other types of political organisations (Klinger et al., 2015; Sanders et al., 2011)[24]. In studies examining how political actors are using digital technologies, government organisations are simply treated the same as other political actors (as highlighted in the literature review in Chapter 2).

Consequently, there has been little theoretical reflection within political communications as to how government organisations are adopting and using digital technologies, how this unique organisational environment shapes the use of digital technologies (and vice versa), and most importantly, the democratic consequences of the digitalisation (or non-digitalisation) of communications within these organisations. Just like other political actors, government organisations must also adapt to the changing organisational and communications environment. However, the democratic legitimacy of governments is dependent on their ability to be able to communicate political decisions to the public and media (Borucki & Jun, 2018). Their primary challenge is "to develop institutions and actors that survive and flourish in the face of changing environmental pressures while maintaining commitment to the primacy of democratic values" (Olsen, 2006, p. 8).

As outlined in Section 4.1, the rise of digital technologies supports new and hybrid organisational forms (Chadwick, 2007). These technologies support organisational forms with flexible and decentralised structures (e.g., network organisations). In contrast to these new organisational forms,

24 While this thesis specifically defines government organisations as being executive government organisations only, however, in this theoretical chapter a broader perspective of government organisations is taken. Literature on communications within public sector organisations is also considered as public sector perspectives help to understand the dual role of government organisations as both public sector and government organisations, and consequently the constraints and tensions faced by communications within these unique organisations. Therefore, in this theoretical section, government organisations and public sector organisations are considered the same.

> government organisations have come to organise their communications through a set of centralised and formal working methods (Yates, 1993). External communication to broad audiences widely came to be seen as an activity that needs to be controlled, to prevent damage to the bureaucratic organisation (Perrow, 1986; Weber, 1968). (Meijer & Torenvlied, 2014, p. 144)

In order to theoretically reflect on, and understand, how government organisations are adapting, the next section examines the unique organisational constraints that they face (Mergel, 2016) compared to other organisations (Liu et al., 2010). It is also necessary to examine some of the important organisational changes that have taken place in the public sector in recent decades. Finally, this section considers the democratic consequences of organisational changes such as the "de-bureaucratisation" of public organisations (Olsen, 2006, p. 8). While the emergence of new organisational forms and logics does not mean that older bureaucratic organisational forms are also becoming more hybrid or are being replaced by digital networks, it means that government organisations face unique challenges in adapting to and maintaining legitimacy (Borucki & Jun, 2018) in this new organisational environment.

4.2.1. Government organisations as unique organisational structures

First and foremost, government organisations differ from other organisations due to their democratic and constitutional[25] duty to communicate government decision-making to the public. Canel and Sanders (2013), for example, define government communications as "the role, practice, aims and achievements of communication as it takes place in and on behalf of public institutions(s) whose primary end is executive in the service of a political rationale, and that are constituted on the basis of the peoples' indirect or direct consent and charged to enact their will" (p. 4). This definition makes clear that the legitimacy of executive government organisations rests on their ability to communicate government decisions to the citizens that elected them (i.e., the government ministers and politicians that are in charge of these executive organisations).

25 As already highlighted in Chapter 3, in Germany, a decision by the Federal Constitutional Court in 1977 ruled that government public relations is a necessity in order to enable the formation of the political will by citizens (Holtz Bacha, 2013, p.48-49).

Government organisations are described as being unique for a number of reasons, for example, due to their public interest function and their central location within the political system (Graber, 2003; Horsley et al., 2010; Liu et al., 2010; Schillemans, 2012). While all organisations are shaped and constrained by the societies in which they are located (Donges, 2008, p. 17), government organisations face a wider array of institutional and environmental constraints than other organisational forms and this influences how they communicate (Graber, 2003; Holtz-Bacha, 2013; Horsley et al., 2010; Kocks & Raupp, 2014; Liu et al., 2010). It also constrains and shapes how they use digital technologies (Mergel, 2016). A number of scholars highlight the lack of theoretical development within this under-researched field (Graber, 2003; Liu et al., 2010). The most significant theoretical contributions to date have been a number of typologies identifying the organisational characteristics that differentiate communications in these organisations from, for example, communications in the private sector. According to Liu et al., while political science and public administration research have long recognised these differences (2010, p. 211), the field of political communications has yet to catch up theoretically in this regard.

Graber (2003) draws on Rainey, Backoff and Levine's (1976) typology which differentiated public and private organisations according to a number of external environmental factors and internal structural factors. Some of the external environmental (system) factors that differentiate public organisations from private organisations include: less open market competition, more legal and formal constraints, stronger political influences, unique public expectations and public scrutiny (Graber, 2003). In terms of structural differences, these organisations are more complex, experience more top-level control (top-level managers are often political appointees who stay in office for a limited period) with employees generally having little decision-making autonomy (Graber, 2003, p. 8). The work of communicators within public agencies is difficult, due to the sheer size of public organisations, the vast array of public organisations and agencies with which they must coordinate information along with the lack of decision-making power and control that communicators have over budgets and personnel (Graber, 2003, pp. 9-11).

Graber (2003) describes bureaucratisation and centralisation as significant barriers to effective communication in government organisations and public sector agencies. Government organisations are organised as bureaucratic structures and this results in a hierarchical approach to communication. This type of communication "impedes the flow of information that does not fit precisely into the formally established patterns" (Graber, 2003,

p. 76). Hierarchical bureaucratic organisations support a de-personalised form of communications. Graber (2003) states that in large organisations with a vast array of functions centralisation of communications is regarded as highly efficient. The central message is how the structure of these organisations shapes the flow of information (2003, p. 89). While Graber's research focuses on internal communications within public organisations in a pre-digital era, the de-personalisation of communications in public organisations could be regarded as a potential obstacle for communicating in a media environment characterised by personalised communications in digital networks.

Liu and Horsley examined the differences between public and private organisations and designed a model for decision making within public sector organisations (Horsley et al., 2010; Liu & Horsley, 2007; Liu et al., 2010). Their model, the *Government Communication Decision Wheel* (Horsley et al., 2010; Liu & Horsley, 2007), focuses attention on the factors that shape communications in the government and public sector organisational environment. The model identifies four microenvironments in which public communications takes place, and nine environmental attributes that constrain the use of communications by these organisations (see Figure 1 below). The microenvironments in Figure 1 represent and draw attention to the complex and multi-level nature of government communications. Government organisations must communicate across, and within, many different levels of government, for example, the federal, state and local level (the model is based on the U.S. federal system). In Figure 1 the four microenvironments include: the multilevel (when two or more levels of government must communicate with each other), inter-governmental (two or more organisations at the same level of government), intra-governmental (communication decisions within a single organisation) and external microenvironment involves communications with other non-government actors (Horsley et al., 2010).

Figure 1. Horsley et al.'s Government Communication Decision Wheel

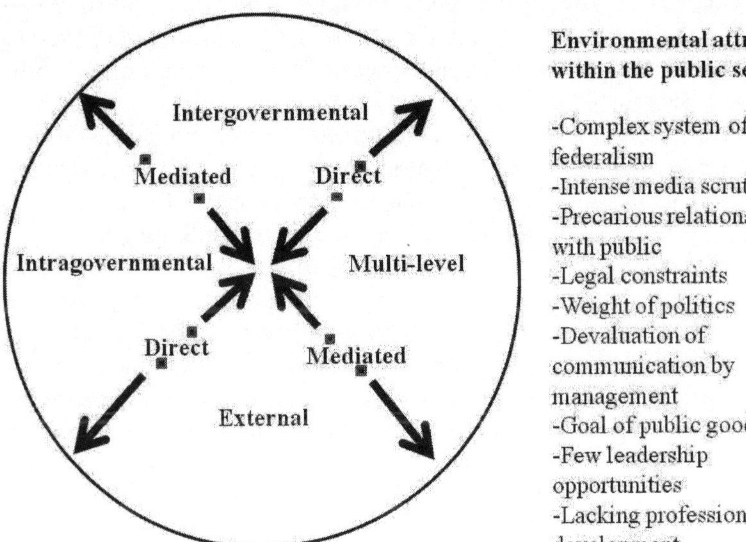

Source: Horsley et al. (2010, p.271)

Each microenvironment is affected by certain environmental attributes more than others, for example, politics affects the intergovernmental and multilevel environment more than the other two microenvironments, while legal constraints affects communications in all four environments (Liu et al., 2010, p. 195). A key finding of their empirical research was that even amongst government communicators at the same level of government, they each faced different constraints and opportunities within their organisations (Liu et al., 2010, p. 195). The most important point of their theoretical model is that government organisations communicate not just with different levels of government, but they must also coordinate and communicate with other government organisations and agencies at the same level. In addition, they each face different constraints and opportunities depending on their organisation. This model is important as it draws attention to the complex multi-level organisational environment in which government organisations communicate. Finally, many of the environmental attributes that they identify as constraining government communications, for example, political influence and legislation, are similar to those attributes identified by Graber (2003).

In a survey of U.S. government communicators and corporate communicators Liu et al. (2010) found support for their hypotheses (and their government communications model, the *Government Communication Decision Wheel*) that the work of government communicators is more strongly influenced and constrained by a number of factors, that is, politics, public pressure, frequency of communication with primary publics, inadequate budgets, interaction with outside organisations, frequency of media scrutiny, perceived negative media coverage and legal frameworks (Liu et al., 2010, p. 204). The findings showed that factors such as the influence of politics and insufficient budgets affected the extent to which government practitioners could be creative in their message development. While Horsley et al.'s (2010) model and Liu et al.'s (2010) survey were specifically designed for understanding government communications in the U.S. federal system of governance, this study assumes that many of these factors and the multi-level and complex organisational environment also affect government communications in other countries.

One of the categories that appears throughout each of these models and typologies is the strong influence of politics within government/public sector organisations. This category refers to the tension that politics triggers within these organisations, a tension that is central to understanding communications within this organisational environment. Government/public sector organisations, and the civil servants working within them, have a mandate to carry out their work in a manner that is accountable, transparent, impartial and in the public interest. They have a mandate to not only communicate government decisions to citizens, but they must do it in a neutral (i.e., non-partisan), factual and comprehensive manner that respects various rules and laws, such as, freedom of information laws and public service codes of conduct (Figenschou et al., 2017; Horsley et al., 2010). However, at the same time these organisations also serve the political interests and demands of the incumbent minister who may require more proactive and persuasive communications in order to paint him/her in a positive light (Figenschou et al., 2017, p.412). Within these organisations public service codes of conduct apply to civil servants, but they do not apply to ministerial staff and politicians (Head, 2007). This brings about a constant tension between the public service and political interests of the organisation, and tensions for those working within it (as was the case in Great Britain as outlined in Chapter 3) (Garland et al., 2017). Figenschou et al. (2017), who examined the increasing personalisation of ministerial communication in Norway, assumed that laws and rules preventing communications that serves the incumbent during election campaigns would constrain, for example, the personalisation of ministerial communications. However, they found that in practice "lines are more blurred, as public service laws and freedom of information acts, even if they define vital constitutional principles that must be respected, do not specify how communication should be organised or directed in practice" (p.415). While previous typologies and models of government communications highlighted "political influence" as a factor that shapes communication within these organisations, Figenschou et al.'s (2017) study drew attention to the fact that it is often the personal motivations, ambitions and media competencies of the minister that influences communications (p.421-422). Most importantly, the study highlights how the line is often blurred between ministerial and party political communications despite legislation and codes of practice attempting to draw a dividing line between the two. As communication professionals work under increasing stress and time pressures in a new media environment, it is becoming increasingly difficult to maintain a clear distinction between the two (Figenschou et al., 2017). In a study by Thorbjørnsrud, Figenschou, and Ihlen (2014), examining the effect of the mediatisation of politics on public bureaucracies in Norway, they found that it is not just the top-down demands of political leaders that influences communications, but it is also civil servants themselves who "perceive it as strategically important to be in the news media to strengthen the reputation and the public perception of the organisation as such, beyond the reputation of the elected government and the party it represents" (p.17). They also found that despite public service codes and laws around the need for neutral, impartial and comprehensive information, civil servants are adapting to the norms and expectations of the media and producing proactive and persuasive communications that paints their work and organisation in a positive light (Thorbjørnsrud et al., 2014).

In the previous section (Section 4.1) on political organisations and digital technologies, there appeared to be an underlying assumption within the field of political communications that new flexible organisational forms are desirable and necessary in order to communicate in a networked media environment. Some studies question whether bureaucratic organisational forms are still relevant in today's communications environment (Meijer & Torenvlied, 2014). However, in the case of government organisations, it is equally questionable whether network organisational forms present a more appropriate or improved form of organisation for the public sector (Olsen, 2006). Olsen questions whether bureaucratic organisations are in fact undesirable and obsolete. He says that questions around what is a desirable form of public organisation are directly connected to normative questions and expectations of government, governance and democracy (Olsen, 2006). Bureaucracy, as a form of organisation goes hand in hand with understandings of democratic governance "administration is based on the rule of law, due process, codes of appropriate behaviour, and a system of rationally debatable reasons. It is part of society's long-term commitment to a Rechtsstaat and procedural rationality for coping with conflicts and power differentials" (Olsen, 2006, p. 3). Bureaucracy signifies rationality and presumes that public organisations and administration operate in a rational manner. Rules, codes of conduct and procedures are key characteristics of bureaucratic organisations (Olsen, 2006).

Olsen (2006) outlines the two dominant, but contradictory criticisms of bureaucracy, one is that organisations are not bureaucratic enough (they are unresponsive and unaccountable) and the other is that they are too bureaucratic (inflexible and inefficient). The second criticism is the charge most often laid before public organisations. In response to these criticisms "Reforms based on neoclassical economic ideology and private management ideology have prescribed privatisation, deregulation, market competition, and commercialisation" (Olsen, 2006, p. 6). These criticisms led to a new organisational perspective within the public sector called *New Public Management* (NPM). According to the NPM perspective "Citizens are a collection of customers with a commercial rather than a political relationship to government, and legitimacy is based on substantive performance and cost efficiency and not on compliance with formal rules and procedures" (Olsen, 2006, p. 6). Compared to the traditional bureaucratic perspective, organisational legitimacy is instead based on flexibility and achieving value-for-money and cost efficiency rather than upholding certain rules and procedures (Olsen, 2009). NPM was first introduced in the U.S. in the 1980 s and then spread throughout the Western world, with the U.S., Great Britain and New Zealand regarded as the pioneer countries (Müller, 2011). NPM was an attempt to de-bureaucratise the public service and it shifted government responsibilities out to semi-public and private organisations blurring the boundary between the public and private sector (Schillemans, 2012).

A number of scholars warn that the risk of NPM, that is, a de-bureaucratisation of public administration, is the politicisation of public organisations, with public servants becoming more behoven to political interests (Müller, 2011; Olsen, 2006). The adoption of new organisational forms or a move away from bureaucratic organisational structures, could lead to a loss of an important separation of powers (Olsen, 2006). This could lead to more politicised communications and a threat to the legitimacy of these public organisations. Dunleavy et al. (2015; 2006) write that the NPM movement stalled in the early 2000 s and a new organisational culture took over, a culture that centred around the integration of information technologies into governance, public management and policy making. Dunleavy et al. (2015; 2006) refer to this new form of public management as *Digital Era Governance* (DEG). However, "the legacies of the Weberian model and NPM have constrained the shift to the digital era" (Dunleavy & Margetts, 2015, p. 5) and instead, public organisations have been left with a mix of organisational structures and forms[26]. They state that DEG remains an ideal type "pursued to varying degrees by different governments and different agencies and departments within governments" (Dunleavy & Margetts, 2015, p. 4)[27]. While Graber (2003) and Horsley et al. (2010) have analysed the organisational factors that shape and influence government communications more generally, in recent years, Mergel (2016; 2013) and Chadwick (2011 a) have examined the factors that shape the use of social media and online citizen engagement initiatives within government organisations. Their findings confirmed that many of the same internal organisational factors also shape the use of new digital technologies. For example, Chadwick (2011 a) who looked at the institutional factors that influenced an online citizen engagement initiative at the local government level in the U.S., found that "budget constraints and general organisational instability, internal policy shifts, political ambivalence, the perception of legal risks, and the tensions created by outsourcing" (p. 35), all strongly determined the outcome of this engagement process within government.

According to Mergel (2016), different government organisations have different goals and they integrate digital technologies such as social media according to their own organisational missions. This means that not every government organisation will institutionalise social media in the same way or to the same degree (2016, p. 146). Through the implementation of rules and regulations, the government organisational setting shapes, constrains and delays the use of social media (Mergel, 2016)[28]. Unlike in political organisations where the adoption of new technologies can emerge from the bottom-up (e.g., by activists or supporters), technology adoption in govern-

26 In a similar vein, Van Dijk and Winters-van Beek (2009) describe three competing modes of governance in the public sector: traditional, market and network modes of governance. Each of these modes have to compete with each other.

27 It is important to note that the authors are referring to public organisations in Great Britain, the U.S., Canada, Australia, New Zealand and the Netherlands.

28 In this paper, Mergel (2016) is specifically referring to the use of social media by executive government departments in the U.S. federal government.

ment organisations "is usually seen as an investment decision that is made top-down and rolled out throughout the organisation. Technology acceptance follows existing policies and guidelines and has to be aligned with the existing technology use paradigm in government organisations" (Mergel, 2016, p. 143). She states that in order to understand technology adoption, we must look at the internal management practices and regulations within these organisations.

Her findings suggest that the more formalised or institutionalised social media becomes within government organisations, the less interaction or experimentation takes place as new regulations and codes of practice are drawn up and implemented (Mergel, 2016; 2013). However, she views this professionalisation of social media in a positive light,

> while formalisation might sound counterproductive to the interactive, fast and furious nature of social networking sites, these professionalisation efforts show mission-driven diversity of communication needs. Social media directors create diverse modes of online interactions and are adapting them based on organisational needs and align them with the mission of the organisation. (Mergel, 2016, p. 146)

Social media appears to diffuse in these organisations in a non-rational way (Mergel & Bretschneider, 2013). Mergel and Bretschneider (2013) describe how social media emerges in a three-step process, in the first phase organisations adopt social media based on what they see other organisations doing in their environment. It is only after they first start to use social media that the organisation reacts and considers the strategic purpose of these technologies (second stage of the diffusion process). It is in this stage that they consider the introduction of codes of practice and guidelines around the use of these technologies. In the final stage, these new rules and guidelines become formalised and constrain interaction or experimentation (Mergel & Bretschneider, 2013). Different organisations are at different stages of this process. It is noteworthy that these bureaucratic – supposedly rational – actors, implement these technologies in a way that appears to be non-rational or strategic. The idea of government organisations as being bureaucratic rational actors seems to be at odds with the reality of how they adopt digital technologies. Despite their bureaucratic organisational nature, government organisations appear to adopt technologies in a non-rational way and this eventually leads to a more formalised use of these technologies as they become institutionalised.

4.2.2. Summary: government organisational perspectives

The previous section demonstrated just how different government organisations are compared to political organisations due to their bureaucratic and inflexible organisational structures. They communicate in an organisational environment that is complex, multi-level and subject to political (influence) and legal constraints, among other constraints. Nevertheless, this thesis argues that they face some of the same challenges as political organisations, such as, how to adapt to and communicate in an increasingly individualised and personalised online communications environment. There also appears to be some similarities, for example, both government and political organisations seem to adopt digital technologies in a non-rational way. Table 4 highlights and compares the key theoretical findings from Sections 4.1 and 4.2. It identifies the various similarities and differences between political and government organisations in how they adopt digital technologies. Table 4 also reiterates the unique constraints that set government organisations apart from other organisations. They not only have different organisational functions, but even amongst government organisations they differ greatly in terms of how they use digital technologies and the constraints they face. This thesis argues that the organisational and institutional environment strongly influences how government organisations adopt technologies in different ways. It will also be characterised by a top-down and controlled approach to communication.

Table 4. Key Features of Technology Use by Political & Government Organisations

Political Organisations	Government Organisations	
Characteristics	Characteristics	Constraints
– Controlled interaction – Mostly top-down, but can emerge bottom-up – Environment scanning/ imitation – Flexible boundaries; individuals can move in and outside these boundaries – Hybrid, flexible identity – Formal and informal organisational practices – Individualised/personalised communication in digital networks – Non-rational adoption of online technologies	– Highly centralised organisational structures – Institutionalisation & formalisation leads to less interaction/innovation – Top-down controlled – Environment scanning & imitation – Definite organisational boundaries – Bureaucratic form – Non-rational adoption of online technologies – Multi-level communications environment	– Complex multi-level communications environment[29] – Political, legal and budgetary constraints at all levels of government – Incomplete public service/ organisational reform e.g., NPM & DEG – New rules, codes of practice, regulations constrain technology use – Differing organisational missions

Source: Own table; information taken from Bennett, 2012; Bennett & Segerberg, 2012; Bimber et al., 2005; Chadwick, 2007; Chadwick, 2011; Chadwick & Stromer-Galley, 2016; Donges & Jarren, 2014; Dunleavy & Margetts, 2015; Graber, 2003; Horsley et al., 2010; Mergel, 2013, 2016; Olsen, 2006; Penney, 2017.

Graber (2003) described bureaucratisation and centralisation as significant barriers to effective communication in government organisations and public sector agencies. Due to their bureaucratic organisational form, they

29 This factor is repeated here as I consider it to be something that differentiates the government organisational environment from the political organisational environment, but it is also something that constrains and strongly influences communications in public/government organisations.

have less flexible boundaries and increasing codes of practice and regulations constraining how government organisational actors use digital technologies. As these technologies become more institutionalised, it seems that their usage is becoming more controlled from the top-down (Mergel, 2016). Public organisations have also undergone significant organisational change over the past twenty years (e.g., NPM and digital government). This has also shaped how communications are structured and used within these organisations (e.g., focus on cost-efficiency and efficient delivery of services rather than interaction and dialogue). However, at the same time there is a constant tension between public and political interests within government organisations, and this can sometimes lead to a blurred boundary between non-partisan public communications and more persuasive political communications (despite the existence of laws and codes of practice regulating a strict divide). In a new media environment, this public service/political tension could lead to an increasing politicisation of government communications as social media supports more personalised forms of communications. Nevertheless, the theoretical perspectives outlined in this section suggest that government organisations will be much slower and resistant to organisational change in a digital age than political organisations.

4.3 Comparing Political Communications in a Digital Age

Comparative research is necessary in order to better understand how different political and media systems (Hallin & Mancini, 2004) or different political communication cultures (Pfetsch, 2003) shape and influence the use of communication technologies by organisations and individuals. Comparative communications is to a large extent about trying to understand how different levels of analysis (typically the macro and micro levels) relate to each other, interact and shape one another (Pfetsch & Esser, 2012). In reference to Blumler, McLeod and Rosengren (1992), Pfetsch and Esser stressed the importance of the systemic or macro context "comparative research guides our attention to the explanatory relevance of the macro-contextual environment for communication processes and outcomes. It aims to understand how the systemic context shapes communication phenomena differently in different settings" (2012, p. 28). While much of comparative communication research has focused on the relationship between traditional mass media and politics, more recent research has highlighted that digital technologies are also shaped by the political and economic interests of media and governments (Castells, 2011 b; Svensson, 2015; Van Dijk, 2012). Newer digital technologies are far from being neutral; they are influenced by the macro and organisational environments (as Sections 4.1 and 4.2 demonstrated) in which they are used.

As the previous sections in this chapter have illustrated, not only are there significant changes taking place within political and government organisations as a result of digital technologies, the government organisational environment is highly complex and faces unique challenges and constraints in this regard. One of the central arguments in this thesis is the need to better understand the meso level of analysis within online political communications. As Donges (2008) states, we need to connect the macro and micro through the analysis of the meso level. This study argues that this theoretical issue also needs to be addressed within comparative communications research. Theoretical development within comparative political communications research has generally overlooked the meso level as a distinct and separate level of analysis. Previous comparative models and typologies (e.g., Hallin & Mancini, 2004; Pfetsch & Esser, 2012) do not sufficiently explain the role of the organisational environment and how it relates to the macro and micro level, how different types of organisations may adapt communication technologies differently and how the relationship between these levels is changing in the new media environment.

While this author is fully aware that comparative political communications is not a theoretical approach, nonetheless, all comparative research requires a certain amount of theoretical reflection around levels of analysis and how they relate to each other. This dissertation argues that there is a need for a theoretical consideration of the meso level and how the meso level should be incorporated into comparative communications models. This section analyses to what extent previous comparative communications models can explain how political or government organisations are communicating in a digital era. In order to do this, this section first provides a critical overview of previous comparative approaches and theoretically reflects on the aspects that are missing from these models.

There have been a number of important theoretical contributions in the field of comparative political communications, mostly in the form of models, heuristics and typologies. These have served as important starting points for theory building within the field (Esser & Pfetsch, 2017). A number of influential comparative approaches take an institutional/macro perspective such as Siebert, Peterson and Schramm's (1956) *Four Theories of the Press* and Hallin and Mancini's (2004) *Three Models of Media and Politics*, which examine how different political ideologies (in the case of Siebert et al.) or different political systems (in the case of Hallin and Mancini) shape media systems. Alongside these typologies, there are also useful heuristic models, such as the *Political Communication System*, which builds on earlier work by Blumler and Gurevitch (1995) and was developed further by Pfetsch and Esser (2012). Finally, there are also a number of comparative conceptual approaches that seek to bring together a macro and micro perspective by examining the attitudes, roles and norms of individuals working within media and political institutions. Substantial theoretical contributions in this regard, include the concept of comparing political communication cultures (Pfetsch, 2003), comparing news cultures (Esser, 2008) and comparing journalism cultures (Hanitzsch, 2012).

As mentioned, one of the most influential comparative communications models is Hallin and Mancini's (2004) *Three Models of Media and Politics*, which takes an institutional approach to comparing media systems. It examines how different types of political systems have shaped the media systems in eighteen different western democracies. Their study provides an important typology for classifying eighteen Western European and North American established democracies into three models of media and politics which they categorise as the Liberal, Democratic Corporatist and Polarised Pluralist models. Although it was, and still is, a significant contribution to the field, it also has many shortcomings. Their typology takes a very narrow view of political systems and they overlook a number of important political characteristics at the macro level. For example, they do not consider whether a political system is decentralised (e.g., a federal system) or centralised (Humphreys, 2012), or whether coalition governments are formed on a mandatory or voluntary basis, or the design of political institutions (Rice & Somerville, 2017). Instead, Hallin and Mancini (2004) narrowly focus on whether a political system is a majoritarian or multi-party system. In addition, their understanding of a media system belongs to a pre-digital era. They attribute too much importance, for example, to the historical development of the mass commercial press and entirely overlook the development of broadcast and digital media (Norris, 2011). According to Hallin and Mancini (2004), the most important categories of a media system are: the role of the state in the media (in the governance of public service broadcasting), the historical development of a mass circulation press (no consideration of TV or Internet), the degree to which journalism is professionalised, and finally, the extent to which political parallelism is on display in the press (focus on party press parallelism). They also overlook other influential factors at the macro level such as the legal system of a country and how media policy is decided, for example, the strong role of a constitutional court as is the case in Germany (Humphreys, 2012, p. 168)[30].

Not only are there a number of missing macro variables within their model, but Hallin and Mancini (2004) draw connections between political and media variables that are questionable. One of their most important assumptions is that the more commercial a media market becomes (i.e., like the Liberal/American media model), the less politicised the media and news reporting will be (Hallin & Mancini, 2004). This assumption appears to be rooted in the convergence thesis (or Americanisation), that is, the idea that all western media systems are moving along a path towards the American model. However, this theory has been proved to be false (Humphreys, 2012), and Mancini (2015) has acknowledged that commercialisation and hyper competitiveness appears to be leading to increased political polarisation rather than a more neutral form of reporting. He says "the new commercial logic has not determined the end of the deeply rooted partisanship and elite orientation. Partisanship has mixed with commercialisation" (2015, p. 10). While this thesis does not doubt that the macro environment still influences communications at lower levels, it is necessary, however, to reconsider previous assumptions around how media and political systems shape each other and the macro factors that are more likely shaping political communications today.

According to Reese and Shoemaker (2016) in their re-conceptualisation of the *Hierarchy of Influences Model* for a networked public sphere, they highlight another weakness in taking an institutional approach to comparative research. While in their paper they are specifically referring to comparing journalism cultures, they point out that an institutional comparative approach often "overestimates the degree of media homogeneity in countries" (2016, p. 25) and overlooks important differences within countries. Comparative research needs to not only reconsider the macro-level factors shaping communications at other levels, it also needs to consider the differences within countries in order to better understand the factors that are shaping the use of digital technologies in today's media environment.

Pfetsch and Esser's (2012) heuristic model, the *Political Communication System*, details how different political settings result in different types of political communication systems. Their model adopts a top-down approach highlighting how the interaction between media and political ac-

30 For a more detailed analysis of the macro environments in Germany and Great Britain, please see Chapter 3.

tors (this includes individuals, organisations and institutions) is shaped by different political and media systems and in turn this shapes message flows to the public and media effects on the public. In this model, they conceptualise political communications as an interplay between communication actors, outcomes and these roles, and these interactions and outcomes are affected by the contexts in which they take place (Pfetsch & Esser, 2012, p. 31). In reference to Norris (2001), Pfetsch and Esser state "the flow of messages operates top-down from political and media actors to the public, horizontally through linkages among political actors through the media, and also bottom up from public opinion toward government authorities and legacy media organisations" (2012, p. 31). Again in reference to Norris (2011), Pfetsch and Esser acknowledge that there has been a "sea change" in political communications due to the role of new digital technologies; they describe "a new era for comparative political communication research" (2012, p. 26). However, in a recent updated version of this heuristic, they said that despite the emergence of a more complex communications environment their heuristic, the Political Communication System, remains as valid as before (Esser & Pfetsch, 2017).

Norris (2011) heavily criticises Hallin and Mancini stating that, due to the fragmentation of the communications environment and the proliferation of information sources, it is questionable whether earlier comparative approaches and classifications are still relevant, approaches that were based on traditional understandings of mass communication and media systems. This thesis believes that these criticisms also apply to other comparative approaches and heuristic models. Current comparative models do not reflect, nor explain, the complexity and scale of the transformations that have taken place in political communication systems in an online age and the various factors at the macro and meso level that shape the use of digital technologies. While the rationale of a heuristic model is to reduce complexity, it could be argued that previous models have simplified media systems to the extent that it is no longer possible to identify the factors that are shaping communications in today's media environment and how the relationship is changing between the different levels of analysis.

In considering the conceptual challenges of comparing media systems in a globalised world, Pfetsch and Esser argue that it is not the levels of analysis that should be changed, but instead, comparative research needs to increasingly examine communication phenomena at all levels of analysis in society, rather than focusing on just one level (2008, p. 122). In a similar vein, Esser calls for,

> a multilevel approach in comparative communication research where the national level is merely one among many levels. The nation-state has long ceased to be the only meaningful category; as such, additional levels of analyses—both above and below the nation-state—must be included, depending on the research question of inquiry. (Esser, 2013, p. 121)

Esser points out that the focus should not only be on the macro level, but on different levels and also examination within levels. This is similar to the criticism of Reese and Shoemaker (2016) who warned against overlooking important differences within countries and differences within levels of analyses.

For example, in a study comparing news cultures in Germany, Great Britain, the U.S. and France, Esser (2008) not only considers how differences in the relationship between media and politics at the national level shape news cultures, but he also compares organisational differences within each news culture. He introduces an important second level of analysis, that is, to look at how different types of media organisations also shape news cultures (e.g., public versus commercial broadcasting organisations) within these countries. Although Esser (2008) found no significant differences between the different types of news organisations in how they shape news content, the consideration of additional levels, in particular, the *within level* analysis and also the organisational level, was nevertheless an important theoretical development for comparative communications research designs[31].

Figure 2 adapts aspects of Esser and Pfetsch's (2017) updated heuristic model of the *Political Communication System*, aspects of Horsley et al.'s (2010) *Government Communication Wheel* (see also Figure 1 in Section 4.2.1) which emphasised the multi-level environment of government communications and the various organisational factors that constrain communications. Finally, this model features a number of new aspects that stem from the findings outlined in Sections 4.1 and 4.2 into how political and government organisations are adapting new digital technologies and the changing relationship between the meso and micro level as a result of more personalised communications. The list of organisational influencing factors listed on the right side of the model are a mix of factors that emer-

31 Esser (2008) also included a third level of analysis, the transnational level, to examine to what extent news cultures are shaped by transnational factors rather than necessarily the macro level.

ged in the theoretical analysis of government organisations in Section 4.2. This list incorporates some that were previously identified by Graber (2003) and Horsley et al. (2010), but also new factors related to digital technologies, such as the increasing use of codes of practice to regulate and manage social media use within these organisations (Mergel 2013; 2016). The list of factors also includes reform measures that took place in public service organisations and also the specific policy focus of a government organisation, a factor that could potentially influence the extent to which an organisation adapts new technologies. Figure 2 seeks to bring together all these aspects to create a model for comparing government organisational communications in an online age.

Figure 2. Model for Comparing Government Organisational Communications in an Online Age

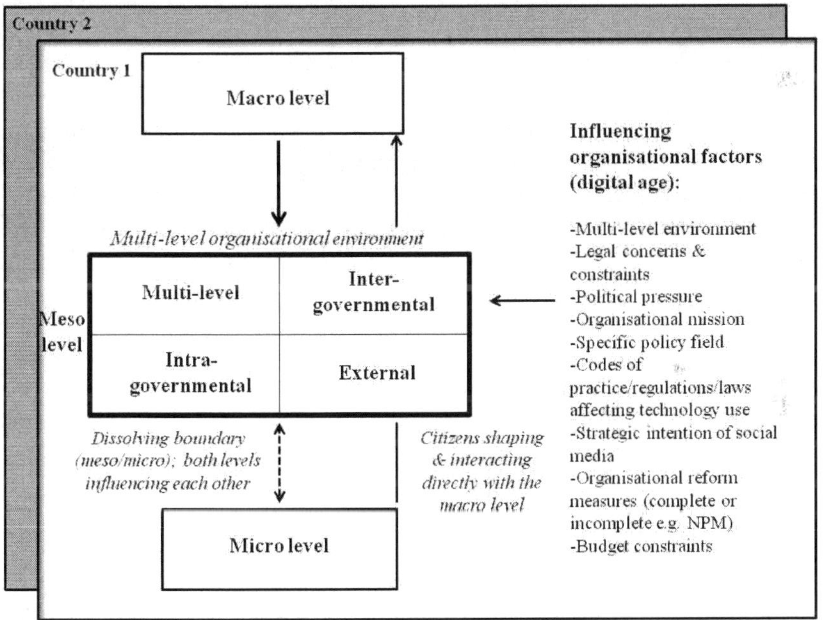

Source: own design; the multi-level organisational environment is taken from Horsley et al.'s (2010) model; the comparative design is taken from Esser & Pfetsch, (2017); the organisational factors are taken from Horsley et al. (2010), Graber (2003) and Mergel (2013; 2016).

Figure 2 emphasises that while the macro level still shapes communication at lower levels, the unique organisational environment of government organisations must also be considered in any comparative study of government communications. This organisational environment is made up of many levels of government as was originally presented in the Government Communication Wheel (Horsley et al., 2010; Liu & Horsley, 2007). The meso level also has a distinctively strong organisational boundary which reflects the bureaucratic organisational form. If this model were to examine political organisations, then the boundary would be presented as being more porous. The model also seeks to highlight the changing nature of the relationship between the meso and micro level. In particular, there is a dissolving boundary between what is organisational and what is individual communications in an online age as social media supports increasingly personalised forms of communications by citizens outside the boundaries of formal political organisations and government institutions (Bennett, 2012).

To summarise Section 4.3, while it is still necessary to consider what macro-level factors are shaping the use of digital technologies, there is also a need to incorporate and examine additional levels of analysis within comparative research designs. Current models don't capture the complexity of the changes in the online political communications environment. The next section in this chapter will continue to examine these changing levels of analysis, but this time from a network theoretical perspective. A central argument of the network perspective is that significant changes are taking place within each level of society (Van Dijk, 2012). Each level is not adapting digital technologies in a uniform way; instead, there are significant differences within levels. Previous studies have already suggested that government and political organisations adopt technologies in a non-rational way (Donges & Jarren, 2014; Mergel & Bretschneider, 2013) and an examination of the macro level alone cannot fully explain similarities or differences found at the organisational level. Instead, comparative research needs to combine additional levels of analysis and also *within-level* analysis. This thesis argues that a network perspective is the most suitable perspective for understanding the complexity of the new media environment, the challenges facing organisational communications and it has the potential to address some of the weaknesses in comparative communications to date.

4.4 Understanding the New Media Environment: A Network Perspective

Section 4.1 previously described some of the fundamental changes taking place in political organising facilitated by digital technologies. It also illustrated changes in how individuals are engaging with formal political organisations. Digital networks are supporting new forms of communication and organisation that has caused a weakening of organisational boundaries as individuals increasingly communicate outside the boundaries of traditional formal organisations (Bennett, 2012; Bennett & Segerberg, 2012; Chadwick & Stromer-Galley, 2016; Penney, 2017). The subsequent section, Section 4.2, outlined the unique organisational constraints that influence communications within government organisations; constraints that set these organisations apart from other types of organisations. Finally, in the most recent section, Section 4.3, examining the theoretical development of comparative political communications, it was argued that current comparative models and approaches do not fully capture the changes that have taken place in the new media environment and the changing relationship between levels of analysis. Comparative models and typologies are "far from adequate to compare the complex, fragmented, and multi-platform digital environment of the third age" (Norris, 2011, p. 330). They continue to take a hierarchical approach to understanding how politics and media interact with citizens. Comparative models have also overlooked the meso level and how the organisational environment shapes political and government communications. For this reason, Section 4.3 presented a comparative model that considers the unique organisational environment of government communications and how this is changing in an online age.

This section argues that the network perspective provides an overarching and relevant theoretical perspective for understanding the changes in the political communications environment as a result of digital technologies. A number of scholars agree that the new political communications environment is fundamentally different to previous eras of political communication (Blumler & Kavanagh, 1999; Chadwick, 2013; Gurevitch et al., 2009; Wright, 2012), and it operates according to a new and distinct logic, that is, a network logic (Castells, 2010; Klinger & Svensson, 2015; Van Dijk, 2012). This thesis argues that a network perspective provides a richer insight into how society, communications and levels of analysis have fundamentally changed as a result of digital networks. It allows us to move away from a hierarchical understanding of how macro social structures shape society. Instead, it draws attention to the complex interactions and relations *between*, and *within*, levels of analysis. This thesis argues that the network perspective not only enriches our understanding of organisational communications and the challenges they face, but it also potentially strengthens comparative communications research by taking a less hierarchical approach and focuses instead on the complex interactions between and within levels of analysis.

Within the network society perspective "attention shifts to the changing organisational forms and (infra)structures of these societies" (Van Dijk, 2012, p. 23). It provides a lens through which, researchers can examine how the structure of society and the relations between society, organisations and individuals are changing. Van Dijk defines the network society as "a modern type of society with an infrastructure of social and media networks that characterises its mode of organisation at every level: individual, group/organisational and societal. Increasingly, these networks link every unit or part of this society" (2012, p. 24). Castells (2011 a) writes that in the network society, networks are our main mode of communication and social power is exercised through multimedia networks of mass communication. Van Dijk (2012) conceptualises this network society with a multi-level theory of networks. Within his model there are different levels of networks. This includes, four different levels and four different networks, all connected with each other: the individual network, group/organisational network, societal network and global network (2012, pp. 30-31). The most distinguishable trait of the network society according to him is "the dissolving of boundaries between the macro, meso and micro levels of social life, between the public and the private spaces and between the spheres of living, working, studying, recreation and travelling" (Van Dijk, 2012, p. 176). One of the key differences between Van Dijk's conception of the network society and Castells's perspective is that Van Dijk still believes that society consists of distinct groups, whereas Castells believes that networks have replaced society entirely, there are no longer individuals or organisations, instead there are just networks (Van Dijk, 1999). Van Dijk (1999) sees networks as being the prime mode of organisation in society, but within these networks individuals, groups and organisations interact with each other.

Reese and Shoemaker (2016) incorporated a network perspective in an effort to re-conceptualise their *Hierarchy of Influences Model* for a networked public sphere. Their aim was to consider the conceptual challenges of the changing media ecosystem and the consequences for their levels of analysis framework. Similar to Van Dijk's (2012) description of the network society, Reese and Shoemaker say that the term network "captures the blurring of lines between professional and citizen, and between one organisation and another, as they develop more collaborative partnerships across digital platforms" (2016, p. 394). The network perspective not only emphasises the blurring of lines between one organisation and another, but also how different levels of analysis connect with one another, such as individuals, organisations and social institutions (Reese & Shoemaker, 2016). However, they make clear that this relational perspective still regards relationships as being shaped by larger systemic factors,

> The network perspective itself, so central to understanding the networked public sphere, does not necessarily run contrary to a hierarchical approach. Social network analysis emphasises relationships among and characteristics of nodes (whether people, news sources, or stories), but these relationships are still conditioned by larger systemic factors. (Reese & Shoemaker, 2016, pp. 405-406)

They argue that we need to understand how different units, such as organisations, are changing and how these relate to larger societal structures:

> Societal changes force a general re-examination of the relationship between individuals and larger structures. That is, the aggregates traditionally signaled by levels – whether community, organisation, or nation – are containers that don't have the same meaning as they once did, as new structures are woven outside of and through institutional frameworks. (2016, pp. 398-399)

This is similar to Van Dijk who also emphasised that the national state is not disappearing in a network society, it is still one of the strongest actors in a society (2012, p. 104). This makes the network perspective particularly appropriate for applying to a comparative study, as it also emphasises the importance of understanding the connection between societal (i.e., macro) structures and other units in society.

Reese and Shoemaker say that the network perspective "does not necessarily run contrary to a hierarchical approach" (2016, pp. 405-406). Instead, the network perspective views relations as being organised as a heterarchy rather than as a hierarchy or a flat mode of communication. According to Van Dijk and Winters-van Beek "the popular view of networks as a flat, horizontal mode of organisation is very one-sided. Networks are only 'flat' in comparison with hierarchies. Networks also have centres and central modes of steering and governance" (2009, p. 242). The network perspective does not mean that there are no longer hierarchies within society or within organisations, rather certain actors will be more central (better connected) in networks than others. Power constellations still exist within society and networks, however, they are organised as a heterarchy (Van Dijk & Winters-van Beek, 2009). This heterarchical understanding of how society is structured could also potentially benefit comparative political communications research which until now has been predominantly based on a hierarchical understanding of the interaction between politics, media and citizens.

The heterarchical perspective emphasises the need to examine the dynamic structures that form across levels of analysis (Reese & Shoemaker, 2016), whereas the comparative approach has typically focused on how higher levels shape lower levels (see Section 4.3). Van Dijk and Winters-van Beek say that "as a mode of organisation networks realise complex interactions within and between levels" (2009, p. 246). Van Dijk (2012) draws heavily from the work of Kontopoulos (1993) who differentiated between hierarchical and heterarchical modes of organisation. Kontopoulos stressed the importance of understanding how levels are rooted with other levels "same-level or intra-level analysis must be supplemented and enriched by cross-level or inter-level analysis" (1993, p. 63). Networks "cut right through all levels, and they connect these levels. Networks realise complex interactions within and between levels" (Van Dijk, 2012, p. 32). Within a heterarchy, power or determination can emerge from both higher and lower levels (Kontopoulos, 1993). This study argues that comparative research needs to move towards such a perspective and away from a solely hierarchical understanding of political communications as this potentially limits our understanding of the changing relationship between macro structures, organisations and individuals. Instead, the network perspective brings into focus the complex interactions between and within levels of analysis.

Another common, and relevant, theme in theoretical contributions on the network society or the network perspective, is the phenomenon of the networked individual (a theme that was also referred to in Section 4.1 on political organisations in an online age). Castells (2007) refers to this phenomenon as "mass self-communication", Van Dijk (2012) describes it as "network individualization", Wellman (2001) calls it "networked individualism" and Svensson (2015) refers to "connective individualism". However, they are all slightly different variations of the same phenomenon. They each emphasise that social fragmentation has resulted in individuals becoming the most important node in the network society (Van Dijk, 2012, p. 24). In order to understand organisational communications in a network society, we need to start with understanding the central role of the individual and individualism in society (Svensson, 2015) and the increasing personalisation of political participation (Bennett, 2012). Monge and Contractor (2003) referred to Giddens (1991) concept of individuation, which refers to how people are relying less on traditional institutions and instead on their own knowledge (p. 6). They say that,

> This leads to individualised patterns of consumption and mass customisation of products, both important challenges for future organisations. It also changes the nature of work expectations and experiences, as well as affiliations within a wide range of social, political, religious, and recreational organisations. Thus, over the next decades we are likely to see substantial global transformations in the ways in which people view themselves, in how they relate to organisations, and in what they are willing to tolerate (Held, McGrew, Goldblatt, & Perraton, 1999). (Monge & Contractor, 2003, p. 6)

Similar to the themes touched on in Section 4.1 in this chapter, Castells describes how people are less engaged with institutional politics and instead align themselves with and become active with more informal forms of organisation "traditional forms of politics and ideological sources of voluntary associations seem to be on the decline almost everywhere" (2008, p. 84). In this way, the network perspective addresses many of the central challenges that organisational communications (including government organisational communications) are facing in today's networked communications environment.

The network perspective also provides an understanding of interaction that differs to previous understandings of interaction between politics, media and citizens. Previous understandings were often based on hierarchical, linear flows of communication and two-way forms of interaction (Young & Pieterson, 2015). Digital technologies have fundamentally changed how individuals interact with each other. Communication and interaction follows an entirely different logic, a *network logic* (Klinger & Svensson, 2015, 2016). Digital technologies such as social networks have changed the way information is distributed and the rationale is to encourage others in the network to share, comment and recommend content to other users (Klinger & Svensson, 2015, p. 1248). Information is distributed through networks. This perspective focuses on the relational rather than dialogic communication. It focuses on the extent to which individuals and organisations are connected with each other and who is central within a network, how they share information and other new means of response afforded to individuals online.

The focus of this thesis is government organisations and so the network society perspective raises questions around how these organisations should respond and how they are responding within this networked environment. However, it is unclear from the literature how governments should network in this environment. For example, Van Dijk argues, that within a network society it is necessary for organisations to open themselves up and adapt to these changes in order to compete economically or meet societal demands (2012, p. 34). Monge and Contractor say that in a network "it might seem reasonable to interpret a high degree of centrality as a positive and desirable feature of the network, but it could also be justifiably interpreted as signalling a strain such as communication overload or a constraint on the node's ability to function effectively" (2003, p. 38). They say that centrality can be both a positive and negative feature. For example, within the context of government networks, a network dominated by just a few government actors could indicate that the network is overly centralised with information flows controlled by just one or two central government actors. Van Dijk says that networks could enable governments to have greater control of information flows and control citizens through networks (2012, p. 105). Accordingly, governments will take a highly controlled approach to networking. This is quite a pessimistic perspective and also assumes that governments adopt a highly rational and strategic approach to networking. However, as previous sections in this chapter indicated government and political organisations appear to adopt technologies (at first anyway) in a non-rational way (Donges & Jarren, 2014), but as these technologies become more institutionalised, organisations take a more top-down controlled approach to communication (Mergel 2013; 2016).

Finally, this thesis is not suggesting that government organisations should transform into network organisations or that they are being replaced by networks. However, the democratic legitimacy of governments is dependent on their ability to be able to communicate political decisions to the public and media (Borucki & Jun, 2018) and this requires that they must adapt and connect with others in this networked communications environment. On the other hand, as Olsen (2006) highlighted (in Section 4.2.1), government organisations have a responsibility to be transparent, uphold democratic values, the rule of law and follow codes of conduct as is expected of bureaucratic organisations. For this reason, this thesis is interested in exploring and empirically examining how governments are networking and connecting with others.

Table 5 summarises some of the most important theoretical conclusions from this section on the network perspective that are relevant for this thesis. These will form part of the research guiding assumptions of this thesis and they will shape the comparative and empirical approach of this study in Chapters 5 and 6. In the empirical part of this study, I will examine and incorporate a number of aspects and themes of the network perspective into the analysis of online government organisational communications in Germany and Great Britain.

Table 5. Summary of the Theoretical Conclusions of the Network Perspective

Characteristics of the Network Perspective
1. The macro level still matters. Relationships are shaped by systemic factors, but the macro is only one of many levels shaping communications.
2. The network society is characterised by a blurring of boundaries between the macro, organisations and individuals in society.
3. Society is organised as a heterarchy rather than a hierarchy. Less focus on how higher levels control lower levels, more focus on relations between and within levels.
4. Communication and interaction follows a network logic.
5. The communications environment is characterised by networked individualism; the individual is the most important node in society.

Source: Own table; information taken from Van Dijk, 2012; Reese & Shoemaker, 2016; Kontopoulos, 1993; Van Dijk and Winters-van Beek, 2009.

For example, this study will examine whether government organisations engage in more individualised forms of communication online, how these organisations present themselves online (whether they present a blurred identity), the extent to which government organisations interact and network with other government actors and non-government actors online and what actors are central within government networks. This author will also examine the similarities and differences not just between countries, but also similarities and differences among government organisations in both countries (*within level analysis*) and between the organisational and individual levels of analysis *(between level analysis)*. In this way, this study will consider not just the macro factors that possibly shape lower levels of communication in a network society, but also the meso-level factors that may be shaping government communications and the changing relationship between different levels of analysis in a digital age.

4.5 Summary & Research Guiding Assumptions II

A recurring theme throughout each section in this theoretical chapter was the missing meso perspective. Each section drew attention to the importance of understanding the organisational level. Within the field of political communications the political and government organisational environment has been overlooked (Donges, 2008). A central argument of this chapter is that in trying to understand how government organisations use digital technologies, we need to understand their unique organisational constraints. We need to understand these as much as we need to understand the macro-level factors that shape communications in different countries. This chapter highlighted that the organisational level has also been overlooked within comparative political communications models and approaches to date. Comparative communications has mostly taken a hierarchical approach to understanding the relationship between politics, media and citizens, that is, how the macro level shapes lower levels. However, the network perspective highlighted that the macro is just one of many levels that shapes communications in a networked sphere. The new communications environment is characterised by a blurring of boundaries between the macro, meso and micro levels, and in order to understand the changing relationships between levels of analysis, we need to examine communications at different levels and within levels of analysis.

Based on the theoretical findings of this chapter, this section seeks to combine these perspectives with some of the macro-level influencing factors identified in Chapter 3 as shaping government communications in Germany and Great Britain. This thesis also incorporates some of the key findings presented in the literature review in Chapter 2. This section seeks to bring together some of the central findings of these three different chapters in order to formulate the research guiding assumptions that will be investigated in the empirical analysis of this study.

One of the key themes in this chapter was the importance of understanding the organisational environment in which government communications takes place. This chapter highlighted many of the unique constraints and challenges that government organisations face in adapting to the new media environment. This study assumes that different government organisations will face different challenges in using digital technologies (Mergel, 2016). I assume there will be *(within-level)* differences between organisations in both countries in how they use websites and social media:

1. Government organisations within Germany and Great Britain will use websites and social media differently. There will be differences between the organisations in the extent to which they use websites and social media for interaction and networking.

As pointed out, the macro/systemic level will continue to shape government organisational communications, but it is not the only level that shapes communications. This study assumes that a number of factors at the macro level will shape the use of digital technologies. Based on the key macro-level influencing factors identified in Chapter 3, this thesis assumes that the centralised organisations for government communications – the BPA and GCS – will both play a prominent role in online government communications in the two countries:

2. Both the BPA and GCS will be central actors within government social networks. They will occupy a central position in social media networks and they will be one of the most active actors on social media in terms of interaction and networking.

In addition, based on another macro-level factor identified in Chapter 3, this study assumes that the PM's Office will also play a central and active role in online government communications in Great Britain due to the centralisation of media resources and power in this office (Dowding, 2013; Heffernan, 2006). Therefore the assumption is:

3. The PM's Office will be a central actor within government social media networks in Great Britain. It will occupy a central position in social media networks and it will be one of the most active actors on social media in terms of interaction and networking.

The findings of the literature review in Chapter 2 highlighted that most government organisations are using websites and social media as an informational tool rather than as a tool for interaction and networking (Gurevitch et al., 2009; Meijer et al., 2012; Mossberger et al., 2013). Therefore, I assume that government organisations in Germany and Great Britain will use websites and social media predominantly for one-way communication. Based on this, I also assume that government actors will rarely network with others, instead, they will mostly network with other government actors on social media.

4. Government organisations in both countries will predominantly engage in unidirectional (top-down) communication on their websites and social media.
5. Government organisations in both countries will predominantly network with other government actors on social media.

However, due to a strictly regulated and formal organisation of government communications in Germany (Kocks & Raupp, 2014; Sanders et al., 2011), this study assumes that government organisations in Germany will be more reserved in using online technologies for interaction compared to Great Britain. This thesis assumes that:

6. Government organisations in Germany will use websites and social media exclusively for unidirectional communication.

The literature review in Chapter 2 and the analysis of the political organisational environment in Chapter 4 both highlighted how political participation is becoming increasingly defined by personalised communications across digital networks (Bennett, 2012; Bennett & Segerberg, 2012). The network perspective in Chapter 4 also described the emergence of networked individualism, that is, the individual is becoming the most important node in society (Svensson, 2015; Van Dijk, 2012; Wellman, 2001). One of the consequences of the increasing individualisation of communications is the blurring of boundaries between individual and organisational communications. This thesis assumes that government organisations will seek to adapt to the demands of the changing media environment by using more individualised communications (i.e., they will engage as networked individuals). I assume that this will also lead to a blurred boundary between what is organisational (official government communications) and individual government communications (non-official personalised political communications). As a result, it is assumed that there will also be less transparency on individual government social media pages compared to government organisational pages. The assumptions are:

7. Government organisations in both countries will engage in individualised communications on social media.
8. Government organisations in both countries, will take similar approaches to the individualisation of organisational communications, that is, they will blur the boundary between organisational and individualised communications.
9. Individual social media pages will be less transparent than organisational social media pages.

The next chapter, Chapter 5, will outline the research questions to be investigated in the empirical part of this dissertation. It will provide an extensive overview of the comparative research and methodological design of this study, including the empirical methods employed and the development of the instrument of analysis and categories of analysis.

5. Methodological Approach

Despite the increasing professionalisation of government communications (Sanders & Canel, 2013; Sanders et al., 2011) and the prevalence of social media in day to day government communications, comparative studies examining online political communications have, over the last fifteen years, focused predominantly on the digitalisation of election campaigning among political parties (e.g., Foot et al., 2009; Gibson et al., 2003; Gibson & Ward, 2000; Russmann, 2011). While some studies have examined how governments are adapting to the digital sphere, these have, for the most part, been single country studies (e.g., Borucki, 2014 a, 2014 b; Chadwick, 2013; Coleman & Blumler, 2009; Garland et al., 2017; Gurevitch et al., 2009; Klinger et al., 2015; Kocks & Raupp, 2014; Kocks, Raupp, & Schink, 2014; Mergel & Bretschneider, 2013).

Some studies found that governments use social media predominantly as another channel for broadcasting information alongside traditional mass media channels (Chadwick, 2011 a, 2013), something that is also the case for political parties. Government has generally proved to be a bad "conversationalist" online (Gurevitch et al., 2009, p. 174)[32]. However, comparative research designs are necessary in order to test whether these findings apply in other political contexts and also to understand and identify the macro-level factors that possibly shape the use of digital technologies. Livingstone says that "in a time of globalisation, one might even argue that the choice not to conduct a piece of research cross-nationally requires as much justification as the choice to conduct cross-national research" (2003, p. 478). In today's digital age, the argument for more comparative research has never been stronger. Comparative research not only allows a deeper understanding of how different governments are using new media technologies, but it also helps to reveal (otherwise hidden) organisational and systemic structures (Blumler & Gurevitch, 1995) that are shaping the use of communication technologies. In single-country studies it is difficult to pinpoint the structures that are shaping communications

32 See the literature review in Chapter 2 for an in-depth summary of the key findings from these studies into how governments and political actors have been adapting and using digital technologies until now.

in that country. It is only by looking outside our own country and comparing it with others that we begin to learn more about ourselves.

As highlighted in Chapter 4, comparative studies typically seek to identify phenomena at the micro level of analysis under different macro conditions (Blumler & Gurevitch, 1995; Pfetsch, 2003; Pfetsch & Esser, 2012). According to Pfetsch, the aim of comparative research is to understand how the macro environment "constrains" communications at lower levels, however, comparative research does not identify causal relationships (2003, p. 66). This study seeks to identify phenomena in relation to the online practices of government actors and to understand these practices within the context of their unique organisational and political environments in Germany and Great Britain. It is not possible within this type of research design, to identify direct causal relationships between the meso or macro environments and their online practices; it is only possible to suggest possible correlations.

This chapter will first present the research questions for this study based on the conclusions of the previous chapters (i.e., Chapters 2, 3 and 4) and it will then outline all aspects of the methodological design and how the empirical analysis proposes to answer these research questions. This chapter will present the empirical methods employed, the development of the sample for the online content analysis, the challenges in defining online government communications, the design of the codebook and the categories of analysis and finally, the development of an additional social network analysis (SNA). It will also describe the many challenges and steps taken to ensure equivalence throughout the methodological design, an essential component for comparative studies.

5.1 Research Questions

The central overarching research question in this dissertation is the following:

RQ1. How are government organisations and individuals in Germany and Great Britain using websites and social media to communicate with citizens and media in their day-to-day communications?

This central research question will be answered through an online content analysis and a SNA of their Twitter (TW) networks. This question is broken down below in to a number of specific sub-questions. These sub-questions will be answered by an online content analysis and they relate to different aspects of interaction in an online age. This study considers interaction in the form of dialogue, sharing information and connections (e.g., hyperlinks) and it also regards personalised individualised communications as a form of interaction in an online age:

RQ1 a. To what extent are government organisations using websites and social media to interact with media and citizens?

RQ1 b. To what extent are government organisations using websites and social media to connect/network with media and citizens?

RQ1 c. To what extent do government organisations have an individual social media page?

RQ1 d. How do government organisations present themselves on these individual social media pages? (e.g., a blurred identity)

RQ1 e. To what extent are these individual pages transparent compared to organisational pages?

Based on the literature review in Chapter 2 and the theoretical considerations in Chapter 4, it is assumed that government organisations in both countries will predominantly engage in unidirectional communication (top-down) on their websites and on social media (RGA 4)[33] (Chadwick, 2013; Gurevitch et al., 2009; Meijer et al., 2012; Mossberger et al., 2013). Although it is assumed that government organisations will predominantly engage in unidirectional communication, it is also assumed that there will be some differences between the countries based on macro-level differences. For example, due to a highly formalised and regulated government communications environment in Germany (Holtz-Bacha, 2013; Kocks & Raupp, 2014; Sanders et al., 2011), the author assumes German government organisations will use websites and social media exclusively for unidirectional communication (RGA 6). In a similar vein, the author assumes that government organisations will rarely use websites and social media to connect/network with media and citizens. Based on the organisational perspective of how political organisations are using social media (see Bennett & Segerberg, 2012; Chadwick & Stromer-Galley, 2016; Penney, 2017) and on the network perspective outlined in Chapter 4 (Svensson, 2015; Van Dijk, 2012; Wellman, 2001), the author assumes that government organisations in both countries will increasingly have an individual presence online (RGA 7) and that these pages will be a mix of personalised individualised communications and government organisational communications (RGA

33 See Section 4.5 at the end of the previous chapter, Chapter 4, for the full list of research guiding assumptions (RGAs).

8). This author also assumes that these individual pages will be less transparent in stating who is responsible for content on these pages (RGA 9).

Based on the theoretical considerations at the macro level in Chapter 3 and the organisational and network theoretical perspectives outlined in Chapter 4, this study seeks to incorporate a number of levels of analysis in to the comparative research design of this study, therefore, similarities and differences at a number of different levels of analysis are examined. There are also a number of sub-questions related to these levels of analysis:

RQ1 f. Are there similarities between Germany and Great Britain in how government organisations and individuals use websites and social media to communicate with citizens and media in their day-to-day communications? (i.e., macro-level perspective)

RQ1 g. Are there differences between government organisations within Germany and Great Britain in how they use websites and social media to communicate with citizens and media in their day-to-day communications? (i.e., inter-organisational/meso-level perspective)

RQ1 h. Are there differences between government organisations and individual government actors in how they use websites and social media to communicate with citizens and media in their day-to-day communications? (i.e., between level analysis/meso-micro level perspective)

In relation to RQ1 g above, it is assumed that government organisations within Germany and Great Britain will use websites and social media differently (Mergel, 2016) and that there will be differences between the organisations in the extent to which they use websites and social media for interaction and networking (RGA 1).

The aim of the SNA is to incorporate the network perspective from Chapter 4 into the empirical analysis, and to analyse to what extent government actors are networking with others on social media (specifically TW) and who they are networking with online, for example, whether it is mostly with media actors, other political actors, with citizens, or simply with other government actors. While the online content analysis allows an examination of how they actually interact and present themselves on social media, the SNA allows the analysis of how they network, which actors are central within these networks and what macro-level factors possibly shape government networks.

The main research question for the SNA is:

RQ2. How are government organisations in Germany and Great Britain using Twitter (TW) to network with citizens and media in their day-to-day communications?

This question is then broken down into three sub-questions:

RQ2 a. Who are government organisations networking with on TW? (e.g., political, media, citizens, or other government actors)

RQ2 b. Which actors occupy central positions in their TW (retweet) networks?

RQ2 c. Are there similarities between the countries in how government organisations use TW to network with citizens and media in their day-to-day communications?

Based on the structural/macro-level analysis of government communications in Chapter 3 and the theoretical assumptions in Chapter 4, the author assumes that the centralised organisations for government communications – the BPA and GCS – will occupy central positions in government TW networks (RGA 2). In addition, this study assumes that the PM's office will play a central role in the TW network in Great Britain due to the centralisation of resources and power in his office (RGA 3) (Dowding, 2013; Heffernan, 2006). It is also assumed that government organisations and individual actors in both countries will mostly network with other government actors (RGA 5).

5.2 Research Design: A Comparative Study

As outlined in Chapter 3, Germany and Great Britain are a suitable comparison due to many similarities in the development and professionalisation of centralised government communications and the digitalisation of government communications in both countries. At the same time, there are a number of notable differences between the two countries. For example, 1) in their political systems (majoritarian vs. federal state; highly centralised political system vs. strongly decentralised political system), 2) media systems (particularly in relation to the press market and media/press relations in Great Britain), 3) approach to the regulation of government communications (non-statutory in Great Britain vs. statutory approach in Germany) and 4) the centralised structures of government communications (GCS in Great Britain organised as a professional body, very different to the BPA in Germany).

The most common approach to sampling countries continues to be Przeworski and Teune's (1970) *most similar systems* and *most different systems* design method. For example, Przeworski and Teune's most similar systems design approach was adopted by Hallin and Mancini (2004) in their seminal work *Three Models of Media and Politics*. Based on the differences and conclusions outlined in Chapter 3, this dissertation adopts a most different systems design for the comparison of these two countries. This study therefore focuses on identifying similarities across Great Britain and Germany. I assume that there will be a number of similarities between them in how they use new digital technologies to engage with media and citizens. For example, I assume they will both use digital technologies largely as an informational tool, but that there will be some differences due to influencing factors at the macro level and different meso-level constraints.

While comparative studies typically focus on inter-country similarities or differences, this study incorporates some of the theoretical conclusions from Chapter 4 and seeks to analyse government organisations' online communications from a number of perspectives and different levels of analysis. This study takes an inter-country perspective (the comparison of online organisational communications between Great Britain and Germany), an inter-organisational or within-level analysis (the comparison of organisations within both countries) and a multi-level (between-level) perspective (the comparison of organisational and individual online communications on social media). In this way, this dissertation seeks to examine whether there are macro, as well as meso-level factors, that are possibly shaping how governments use social media and websites.

5.3 Conceptual and Methodological Challenges: Establishing Equivalence

Comparative studies involve unique methodological and conceptual challenges that don't arise in single country studies (Esser & Hanitzsch, 2012, p. 6; Murphy, 2018). The most important challenge for comparative research is the establishment of equivalence throughout the methodological design (Rössler, 2012; Wirth & Kolb, 2004), or which can be more easily understood as the removal of bias (Van de Vijver & Tanzer, 2004). Equivalence is essential for achieving reliable and valid results. Bias can emerge at different stages of the methodological process, for example, during the development of the concept of analysis (for example, researchers from different countries could have different understandings of what constitutes online government communications), sampling (they could also have different understandings of what a government organisation is and what organisations should be included in the sample), the selection of the empirical method and the development of the instrument of analysis. According to a number of studies on comparative methodological designs, there are three different levels on which equivalence should be established: the construct, method and item level (Van de Vijver & Tanzer, 2004; Wirth & Kolb, 2004). Table 6 below, lists the various steps taken in this study to ensure equivalence throughout the methodological design.

Table 6. Key Methodological Considerations around Equivalence and Reliability

1. Construct Equivalence	2. Method Equivalence	3. Item Equivalence	Reliability & Validity
Is the object of analysis (i.e., government communications) equivalent? Define government and government communications	Is the sample and codebook equivalent in both countries? Developing the codebook: cultural & language considerations – emic or etic approach; native, project or multilingual language approach?	Are the categories /questions within the instrument equivalent?	1. Coder training & coder protocol 2. Informal reliability tests (pre-tests) 3. Formal reliability test

Source: Own table; replication of a table published in a previous publication by the author of this dissertation (see Murphy, 2018, p. 204); information in this table taken from Van de Vijver and Tanzer, 2004; Wirth and Kolb, 2004; and Rössler, 2012.

This chapter will outline the steps taken to ensure equivalence in defining government and government communications in both countries, the sampling of government actors and websites and social media pages, the design of the codebook for the online content analysis, the categories of analysis in the codebook, the choice of languages for the empirical analysis and finally, equivalence in data collection and analysis. All four steps outlined in Table 6, were considered in the methodological design of this study.

5.4 Methodological Approach: Online Content Analysis & Social Network Analysis

In recent years there has been an increasing number of political communications studies combining quantitative online content analysis and SNA methods in order to investigate different aspects of online practices by media, political and non-government actors (e.g., Adi et al., 2014; Anstead & Chadwick, 2017; Maier et al., 2017; Nuernbergk & Conrad, 2016), and to consider online interaction and political participation from a number of different perspectives, including a network perspective. Based on these approaches, this study also employs an online content analysis and SNA in order to carry out a broader investigation of interaction and networking by government actors. The main empirical method is a quantitative online content analysis of the organisational websites and social media pages – Twitter (TW), Facebook (FB), and YouTube (YT)[34] – of government organisations (ministries) and government individuals (ministers) in the two countries. Alongside the content analysis, the methodological approach combines an additional SNA of government TW networks using retweet data collected as part of the online content analysis. The online content analysis in this dissertation was designed and carried out as part of the DFG Project "Networked Media Government Relations" (previously referred to in Chapter 1). The additional SNA was designed by this author specifically for this dissertation.

While much of the focus of this chapter will be on the development of the sample and codebook for the content analysis, the design of the SNA will also be explained in detail in Section 5.10. It is important to emphasise that it was not the main empirical approach of this dissertation, but it was employed to complement the content analysis and allow an analysis of government interaction online from a network perspective. It allowed the author to analyse in greater detail who government actors network with online and who is central within government (TW) networks.

In relation to the choice of social media platforms for the online content analysis, it was decided to focus on those platforms that were the most commonly used social media platforms in the two countries at the time that the online content analysis was being designed and the online content was being saved (first half of 2015). TW, FB and YT were the most popular platforms regarded as supporting citizen interaction and political participation, compared to other platforms that were also in use at the time.

34 For the rest of this chapter, and also in Chapter 6, Twitter, Facebook and YouTube will be abbreviated as TW, FB and YT in order to avoid repetition.

5.5 Definitions & Sampling

According to Wirth and Kolb "the functionality of the research objects within the different system contexts must be equivalent" (2004, p. 88). In order to establish construct equivalence, it was necessary to first define government and government communications in the two countries. It was only by doing this that the author could then identify and build an equivalent sample of government organisations for both countries. The usual sampling approaches that apply in empirical studies, such as representative, random, or probability sampling, among others, did not apply to this study. Instead, the approach to sampling in this dissertation could be described as "non-random" (Enli & Skogerbø, 2013), that is, I created a sample of all government organisations and individual actors at the executive level that are relevant for the analysis of online government communications in the two countries.

5.5.1. Defining online government communications

Before creating the sample, this thesis looked to different studies from political science and political communications for a suitable definition of government and government communications for Germany and Great Britain. Different disciplines, from legal studies, to political science, to political communications, define government in different ways. According to Vogel, who compared the structures of government communications in Germany, Great Britain and Switzerland, there is a general lack of consensus across these fields as to the definition of government and government communications (2010, p. 11). Andeweg (2003) also referred to this lack of agreement among political scientists on the meaning of government and pointed out that government is understood differently in different countries.

In attempting to define government, the most typical approaches within political science involve defining government as "cabinet government" or using the concept of the "core executive" (Dunleavy & Rhodes, 1990). There are criticisms of both approaches, in particular, the cabinet approach, which often fails to capture where the real power in government lies (Andeweg, 1993). Döhler, Fleischer and Hustedt (2007) point out that there are many important differences between where the centre of power lies in modern democracies. In reference to Mayntz and Scharpf (1975, pp. 42-43), Döhler et al. (2007) maintain that the cabinet in Germany "should be understood as an assembly of heads of department which must formally ratify important policy proposals originating from the departments" (p. 12). While in Great Britain, the important policy decisions are carried out by a number of cabinet committees rather than by the cabinet (Döhler et al., 2007, pp. 12-13). There are also difficulties using the core executive as a definition of government as this concept is based on the British model of government and it is not applicable, for example, to the system of governance in Germany (Vogel, 2010). However, governments do not have to have identical organisations, actors and structures in order to be comparable, as this would render comparative studies redundant (Murphy, 2018, p. 207). Instead, the idea is to capture an aspect of government's behaviour rather than every government organisation and actor (Korte, 2002). It is more important that, in the end, the sample (which is determined by the definition) contains actors embedded equivalently at the same level within the political system (Murphy, 2018; Wirth & Kolb, 2004, p. 88).

Within the field of government communications, Sanders and Canel (2013) defined government communications as the following,

> The role, practice, aims and achievements of communication as it takes place in and on behalf of public institution(s) whose primary end is executive in the service of a political rationale, and that are constituted on the basis of the people's indirect or direct consent and charged to enact their will. (p. 4)

This definition is a useful starting point as it emphasises executive government institutions with an explicit political rationale. Although it excludes non-executive government agencies, it still includes executive organisations at the national, regional and local level. As a result, this definition was considered to be too wide for this dissertation; it would have captured too many government actors, particularly in Great Britain where government is much larger and there are hundreds of government agencies. Instead, this dissertation created a definition that restricted the analysis to the most important government organisations at the national executive level and the centralised organisations that play a key role in government communications (i.e., the BPA and GCS).

In addition, due to increasing personalised forms of communication and the individualisation of participation within organisations (see Bennett & Segerberg, 2012; Gibson & Ward, 2009; Nitschke & Murphy, 2016), this study sought to include all those individual actors at the executive government level that also play an influential role in government communications. Therefore, government communications (specifically online government communications) was defined as[35]:

> The websites and social media pages of the government, office of the head of government, cabinet office, ministerial government departments/ministries, offices of cabinet ministers without portfolios, central government communications office and the individual social media pages of the main representatives of these ministerial government departments/offices/ministries. This includes the head of government, all members of the cabinet and the chief spokesperson of the central government communications office. (Murphy, 2018, p. 207; Murphy, Kocks, & Raupp, 2016, p. 13)

One of the research guiding assumptions of this thesis (see Section 4.5 in Chapter 4) is that government organisations will increasingly use more individualised communications. The author assumes that some individual government actors, such as government ministers, will have an individual social media page (e.g., on TW or FB) in addition to a ministerial (organisational) social media page. For this reason, the definition above includes all individual government actors who are full members of the cabinet and who are the main representatives of ministerial government departments/ offices and central government communications offices. One of the central aims of the empirical approach is to analyse to what extent and how, government organisations are using individualised communications in their day-to-day communications, whether there is a blurring of the boundary between the two and what are the potential democratic consequences in terms of the transparency, accountability and impartiality of government communications.

5.5.2. Sampling

Based on the definition of government communications above, it was possible to build an equivalent sample of organisational and individual actors for both countries. Firstly, the author identified all organisations listed as "ministerial departments", "government ministries", "bundesministerien"

35 Please note that the author of this dissertation wrote this definition for the DFG Project "Networked Media Government Relations" and it has previously featured in a conference paper and book chapter written by the author (see Murphy, 2018; Murphy, Kocks, & Raupp, 2016).

on the main government websites www.bundesregierung.de and www.gov.uk. Additional government organisations like the Chancellor's Office (KA) and the BPA in Germany and the PM's Office and GCS in Great Britain were added to the sample[36]. The author included all organisations that are represented by a member of government at the cabinet (the only exception to this rule were the BPA and GCS who are not represented in the cabinet). The list of organisations on the two government websites were cross-checked numerous times with those listed on the parliamentary websites for Great Britain and Germany.

In a second step, the author identified all the relevant individual government actors by referring to the list of cabinet members on both government websites www.bundesregierung.de and www.gov.uk. The list of individual actors listed on the government websites were cross-checked with the most recent government announcements or press statements on the make-up of the cabinet, changes to the cabinet or changes to government departments or ministries. This resulted in a sample of 27 government organisations for Great Britain and 17 organisations for Germany (see Appendix 1 and 2 for the full sample of organisations). It was then possible to create the sample of websites and social media pages for analysis. Based on the definition of government communications this included:

- The main websites and social media pages for both governments (www.bundesregierung.de and www.gov.uk).
- The website and social media pages of the Cabinet Office in Great Britain.
- The websites and social media pages of the offices of the head of government, that is, the PM's Office in Great Britain and the KA in Germany.
- The website and social media pages of the central government communications offices, that is, the GCS and the BPA.
- The websites and social media pages of all ministerial government departments\ministries.
- The individual social media pages of all cabinet ministers (including those who don’t have responsibility for a full government department, for example, the head of the KA), the heads of both governments (e.g., the German Chancellor and the British Prime Minister) and the heads

36 While these organisations are not listed as government ministries, they are the offices of the heads of government and the main centralised government communications offices and therefore, were considered to play a central role in government communications.

of both central government communications offices (e.g., Steffen Seibert and Alex Aiken).

This resulted in a sample of 44 organisational websites (i.e., all 44 organisations had a website), 88 organisational pages on FB, TW and YT and 32 individual pages on FB and TW (120 social media pages in total). While nearly all organisations had a presence on at least one or more social media platforms, some individual actors didn't have any social media pages. In the end, the total sample for the empirical analysis was 164 online platforms.

As this dissertation seeks to analyse the day-to-day communications of government organisations (i.e., non-electoral or party political communications), any individual social media page that was explicitly a party political or electoral page, was excluded from the sample. The author considered pages to be party political or electoral that contained one or more of the following features:

- The logo or name of the political party in the background photo or profile picture (e.g., CDU, SPD or the Conservative Party).
- If the profile/information box on the TW/FB page contained a link to the website of a political party.
- If the minister states in the information box on their TW/FB page that they are an electoral candidate for a specific political party.

For example, German Chancellor Angela Merkel's individual FB page was not included as it was clearly a party political page. It contained the CDU logo in the cover picture of her page. However, some individual pages were included where it was unclear whether the page was a government (organisational communications) or personal social media account (individual communications). These pages usually contained a link to a personal website (rather than a link to a political party), but the individuals often identified as being both a government and political actor (e.g., they mention that they are a member of parliament for a particular constituency).

5.6 Saving Content: Technological Considerations

As previously outlined, this thesis focuses on the analysis of day-to-day online government communications. However, due to a general election in Great Britain in early May 2015, it was necessary to save the online content for the content analysis in two phases to ensure electoral communications were excluded for Great Britain and to ensure the comparability (i.e., equivalence) of the content in both countries. The author began to save the content for both countries in early March 2015, but it quickly became clear that the British government was already in election campaigning mode two months ahead of the election. Therefore, the online content for Germany was saved in early March 2015 and the British content was saved two months after the general election from the end of June to early July 2015. It was important to allow sufficient time after the general election in order to ensure a return to normal routine government communications.

All government organisational websites and YT pages were saved using the website copier HTTrack (Version 3.49-2) in early March 2015 (Germany) and late June/early July 2015 (Great Britain). The FB and TW pages were saved as Fireshot images in early March 2015 (Germany) and early July 2015 (Great Britain). Additional data from FB and TW was saved using an open source software called Facepager[37] (Version 3.6) (Keyling & Jünger, 2013). This data was downloaded from Facepager and saved in Microsoft Excel. The following content was saved with Facepager: all government responses to user comments on FB and all tweets, retweets and direct responses by government actors to other TW users over a two-week period. For example, if a FB and TW page had been saved with Fireshot on March 10, 2015, then all government responses to user comments on FB and TW during the previous two weeks were saved. The value of using Facepager to collect and analyse data, is that it allows coders to more accurately quantify the number of tweets, retweets and responses to comments as the data is downloaded and saved in Microsoft Excel. This means that coders don't have to continuously scroll through a Fireshot image of FB and TW to count the number of posts, retweets and responses to comments (which are not visible on Fireshot images as it is not possible to click on all the comments). Instead, the number of tweets/posts can be counted quickly and accurately in an Excel document. This ensured higher reliability results in the final coding.

Not only was the content saved during two different phases, but it was also decided to carry out the online content analysis (i.e., the coding) in two phases. The coding was conducted for Germany in August 2015 and for Great Britain between December 2015 and January 2016. The decision to carry out the content analysis in different periods was due to a decision

37 Facepager is an open source software that allows researchers to take publicly available data from Facebook, Twitter and other JSON-based API. All data may be exported into csv files.

taken within the DFG project[38]. While it is important in a comparative study to use content/data from a similar period of analysis, the phased approach did not cause any problems for this study as all websites and social media pages had already been saved between March-June 2015. This phased approach had the added advantage of allowing more time to achieve a high level of language, method and item equivalence in both the German and English codebooks and in the reliability tests before beginning final coding (this will be elaborated upon in the next section).

5.7 Cultural and Language Considerations in the Codebook

Section 5.3 outlined the importance of establishing construct equivalence at the outset of a comparative research design. This study's definition of government communications in Section 5.5.1 helped to establish an equivalent understanding of government and online government communications in the two countries. Once this was established, careful attention was paid to establishing method and item equivalence throughout the development of the instrument of analysis, that is, a codebook for a cross-country online content analysis (Van de Vijver & Tanzer, 2004; Wirth & Kolb, 2004). Approaches to language play a particularly critical role in ensuring equivalence in a comparative study (Murphy, 2018, pp. 207-208). This section will expand on a number of cultural and language considerations that were made throughout this study's methodological design.

Firstly, it was necessary to decide on the cultural approach to developing the codebook for the online content analysis. According to the literature on comparative methodologies, there are two approaches that can be taken, an *emic* or *etic* approach (Wirth & Kolb, 2004). The emic approach is a culture-specific approach and this means a codebook is developed in each country, usually by research partners in those countries (Wirth & Kolb, 2004). Whereas an etic approach involves developing the instrument nationally and then applying this across each country (Wirth & Kolb, 2004). However, it is important to point out that when a codebook is developed for each country it does not mean that the instrument must be identical. It is imperative that the researcher adapts terms in each codebook to reflect differences in meaning across different cultures (Van de Vijver & Tanzer,

38 It was decided that it would make sense to coordinate the online content analysis at the same time that interviews were taking place with government spokespeople in each country.

2004). These cultural adaptations help to avoid methodological bias and potential false "differences" in the final results (Murphy, 2018; Rössler, 2012, p. 461; Wirth & Kolb, 2004, p. 95). Wirth and Kolb (2004) point out that an etic approach is suitable when construct equivalence has already been established within a study (p. 94). As this was the case in this study (i.e., there was a similar understanding of government communications in both countries), the author opted for an etic approach to the development of the codebook. This also made sense as the DFG project team was made up of a mix of native German and native English speakers with strong cultural understandings of both countries. It was not necessary to have research partners in other countries develop the codebook.

The next step in designing the codebook was the approach to languages. According to Rössler (2012), there are three language approaches that can be used in a cross-country content analysis, that is, a *native language*, *project language* or *multi-lingual* approach. The three approaches that he presents are in reference to those previously presented by Lauf and Peter (2001). Within comparative research, the project language proceeding is most often used, with one common language (mostly English) used for the codebook and each coder codes content in his/her native language (Murphy, 2018; Rössler, 2012). However, in order to achieve a higher level of language equivalence, this study opted for the multi-lingual approach[39]. An English and German language codebook was used along with native bilingual coders, that is, native English and native German speakers fluent in both languages.

The codebook was first developed as an English language codebook, written by a native English speaker (the author of this study) and it was then translated into German by a native German speaker fluent in English (see Appendix 3 for the English codebook). However, translating a codebook into another language is more than simply rewriting the text in another language (Van de Vijver & Tanzer, 2004, p. 122). Many categories or questions can have different meanings in different contexts and certain terms may not exist in the other country (Murphy, 2018; Rössler, 2012). For example, a term like "online public consultation" was a commonly used term on government websites in Great Britain, but if it is directly translated into German it has no meaning. Instead, the equivalent term was "Online Dialog" or "Bürger Dialog" (citizen dialogue) (Murphy, 2018, p. 208). This study was able to identify these types of misunderstandings or differences in language by carrying out a number of reliability pre-tests us-

39 This approach was possible due to resources available within the DFG project.

ing native German and English speaking coders prior to the formal reliability test (see Section 5.9 for more information on the reliability tests). All of these measures played an important role in ensuring method and item equivalence throughout the development of the codebook.

5.8 Developing the Categories of Analysis

The codebook was divided into two parts: 1) formal and content questions related to organisational websites and 2) formal and content questions related to external pages (i.e., organisational and individual social media pages). Coders first coded the website of a government organisation and then coded the organisational and individual TW and FB pages and finally the organisational YT page (there were no individual YT pages). All of the questions in the codebook were quantitative apart from one qualitative question related to government posts and tweets encouraging political participation on TW and FB.

In relation to the analysis of the websites there were four categories of analysis: 1) interaction/participation, 2) networking, 3) transparency and 4) press relations. The first category (i.e., interaction/participation) examined to what extent communications features on websites are unidirectional, two-way asymmetrical and two-way symmetrical (Grunig & Hunt, 1984). This category formed the largest part of the analysis of government websites and the main aim was to ascertain whether government organisations continue to engage in top-down communications online or whether they provide citizens with the opportunity to engage directly with governmental organisations and respond directly to citizens. One of the research guiding assumptions of this thesis is that government organisations in both countries will predominantly engage in unidirectional (top-down) communication on their websites and social media (see assumptions in Section 4.5 in Chapter 4). The second category on websites, that is, networking, consisted of just one question and also formed part of the section on interaction/participation (as outlined in Chapter 4, networking was considered to be an important aspect of interaction). In relation to networking, it was investigated to what extent government websites networked with other government actors. The third area of interest was the extent to which there was transparency on government websites in terms of the availability of government publications and information about the right to access government information (e.g., freedom of information laws, social media policies etc.). The questions in the category on transparency were measured on a scale of zero to three (*0* meaning there is no information available and *3* meaning information can be easily found). Fourth and finally, the content analysis examined to what extent the content on websites is directed at the press/media[40]. In this section, the codebook examines the press/media section on websites to see what kind of information and services are provided for journalists (see Table 7 for more information on all these categories).

The analysis of the social media pages involved similar categories of analysis, but the questions were adapted to take account of the fact that each platform operates differently and encourages different types of interaction. The analysis of FB, TW, and YB also included categories such as interaction, participation, networking and transparency. However, a new category of analysis was added for the analysis of the social media pages, that is, individualisation. This category specifically applies to the analysis of individual TW and FB pages. One of the research guiding assumptions of this thesis is that government organisations in both countries will take similar approaches to the individualisation of organisational communications blurring the boundary between what is organisational and individualised communications (see Section 4.5 in Chapter 4). Therefore, it was examined whether the main individual actors from these organisations (i.e., government ministers) have an individual presence online, and secondly, how they represent themselves online and if they blur the boundary between personal private communications and organisational government communications. Questions within this category (individualisation) examined whether government individual pages were presented as "official government" or "non-official government" (i.e., private) social media pages (see Section 6.1.9 in Chapter 6 for a more detailed explanation).

Table 7 provides a full list and overview of the categories of analysis within the codebook and lists these categories according to each online platform analysed: websites, TW, FB and YT. This shows that while there are similar categories for each platform, the focus is slightly different for each platform.

40 The category "press relations" was included as part of the DFG project. A central focus of the project was the examination of changing government media relations under the conditions of digitalisation. While this section features in the codebook presented in Appendix 3 of this thesis, however, it was not a central focus of this dissertation. This thesis focuses more generally on how governments are using websites and social media for interaction and networking with citizens and media.

Table 7. Overview of the Categories of Analysis for the Online Content Analysis

Online Content Analysis Categories of Analysis	Websites[41]	TW	FB	YT
Interaction	3 levels of analysis: – Unidirectional – 2-way asymmetrical (e.g., social media sharing options, download an app) – 2-way symmetrical (direct dialogue e.g. online public consultations, E-petitions)	3 levels of analysis: – Unidirectional (e.g., posting information, but no response) – Encourage active participation online – Respond directly to other TW users	3 levels of analysis: – Unidirectional (same as TW) – Encourage active participation online – Respond directly to user comments	3 levels of analysis: – nidirectional (same as FB/TW) – Allow users to leave comments under videos – Respond directly to comments/ videos feature interaction between government and citizens
Networking (form of interaction/ participation)	– Hyperlinks to the websites/ social media pages of other government organisations – Social media sharing icons	Actively network with citizens/ media/other government actors (i.e., follow other TW users, retweet information)	Actively network with citizens/ media/other government actors (i.e., share other FB posts)	Not applicable
Individualisation	Not applicable	– Presence of a social media page of an individual government actor – "Official" government page or "non-official" personal page	– Presence of a social media page of an individual government actor – "Official" or "non-official" government page	Not applicable

41 Each government organisation in GB has its own webpage rather than its own individual website. Their webpages are part of the main government website www.gov.uk. This study counts each organisations' webpage as a website.

Online Content Analysis Categories of Analysis	Websites[41]	TW	FB	YT
Press	– Presence of a clear press section – Services for journalists	Not applicable	Not applicable	Not applicable
Transparency	Accessibility of information related to: – Freedom of Information/ transparency laws – Government publications – Organisational information (e.g., Organigramm) – Social media policy (e.g., netiquette) – Media spokespersons (e.g., contact info)	Accessibility of information related to: Who is responsible for content on Twitter	Accessibility of information related to: Who is responsible for content on Facebook	Not applicable

5.9 Reliability & Validity

Coder training, a coder protocol (with definitions and directions in the codebook) and inter-coder reliability tests (including both informal pretests and a formal inter-reliability test) were the critical final steps taken to ensure there was no remaining bias in the methodological design (Murphy, 2018; Rössler, 2010, 2012; Van de Vijver & Tanzer, 2004; Wirth & Kolb, 2004). If method and item equivalence have been successfully established throughout the research design, then coders should be able to produce reliable and valid results (Rössler, 2012). Before beginning the content analysis, a number of informal inter-coder reliability pre-tests and a formal in-

41 Each government organisation in GB has its own webpage rather than its own individual website. Their webpages are part of the main government website www.gov.uk. This study counts each organisations' webpage as a website.

ter-coder reliability test were carried out in order to ensure there was the required level of agreement among coders.

The purpose of the informal inter-coder reliability pre-tests were to test which items/questions within the codebook didn't function (e.g., if coders simply didn't understand a question), identify misunderstandings and the need for additional definitions within the codebook, measure the length of time it took to code, identify any technical issues in relation to the saved data and the need for additional filter questions. Each test was carried out without any consultation between the coders during the coding itself. After each informal pre-test, the coders circulated a list of problems and these issues were then compared and discussed and solutions agreed upon. The codebook was then refined to take account of any new terminologies, additional definitions and filter questions. These pre-tests were critical in removing any cultural/linguistic bias in how the items/questions had been designed or worded. The author proceeded with the formal inter-coder reliability test only after sufficiently high reliability values had been achieved.

In total, three informal pretests and one formal reliability test were carried out for Germany (May-July 2015) and for Great Britain (November-December 2015). Two to three coders were used for the informal pretests and three coders for the formal inter-coder reliability test. The coders included two native German speakers and a native English speaker (the latter being the author of this thesis). It is recommended that at least 10% of the overall sample is tested for inter-coder reliability which equates to typically 200-300 items (Lombard, Snyder-Duch, & Bracken, 2002; Rössler, 2010). The sample for Germany included 17 government organisations, therefore, the websites and social media pages of two government ministries were coded as part of the formal inter-coder reliability test (this equated to 238 items/questions). The sample for Great Britain included 27 government organisations, therefore, the websites and social media pages of three government organisations were coded (equating to 357 items). For the informal and formal inter-coder reliability tests the Holsti coefficient was employed. The reliability threshold for all inter-coder reliability tests was set at the recommended minimum threshold of .8 (Lombard et al., 2002; Rössler, 2010). However, the pretests were carried out until coders had reached a Holsti value of more than .9. In the final formal inter-coder reliability test a reliability value of .9 for Germany and .93 for Great Britain was achieved. These values were significantly above the minimum threshold (see Appendix 4 for the breakdown of the results of the formal reliability tests).

The data was collected and analysed in SPSS (Version 21) and this resulted in two datasets, one for Great Britain and one for Germany. The datasets were cleaned by the author over a number of weeks after the coding had been completed. Any inconsistencies in the answers or missing values were discussed with the other coders to ensure all data had been inputted correctly and the data was clean. Finally, a quantitative evaluation of the results was carried out using SPSS. The two datasets were also combined in order to allow a comparative analysis of the results in SPSS.

5.10 Social Network Analysis

As outlined in the description of the methodological approach in Section 5.4, there are two empirical methods employed in this dissertation. The main empirical method is the online content analysis as outlined in the previous sections of this chapter. This study carried out an additional SNA using the retweet data collected during the online content analysis. As part of the online content analysis, this thesis analysed how many times a government organisation and individual retweeted other TW users. The purpose of this question was to examine to what extent government actors engage in networking behaviour online. Retweets suggest that actors pay attention to what others are saying online and it can be regarded as a form of interaction and networking behaviour (Nuernbergk & Conrad, 2016). Retweets also display a higher level of connectivity than simply following someone online as it suggests that they actively follow and listen to others[42].

The SNA draws on this retweet data in order to examine in greater detail the networking behaviour of government organisations and individuals. In reference to Borgatti (2013), Anstead and Chadwick (2017) state that network analysis "is based on the assumption that an actor's location in a network reveals his/her relational power vis-a-vis other actors" (p. 7). The SNA allowed this study to not only examine the extent to which they network with others, but to also examine which actors occupy a central position in government TW networks. The SNA is exploratory in design and the main aim was to examine whether there are any similarities or differences between the government networks (in terms of which actors are central) and

42 It must be pointed out that retweets are not considered to mean that there is a reciprocal relationship, nor does it reveal anything about the strength of the relationship.

whether certain macro-level factors possibly shape these networks. Some of the assumptions of this thesis (see Chapter 4) were that certain actors would play a prominent/central role in government networks (e.g., the centralised offices for government communications in both countries and the PM's Office in Great Britain).

Before carrying out the SNA, that is, creating the network, it was necessary to collect additional background information on the retweets. This involved analysing all the retweets by government organisations in order to identify who they had retweeted. In order to do this, an additional short codebook (in English) was designed by the author of this thesis for this purpose (see Appendix 5 for the SNA codebook used for both countries) and it contained a number of formal categories and one content category of analysis. Table 8 lists the categories included in the codebook. The point of this additional analysis was to identify *which* government actors retweeted and *who* they retweeted. This was necessary in order to be able to create the matrix and identify all actors in the network in both countries. Until now, the online content analysis had only analysed how many retweets there were over a two-week period, but it did not identify who they retweeted. This additional data had to be collected in order to create the network and identify everyone in the network.

Table 8. Overview of the Social Network Analysis Categories of Analysis

Formal Categories	Content Categories
– Name of the government organisation(e.g., the Cabinet Office) – TW name of the government organisation (@CabinetOffice) – Name of the actor being retweeted (e.g., BBC News) – TW name of the actor being etweeted (@BBCnews)	– Type of actor being retweeted (e.g., political, media, government actor or citizen)

All retweets by government actors in GB were coded by the author, while a native-speaking German coder examined all retweets by government actors in DE during the two-week period of analysis. This additional analysis also enabled the collection of important attribute information (such as whether an actor is a politician, or a journalist, or an ordinary citizen) that could potentially be used in the visualisation and analysis of the networks.

Once this data was collected, the matrix for the SNA was created in Microsoft Excel (one matrix for Germany and one for Great Britain). The networks were first designed as two-mode networks. However, after exporting them into the social network analysis software UCINet (Borgatti, Everett, & Freeman, 2002), it was discovered that the visualisation of the network didn't function due to a mistake in the design of the matrix as a mix of a one-mode and two-mode network. Nevertheless, it was possible to calculate the degree centrality values of the actors within the networks using UCINet. In order to successfully visualise the network, however, it was necessary to convert the network from a two-mode network into a one-mode network using the open source statistical software *R* (Version 3.4) (R Core Team, 2013). *R* produced a matrix in Microsoft Excel that could then be exported into the network visualisation software Gephi[43] (Version 0.92) (Bastian, Heymann, & Jacomy, 2009). The networks were finally visualised in Gephi using the layout algorithim "force atlas".

The next chapter, Chapter 6, will present the results of the online content analysis and SNA in Germany and Germany. These results will be presented according to the different empirical methods, categories of analysis and online platforms employed.

43 The format of the matrix that is produced by *R* in Microsoft Excel does not function in UCINet. It was necessary to use Gephi for visualising this type of matrix. Gephi also has the added advantage of producing higher quality network visualisations.

6. Results

This chapter presents the findings of a content analysis of the websites and social media pages of government organisations and individuals in Germany (DE)[44] and Great Britain (GB) and a SNA of the retweet networks of government organisations in both countries. The results will be divided up according to the two empirical methods, that is, the online content analysis and social network analysis. The results of the online content analysis will be divided up and presented according to the main categories of analysis: *interaction*, *networking*, *individualisation* on social media and *transparency*. Within each of these categories, this chapter will present the results for each platform, that is, websites, organisational Twitter (TW) pages, organisational Facebook (FB) pages, individual Twitter (TW) pages, individual Facebook (FB) pages and YouTube (YT) pages.

Chapters 3 and 4 of this dissertation outlined the need to understand how the macro level as well as the organisational level shapes and constrains communications. Chapter 4 argued that there is also a need to understand the changing relationship *between* and *within* different levels of analysis in the new media environment (see comparative and network perspectives in Chapter 4). This chapter, therefore, seeks to present the findings from a number of perspectives. This author will examine both similarities and differences across the two countries for each category of analysis and platform (the macro-level perspective). At the macro level, it is assumed that there will be a number of similarities between the countries, that is, they will use websites and social media predominantly for unidirectional communication, they will engage in little networking (other than with each other), and will increasingly have an individual presence on social media.

But the similarities and differences between government organisations within both countries are also examined (the inter-organisational/within-level perspective). At the organisational level, this author expects to find more differences than similarities due to different organisational cons-

44 For the purposes of this chapter only, this author will abbreviate Great Britain as GB and Germany as DE in order to avoid repetition, as the country names will be used continuously throughout. Social media pages will again be abbreviated as: Twitter (TW), Facebook (FB) and YouTube (YT) throughout for the same reasons.

traints within government organisations. Finally, this study also compares organisational and individual communications on social media (meso-micro perspective/between-level analysis) to establish if there are differences and similarities in how organisations interact online compared to individuals. Finally at the end of this chapter, the key findings of the empirical analysis will be summarised and it will be outlined whether the research guiding assumptions (RGAs) of this thesis were correct.

6.1 Online Content Analysis: Research Questions

As presented at the beginning of Chapter 5, the overarching research question for this study is the following:

RQ1. How are government organisations and individuals in Germany and Great Britain using websites and social media to communicate with citizens and media in their day-to-day communications?

The results of the online content analysis seek to answer this central RQ together with a number of sub-questions related to how government organisations and individuals use websites and social media for interaction, networking and individualised communications on social media. The online content analysis also seeks to answer a number of sub-questions related to similarities and differences at different levels of analysis. The sub-questions for the content analysis along with their corresponding research guiding assumptions (RGAs) are listed in full below (the full list of sub-questions and corresponding RGAs for the SNA will be summarised in Section 6.3):

RQ1 a. To what extent are government organisations using websites and social media to interact with media and citizens?

RGA4. Government organisations in both countries will predominantly engage in unidirectional (top-down) communication on their websites and social media.

RGA6. Government organisations in Germany will use websites and social media exclusively for unidirectional communication.

RQ1 b. To what extent are government organisations using websites and social media to connect/network with media and citizens?

RGA5. Government organisations in both countries will predominantly network with other government actors on social media.

RQ1 c. To what extent do government organisations have an individual social media page?

RGA7. Government organisations in both countries will engage in individualised communications on social media.

RQ1 d. How do government organisations present themselves on these individual social media pages? (e.g., a blurred identity between personal and government communications)

RGA8. Government organisations in both countries, will take similar approaches to the individualisation of organisational communications, that is, they will blur the boundary between organisational and individualised communications.

RQ1 e. To what extent are these individual social media pages transparent compared to organisational pages?

RGA9. Individual social media pages will be less transparent than organisational social media pages.

RQ1 f. Are there similarities between Great Britain and Germany in how government organisations and individuals use websites and social media to communicate with citizens and media in their day-to-day communications? (i.e., macro-level perspective)

RQ1 g. Are there differences between government organisations within Germany and Great Britain in how they use websites and social media to communicate with citizens and media in their day-to-day communications? (i.e., inter-organisational/meso-level perspective)

RGA1. Government organisations within Germany and Great Britain will use websites and social media differently. There will be differences between the organisations in the extent to which they use websites and social media for interaction and networking.

RQ1 h. Are there differences between government organisations and individual government actors in how they use websites and social media to communicate with citizens and media in their day-to-day communications? (meso-micro/between level analysis)

The results presented below in relation to the online content analysis will seek to answer each of these research questions and identify whether the research guiding assumptions were accurate. Section 6.1.1 will begin with presenting the results of a structural analysis of a number of formal content categories in the online content analysis.

6.1.1. Structural analysis government websites & social media

The collection and saving of government websites and social media pages for the online content analysis, facilitated an extensive structural analysis of the online platforms of government organisations and individual government actors in DE and GB. The codebook consisted of a number of formal content categories related to the extent to which government organisations and individuals have a website and their own social media pages. Table 9 lists the breakdown of government online presences across each platform in the two countries.

Table 9. Structural Analysis Websites (n=44) and Social Media Pages (n=120) per Country; absolute numbers

Platforms	DE	GB	Total (n)
Websites	17	27	44
TW Organisation	16[45]	22	38
TW Individual	4	14	18
FB Organisation	8	12	20
FB Individual	6	8	14
YT	12	18	30
Total	63	101	164

Table 9 and Figure 3 show that government organisations in DE and GB are ubiquitous online in terms of websites (DE & GB: 100%), their use of TW (DE: 94%; GB: 81%) and YT (DE: 71%; GB: 67%). However, Figure 3 shows that government organisations use FB much less with only half of the organisations using FB (DE: 47%; GB: 44%).

45 There are 16 government organisations with a TW account. Three of these organisations share the same TW account. @Regsprecher is the TW account for the German Federal Government (BR), the BPA and the Chancellor's Office (KA). In analysing the results of TW use in Germany, this study calculates 14 TW accounts rather than 16 accounts.

Figure 3. Percentage of Websites (n=44), FB (n=34), TW (n=56) and YT (n=30) Pages

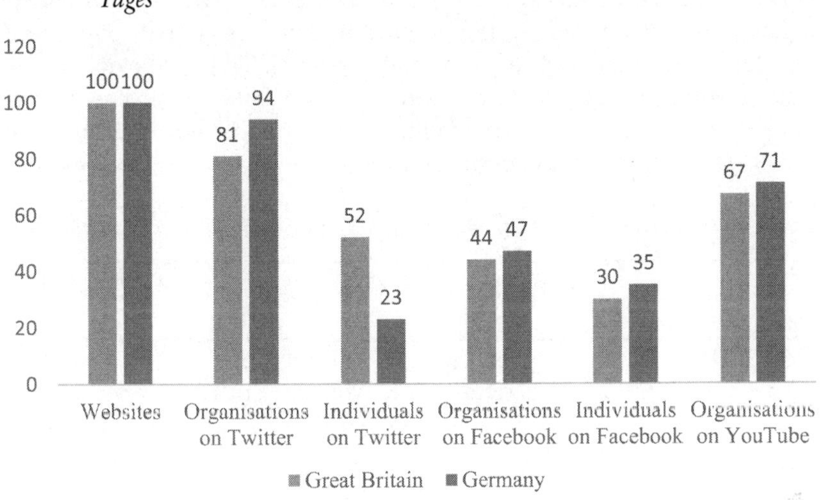

Overall, government organisations in both countries have a similar percentage of TW, FB and YT accounts. As part of the structural analysis, this study also examined to what extent government organisations have an individual presence on social media. The results in Figure 3 show that individual TW and FB pages also play a role in government communications, but they are less prevalent than organisational pages. However, there are some differences between GB and DE in this regard. For example, twice as many individual government actors in GB have a TW account compared to in DE (GB: 52%; DE: 23%). In addition, it is noteworthy that in GB there are more individual presences on TW (52%) than organisational presences on FB (44%). Overall, TW is the most dominant social media platform used by government organisations in the two countries.

6.1.2. Interaction on government websites

The content analysis analysed interaction on websites according to whether certain features were *unidirectional* (top-down, i.e., no interaction), *two-way asymmetrical* (citizens can interact in some way, but there is no dialogue or direct response from government) and *two-way symmetrical* (there is a dialogue/government responds) (Grunig & Hunt, 1984). This study assumes that government organisations in both countries will engage predominantly in unidirectional communication on their websites and social media. However, this study also assumes that in the case of Germany, government organisations will engage almost exclusively in unidirectional communication (due to a number of macro-level differences). Table 10 below lists the features found on government organisational websites according to each category of interaction in both countries. The results show that unidirectional features dominate in both countries.

Table 10. Overview of Interactive Features found on Government Websites

	Unidirectional	Two-way Asymmetrical	Two-way Symmetrical
Great Britain	1. News articles 2. Press releases 3. Publications 4. Speeches 5. Videos 6. Audio 7. Photos 8. FAQs 9. Microsites	1. Subscriptions 2. Volunteer in a government project/ campaign 3. Social media sharing icons 4. E-petition 5. Contribute to a public consultation	1. Government report on the outcome of a public consultation
Germany	1. News articles 2. Press releases 3. Publications 4. Speeches 5. Videos 6. Audio 7. Photos 8. Event calendar 9. Livestreaming 10. FAQs 11. Microsites	1. Subscriptions 2. Volunteer in a government project/ campaign 3. Social media sharing icons 4. E-petition 5. Apps 6. Survey 7. Contribute to a public consultation	1. Receive a report/response to a public consultation 2. Video featuring discussion between citizens & government actors 3. Forum 4. Submit a question/ comment/ receive a response

This study assumed that government organisations in both countries would engage predominantly in unidirectional communication. Table 10 above demonstrates that although there are more unidirectional features on websites than other interaction categories, there are also a number of two-way asymmetrical features in both countries. While there appears to be a larger selection of two-way asymmetrical features in DE compared to GB, there are, however, just a few government organisations that offer a number of these interactive features. These features are not available on every government website, whereas in GB, public consultations, e-petitions and options for volunteering appear on the website of every government organisation[46]. There are very few two-way symmetrical features on government websites in both countries. Once again, German organisations may appear to offer more two-way symmetrical features, but these are limited to just a few organisations. It was found that the KA[47] and the Federal Ministry for Agriculture and Food (BMEL) offered the widest selection of two-way asymmetrical and symmetrical features in DE. Overall, the results in this section demonstrate that organisational websites in both countries mostly offer unidirectional features, but they also offer a selection of two-way asymmetrical features. For example, social media sharing icons, apps, e-petitions and online public consultations. In the case of DE, these asymmetrical features are limited to just a few organisations; there is no consistency between the organisations.

46 An explanatory factor for this difference is the structure of government websites in GB. Each organisation in GB has a webpage rather than its own unique website. These webpages are part of the www.gov.uk website. This means that the same tabs/options appear at the top of every webpage e.g., public consultations, e-petitions etc. This website structure means that these features appear consistently across each organisational page, whereas government organisations in Germany have their own websites and their own unique design. Some websites are more modern than others.

47 Please note that the German abbreviations for German government ministries will be used throughout this chapter. The first time that a ministry is mentioned, it will be written in full in English, for example, "the Federal Ministry for Family, Seniors, Women and Youth". Subsequently it will be referred to using the German abbreviation "BMFSFJ". Please refer to the abbreviation list at the beginning of this dissertation.

6.1.3. Government organisations on Twitter: interaction

Previous studies on political participation on social media emphasise the changing nature of political participation (Bennett, 2012; Klinger & Svensson, 2015; Papacharissi, 2010). These studies argue that social media is facilitating new forms of political participation and that participation and interaction with politics takes place at different levels and in different ways (Chadwick, 2013; Klinger & Svensson, 2015; Svensson, 2015). This study views interaction as containing a number of different features and levels of analysis. Similar to interaction on websites, this study defines interaction according to three different levels of analysis. However, interaction on social media has a number of different characteristics due to its networked character. Table 11 below lists the different aspects of interaction that were examined and which category of interaction each feature belongs to. These categories apply to the analysis of all organisational social media pages.

Table 11. Interaction on Social Media: Categories of Analysis

Unidirectional	Two-way Symmetrical	Two-way Symmetrical
Top-down communication: – How many posts/ tweets in total? – How many posts/ tweets in two-week period of analysis? – How many followers?	Interactive elements: – Network with others (actively follow others) – Share/retweet information of other FB/TW users[48] – Encourage participation online (e.g., use language like "send us your comments" and "get involved")	Highest form of interaction: – Respond directly to the comments of other TW/FB/YT users (direct dialogue) – Include dialogue with citizens within multi-media content (applicable to videos on YT)

This study assumed that government organisations in both countries will engage predominantly in unidirectional communication. The results show

48 Networking is viewed as an important form of online interaction in this study. The results for this category will be dealt with in a separate section called "networking" and also as part of the additional SNA of retweets by government organisations.

that government organisations in GB and DE engage very little in direct conversation on TW, nor do they encourage participation on TW. The mean number of direct responses to other TW users in a two-week period was 4,55 in GB and 3,44 in DE. However, 32% of organisations in GB and 50% of organisations in DE failed to respond to other users over the period of analysis. A further 32% of organisations in GB and 19% of organisations in DE responded as little as 1-2 times during the two-week period. In relation to how often organisations encouraged participation on TW (e.g., call to action), the results were negative for both countries[49]. TW does not appear to be used for participatory purposes.

However, there were large differences between the organisations in both countries in terms of their unidirectional communication. Table 12 below and Table 13 show that there were extreme standard deviations between the organisations in terms of how many followers they had, how many users they followed, and how often they tweeted. There are significant differences between the mean and the median. Due to extreme values (e.g., the minimum number of followers was 5,203 and the highest was 3,450,000), the median is a better representative of how many followers they have and how many they follow.

Table 12. Organisations in GB: Number of Followers, Following and Tweets

Organisations on TW (GB)	Minimum	Maximum	Mean	Median	Standard Deviation (SD)
How many followers does the organisation have?	5203	3450000	278659	124000	716595,454
How many actors does the organisation follow?	85	29700	3904	954	8123,607
How many tweets in a fortnight (2 weeks)?	10	267	85	79	65,456

49 These results could not be represented in a graph as the results were too low.

Table 12 shows that the TW accounts in GB have a much higher number of followers (median: 124,000) than in DE (median: 15,900)[50]. However, the Standard Deviation (SD) for the number of followers is extreme in both countries. This means that some organisations have very few followers, while others have a huge following. However, the SD in GB is the most extreme and the main reason for this is that the prime minister's TW account (@number10gov), has a much larger following (3,450,000 followers), than any other TW account in GB. In DE, no TW account comes close to this number of followers. Table 13 shows that the maximum number of followers in DE is 345,000 for the TW account of the BPA (@RegSprecher)[51]. Steffen Seibert, the Head of the BPA, is responsible for this TW account and it is the main TW account for three government organisations: the German Federal Government (Bundesregierung), the BPA and the Chancellor's Office.

Table 13. Organisations in DE: Number of Followers, Following and Tweets

Organisations on TW (DE)	Minimum	Maximum	Mean	Median	Standard Deviation (SD)
How many followers does the organisation have?	1194	345000	90063	15900	140817,138
How many actors does the organisation follow?	2	1184	279	123	315,465
How many tweets in a fortnight?	7	192	62	64	46,057

There are also differences between the organisations in both countries in relation to how actively they tweet (unidirectional communication). The mean number of tweets in a two-week period in GB was 85,55 (SD: 65,456), whereas the mean number in DE was 62,81 (SD: 46,057). Again

50 It is important to point out that this higher number of TW followers in GB could be due to the fact that there is a higher number of TW users in GB compared to DE (www.statista.com; www.wearesocial.com).

51 As of March 15, 2018 @Regsprecher has 905,000 followers, triple the number of followers since this TW account was saved in March 2015. In GB @10downingstreet (formerly called @number10gov) still has significantly more followers than @Regsprecher in DE. It has 5,540,000 followers (March 15, 2018).

the standard deviations are large in both countries, but larger in GB. Figure 4 and Figure 5 show the distribution of tweets per fortnight in DE and GB. These figures demonstrate that there is no normal distribution in DE or GB, the values are widely spread and uneven between the organisations in both countries.

Figure 4. Frequency Histogram: Number of Tweets (n=1882) per Fortnight Government Organisations (n=22) in GB

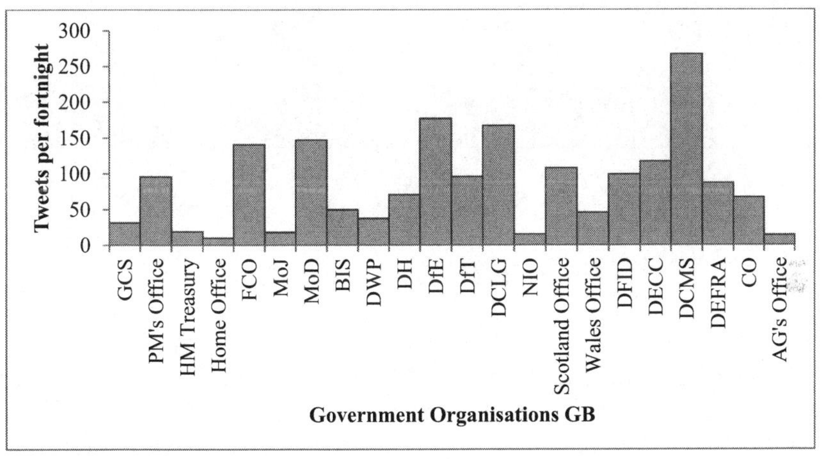

Figure 5. Frequency Histogram: Number of Tweets (n=1005) per Fortnight Government Organisations (14) in DE

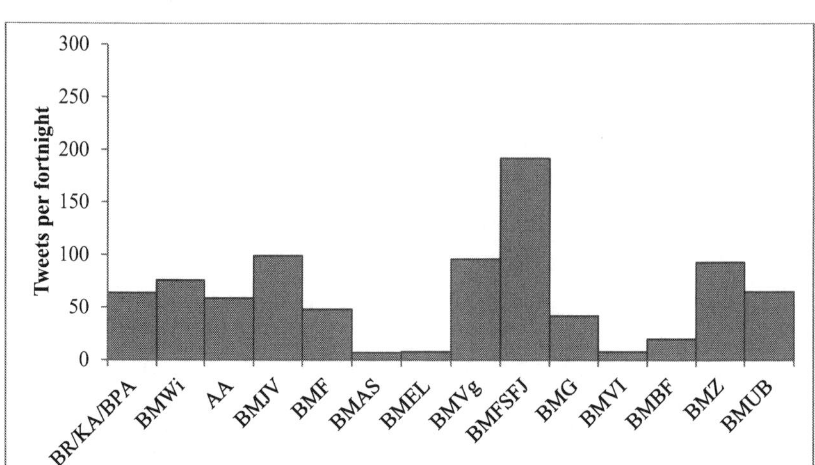

While Figure 4 and 5 demonstrate the uneven distribution of tweets over the two-week period, there is one organisation in both countries that stands out as tweeting significantly more than all other organisations. In DE, the Federal Ministry for Family, Seniors, Women and Youth (BMFSFJ) tweeted 192 times in two weeks, and in GB, the Department of Culture, Media and Sport (DCMS) tweeted 267 times in the same period. Figure 4 shows that although the values are spread more widely in GB, there are more organisations who tweet more often in GB[52].

Those organisations that tweeted most during the period of analysis also responded the most to other TW users. In DE and GB, there were two organisations that tweeted the most and also responded the most (please note that the number of responses are still very low). Table 14 shows that in DE it was the BMFSFJ and the Federal Ministry for Justice (BMJV). In GB it was the Department for Culture, Media and Sport (DCMS) and the Department for Education (DfE).

52 It was not possible to represent in a graph the results for the number of *followers* and *following* for both countries due to such extreme values. Therefore, the results for the number of tweets in a fortnight were presented as the values were less extreme.

Table 14. Organisations on TW: who Tweeted and Responded the most

	DE		GB	
	BMFSFJ	BMJV	DCMS	DfE
Number of tweets per fortnight	192	99	267	177
Number of responses per fortnight	11	9	39	17

This similarity suggests a possible connection between two variables, *number of tweets per fortnight* (i.e., how active they are) and *number of responses per fortnight* (i.e., how responsive they are). In addition, it is important to note that none of these organisations had a particularly high number of followers suggesting that there is no connection between the variable *number of followers* and how active organisations are online in terms of tweeting and responding.

While these results appear to support the assumption that government organisations in both countries engage predominantly in unidirectional communication, these results do not show that government organisations in DE are less interactive online. This study assumed that due to stronger regulation and more formalised structures of government communications in DE, German organisations will engage exclusively in unidirectional communication on social media. The mean number of direct responses to other TW users in a two-week period was 4,55 in GB and 3,44 in DE. The difference in the mean response rate is so small that it is not possible to conclude that government organisations in DE are less interactive on TW.

The next section will examine interaction by individual government actors on TW and whether there are differences in how individual government actors engage on social media compared to government organisations.

6.1.4. Government ministers on Twitter: interaction

This section presents the findings of how individual government ministers, in their capacity as the public face and main representative of their organisation, used TW for interacting with citizens and media online. It also compares both how individual government actors use TW across the two countries and how individual government actors use TW compared to government organisations within the countries.

While 52% of government ministers in GB (n=14) have an individual TW page and only 23% of ministers in DE (n=4) have an individual page, the results show that the few individual ministers in DE who have their own page have a higher following, are more active and responsive on TW than in GB. For example, the mean number of followers in DE is 39,650 (Median is 30,300) compared to 25,514 in GB (Median 15,000). The small number of ministers who use TW in DE are also more active in terms of tweets per fortnight and responses per fortnight. The mean number of tweets per fortnight is 62,75 in DE compared to 19,14 in GB, while the mean number of responses in DE is 11,25 compared to negative results in GB.

Table 15 lists the two government actors that are most active in both countries. When the organisational (i.e., organisations on TW) and individual levels of analysis (i.e., individuals on TW) are compared, there are similarities between those organisations that are most active on TW and the individual ministers that are most active on TW. In DE, the results show that Manuela Schwesig and Heiko Maas are the most active and responsive on TW[53]. Their respective ministries – BMFSFJ and BMJV – are also the most active and responsive on TW. In GB, Nicky Morgan is the most active and responsive government minister on TW and her organisation – DfE – was also the most active on TW (see Table 14 in the previous section for more information on these organisations).

Table 15. Individuals on TW: who Tweeted and Responded the most

	DE		GB	
	Manuela Schwesig (BMFSFJ)	Heiko Maas (BMJV)	Elizabeth Truss (DEFRA)	Nicky Morgan (DfE)
Number of tweets per fortnight	133	105	40	51
Number of responses per fortnight	32	13	0	4

53 Both were SPD Ministers within the coalition government at the time of the analysis. The SPD was the smaller party within the coalition.

In addition, when the overall number of followers, tweets per fortnight and responses per fortnight between the organisational and individual levels of analysis are compared, there are some interesting findings for DE. Table 16 shows that the individuals in DE have a higher following (median: 30,300) than the organisations in DE (median: 15,900). In DE, government individuals also respond more often (mean: 11,25) than government organisations on TW (mean: 3,44).

Table 16. Comparison of Individuals (n=18) and Organisations (n=38) on TW

	Individuals on TW		Organisations on TW	
	DE (n=4)	GB (n=14)	DE (n=16)	GB (n=22)
Followers (median)	30,300 SD: 25678,720	15,000 SD: 34126,504	15,900 SD: 140817,138	124,000 SD: 716595,454
Tweets per fortnight (mean)	62,75 SD: 66,012	19,14 SD: 14,832	62,81 SD: 46,057	85,55 SD: 65,456
Responses per fortnight (mean)	11,25 SD: 15,130	0,79 SD: 1,369	3,44 SD: 4,633	4,55 SD: 8,744

In summary, these results demonstrate that although there are fewer individual TW pages in DE, those few that are on TW have a higher following and are more active in terms of tweets and responses per fortnight than in GB. When the organisational and individual levels of analysis were compared, these results show there is a connection between those organisations that are most active on TW and the individual ministers that are most active on TW, in both countries. In DE, the results show that the TW accounts of individual ministers in DE have a higher following and higher response rate than organisations on TW. These findings suggest that some government individual actors use TW for direct interaction online and are not restrained by the more formalised structures of government communications in DE. The findings also highlight that it is not the most high-profile ministers or ministries that are most active and interactive on TW. In fact, it is lower-profile ministers and ministries that are more active on TW and they use it for two-way symmetrical interaction.

6.1.5. Government organisations on Facebook: interaction

A previous section on government organisations on TW (see Section 6.1.3) demonstrated that organisations in both countries engage predominantly in unidirectional communication on TW, they rarely respond to other TW users (low mean response rate) and do not encourage participation on social media (negative results). This top-down communication was also characterised by large deviations between the organisations in both countries in terms of how often they tweeted. However, the results in this section show different patterns of usage on FB.

The results of the structural analysis (see Section 6.1.1) show that FB is used by government organisations in both countries almost to the exact same extent. In GB, 44% (n=12) of organisations have a FB page, DE 47% (n=8). However, German organisations are more active in how they use FB. Table 17 shows that organisations in DE post more regularly on FB (mean: 19,63) compared to GB (mean: 12,17), they also respond significantly more in DE (mean: 69,25) compared to GB (mean: 0,67). While they post and respond more, the standard deviation in DE is larger than in GB (particularly in relation to the number of direct responses per fortnight). However, the standard deviations are not as large as on TW. These results suggest once again that government organisations in DE use social media, not just for unidirectional communication, but they use it in some cases for direct interaction and they are not restrained by the regulations or formal centralised structures in DE. The results show that government organisations in GB don't respond at all on FB; the results in Table 17 show negative results in this regard.

Table 17. Activity Levels of Organisations on FB in DE (n=8) and GB (n=12)

	Organisations on FB	
	DE	GB
Likes (median)	22,589	14,665
Posts in a fortnight (mean)	19,63 (SD: 13,928)	12,17 (SD:7,322)
Responses per fortnight (mean)	69,25 (SD: 122,597)	0,67 (SD: 1,497)
Participation on social media	1,00 (SD: 1,195)	0,67 (SD: 1,073)

While German organisations appear to use FB for direct interaction, of the eight organisations that have a FB page, there are just three organisations that post and respond regularly (this explains the large SD for German organisations in Table 17). The results in Figure 6 below show strong direct engagement by the German Federal Government (BR)/BPA[54] (348 direct responses), the Foreign Office (AA) (135 direct responses) and the Ministry for Defence (BMVg) (65 direct responses) on FB in DE. These organisations not only post regularly, but they also regularly engage in two-way symmetrical communication on FB, that is, they responded directly and regularly to user comments during the period of analysis.

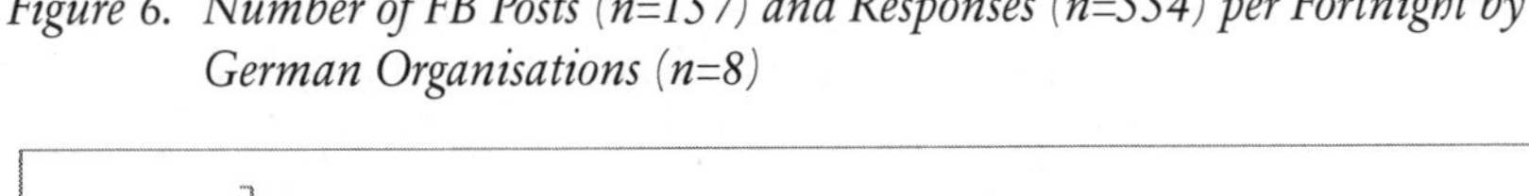

Figure 6. Number of FB Posts (n=157) and Responses (n=554) per Fortnight by German Organisations (n=8)

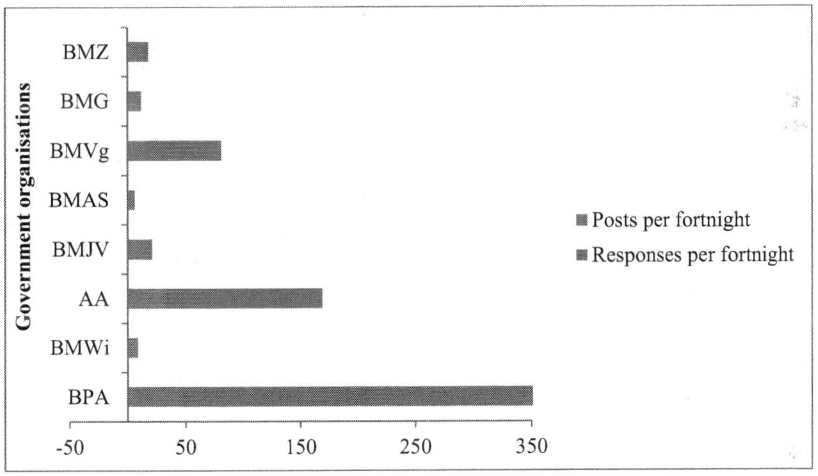

The assumption that government organisations will engage predominantly in unidirectional communication on websites and social media seems to be true for GB. In fact, British organisations appear to engage almost exclusively in unidirectional communication on social media. However, this assumption is less true for DE. A small group of organisations on FB (and individuals on TW) show a tendency towards using social media for interaction. The results show tendencies towards two-way symmetrical communication on social media in DE, albeit by a limited number of individuals

54 The BR and the BPA share the same Facebook organisational account.

and organisations. Another assumption of this study was, both the BPA and GCS would be two of the most active actors on social media in terms of interaction and networking. It is notable, that in the case of DE, the BPA is the most active and responsive government organisation on FB, but GCS doesn't feature as an active actor on social media.

6.1.6. Government ministers on Facebook: interaction

In GB, there is an overall low level of activity among government organisations (n=12) and individual government actors (n=8) on FB. The mean number of posts per fortnight among organisations in GB was 12,17, while for individuals it was only 5,13 (SD: 5,384). In fact, a number of individuals in GB didn't post at all on FB during the period of analysis, whereas all organisations on FB in GB posted during the period of analysis.

Ministers in DE are more active on FB (n=6), the mean number of posts in a fortnight is 18,33 (SD: 22,958) (similar to the rate of posts among organisations on FB). This is compared to a mean of 5,13 among individuals in GB. There is only one government minister in DE who stands out as posting regularly on FB, that is, Frank Walter Steinmeier (AA) who posted 62 times over two weeks (this explains the higher SD in DE). He also responded to some user comments (5 times). He was the only example of a minister in either country responding to any user comments on FB. Overall, the results for how often the ministers in both countries respond to comments on FB, share content from other government organisations and encourage participation on social media were negative. Individuals on FB appear to make no effort at interacting with others.

6.1.7. Government organisations on YouTube: interaction

In DE, 71% (n=12) of organisations and 67% of organisations in GB (n=18) have a YT page. The mean number of posts on YT in a two-week period was 4,82 (SD: 2,523) in DE and 3,50 (SD: 1,000) in GB. In GB, 50% of organisations didn't post any videos at all during the period of analysis. Overall, 83% of organisations with a YT page allow users to leave comments under their video posts. Only one government organisation stands out as being highly active in terms of posting videos and responding to user comments. For example, the BMVg in DE posted 11 videos during the period of analysis and responded 96 times to user comments. There was no organisation in GB that posted regularly or responded to user comments.

The content analysis also analysed the actual content of videos posted on YT over the two-week period of analysis to examine whether the videos featured any interaction with citizens, such as, discussions or interviews between citizens and government actors or government actors answering questions submitted by the public. The only organisation that featured this kind of interaction was the video blog of the KA called "Kanzlerin Direkt". In these videos, the Chancellor is interviewed by a member of the public and answers a number of questions submitted by citizens. No government organisation in GB posted video content that featured such interaction. Government organisations in GB appear to simply have a presence on YT, but it is not used for any form of interaction.

6.1.8. Government networking online

One of the central assumptions of this thesis is that government organisations in both countries will predominantly engage in unidirectional (top-down) communication and that they will rarely interact or network with citizens and media. Within this study, networking and connecting with others is viewed as another important aspect of interaction online (e.g., sharing/retweeting information, connecting with others through weblinks). This study considered networking to be a form of two-way asymmetrical communication (see Table 11 in this chapter). This study considers that interaction can emerge in different forms and it should not be viewed solely from a dialogic perspective. For example, the following was examined: the extent to which government organisational websites linked to each other, the extent to which websites allowed users to share information using social media sharing icons on their websites, the extent to which government actors actively followed other actors on TW (rather than simply being followed), and finally, the extent to which government actors retweeted or shared information by other actors on TW and FB[55]. While the findings of the previous sections suggest that government organisations in both countries engage predominantly in unidirectional communication online (apart from a few best practice examples, mostly in DE), this as-

55 In Section 6.3, this study will present a further aspect of government networking online, that is, the results of the SNA of government retweet networks.

sumption however, cannot be fully answered until networked forms of interaction are also examined.

Networking on websites

This study examined the extent to which government organisational websites connect with each other. In terms of connectivity, websites in GB were better connected to other government organisations. This means that they all connect to the websites/web pages of other government ministries, the cabinet office, the main government website (www.gov.uk or www.bundesregierung.de), and the office of the head of government. In GB, 96% of government organisations are connected with other government ministries, whereas only 53% of websites in DE contained links to other ministries. While 96% of organisations in GB linked to all ministries and agencies across the entire government, 82% of government organisations in DE linked only to those government agencies that are under the remit/responsibility of their department, rather than to the wider government. The results suggest that Government websites are not networked with each other in DE compared to GB.

These differences can be explained by the way in which government websites are structured in GB. There is an overarching government website www.gov.uk and each government organisation has its own webpage as part of this website. This means that each organisational webpage has the same design and tabs at the top of each page. For example, each webpage contains a tab called "departments" and this connects to the same central webpage which contains links to all government ministries and agencies. This overarching structure means that all government actors are better connected as all information is located within one overarching website, whereas in DE, each organisation has its own unique and separate website with a different design and content.

Finally, 100% of government websites in GB featured social media sharing icon options at the end of government announcements (e.g., news articles or press releases) which allow users to share government content on their own social media channels. 59% of government organisations in DE featured social media sharing icons on their websites, notably less than in GB.

Following others on Twitter

A central concept of TW is to be followed as well as to follow others (Jackson & Lilleker, 2011, p. 96). This allows for the expansion of a network and a reciprocal connection with other actors. In order to examine the networking practices of government actors, this study examined the extent to which government actors actively follow other actors on TW. This was viewed as another important aspect of networking. According to Jackson and Lilleker, the measurement of the follower-following ratio provides a good indication of whether a political actor is simply speaking or also listening to others (2011, p. 92). This study adopts the same approach taken by Jackson and Lilleker who "divided the number of tweeters following them by the number of tweeters they followed" (2011, p. 92). According to their approach, a ratio of ten or under indicates that the actor is also listening to the views of other tweeters. It does not mean, however, that they are engaging in a conversation. Instead it indicates a form of interaction, albeit, a low-level form of interaction.

Table 18 shows that in GB there were four government organisations and three ministers with a ratio of 10 or less. The organisation with the highest ratio (not included in the table below) was the PM's office with a ratio of 4971.

Table 18. Organisations & Individuals with Follower-Following Ratio of 10 or less in GB

Government Actor	Followers	Following	Ratio
GCS	5203	567	9
DCLG	84500	27400	3
NIO	6320	2090	3
Scotland Office	10500	1009	10
Tina Stowell (House of Lords)	3021	784	4
Stephen Crabb (Wales Office)	8130	975	8
Amber Rudd (DECC)	10600	1696	6

Similar to findings in previous sections, the results above suggest once again that lower-profile government ministries and ministers possibly take a more active approach to interaction and networking on TW. There is no high-profile ministry (e.g., the Home Office, HM Treasury or the PM's Office) that appears in the table above. Instead, lower-profile ministries and ministers appear to use TW not just for self-representation/unidirectional communication, but also as a means of interaction. It seems that it is more important for them to connect with others in comparison to larger ministries who (possibly) automatically receive a large following due to their higher profile within government. In DE, there was only one government organisation with a ratio of less than 10, that was the BMJV with a ratio of 6, while the BMVg had the highest (i.e., worst) ratio, a ratio of 10850.

These results suggest some differences between GB and DE in terms of how they use social media to network with others. Government actors in GB more often connect with others and follow what others are tweeting. However, there were larger differences between the organisations (inter-organisational comparison) than there were between the countries (macro-level comparison). In both countries, there were large variations in the follower-following ratio among all organisations. While these results may indicate some patterns (such as government actors in GB placing greater importance on connecting/networking with others), it would be wrong to read too much into the significance of the follower-following ratio. It could simply be the case that the higher the following a TW account has, the higher the ratio naturally becomes. It is not possible for social media accounts with millions of followers to also actively follow hundreds of thousands of other TW users. It is easier for those accounts with a smaller following to actively follow others.

Information sharing on Twitter

This study examined how often government organisations and individuals retweeted other TW users during the two-week period of analysis. This study regarded retweeting as a form of 2-way asymmetrical communication (see Table 11 in this chapter for a full list of categories regarding interaction). The findings show some differences between the organisations in both countries in relation to how often they retweet others. The mean number of retweets in a two-week period in GB was 33,73 (SD: 35,199) and in DE the mean was 22,50 (SD: 24,298). Again, the standard deviations are relatively big in both countries, but larger in GB. The government ministry that retweeted most often in GB was the DCMS (126 retweets), in DE it was the BMFSFJ (82 retweets). However, individuals in DE retweet more often than individuals in GB. In DE, there was a mean value of 33,75 retweets (SD: 36,909) compared to just 5,93 retweets (SD: 6,354) in GB. The individual that retweeted most often in DE was Manuela Schwesig (BMFSFJ) (80 retweets) followed by Heiko Maas (BMJV) (46 retweets). This retweet data will be analysed in greater detail in Section 6.3, where this author will examine which actors were retweeted and who was most central in government retweet networks.

6.1.9. Individualised communications on social media

One of the assumptions of this study is that the networked media environment is resulting in a changing boundary between the public and private domain of communication (Papacharissi, 2010), which is resulting in a dissolving boundary between individual and organisational communication (Bimber et al., 2009; Van Dijk, 2012). According to these perspectives, individuals are increasingly engaging in politics in a private sphere outside the realm of traditional politics (Bennett, 2012; Dahlgren, 2005; Papacharissi, 2010). This study assumes that government organisations will also seek to adapt to this characteristic of the new media environment and engage in more individualised communications on social media. This study also assumes that individual government actors will use social media in a way that blurs the boundary between their personal private communications and organisational government communications.

This category of analysis – individualisation on social media – examines two aspects in relation to the individualisation of organisational government communications. First, it examines the extent to which government ministers (as the main representatives of government organisations) have an individual presence on TW and FB. Secondly, it examines how these individuals present themselves online, whether their individual TW or FB page is presented as an "official government page" (i.e., a government organisational page) or a "non-official government page" (i.e., a personal page)[56]. A page was considered to be an official government page if it stated clearly in the infobox (information box in the top-left corner) that it was connected to the government or a particular government organisation. An individual page was coded as an official government page if there was a weblink in the infobox to his or her government ministry or to the main government website, if it clearly stated that it was an official government page, if it stated that the press office of the ministry was responsible for the content, or if it was linked from the ministry's website. If none of these features were present then it was coded as a non-official government page. Non-official government pages typically included a link to a personal web-

56 Individual pages that were clearly party political pages were excluded from the sample. This included any page in which the party logo or the name of the political party appeared in the profile photo or background photo, if there was a direct link to the website of a political party in the infobox, or if it stated in the infobox that a political party was responsible for the social media page. This study analysed those individual pages that were a mix of government, political and personalised communications.

site and the actors also often identified themselves within the infobox as being both a government actor, a political actor and an individual.

While the results of the structural analysis (Section 6.1.1) demonstrated that there are more organisational pages than individual pages on social media, a number of government actors have an individual presence on social media. Figure 7 below shows the percentage breakdown of organisational and individual accounts on TW and FB in both countries. The graph shows there is a significant number of individual TW accounts in GB with 52% (n=14) of individual government actors on TW. In DE, fewer government actors have an individual presence on TW with only 23 % (n=4) having their own TW page.

Figure 7. Percentage of Organisational (n=56) vs. Individual (n=32) Social Media Pages

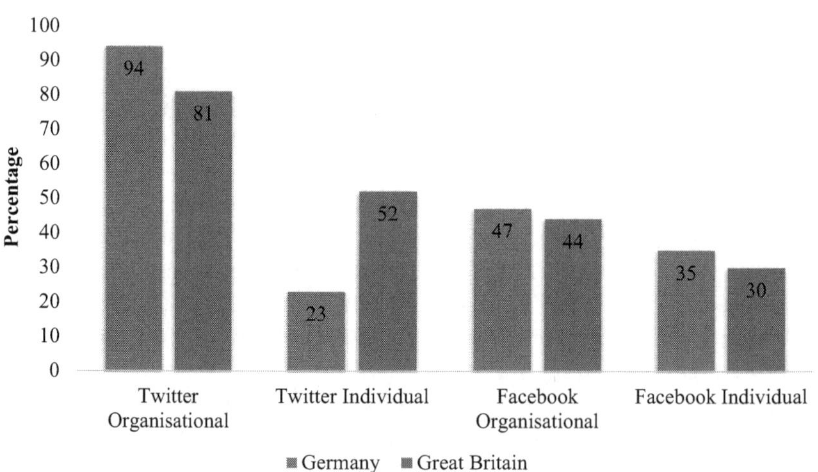

Section 6.1.4 previously described that although only a few individual ministers in DE have their own TW page, these ministers have a higher following, are more active in terms of tweeting and more responsive in replying directly to other users than individual ministers in GB. In fact, individual ministers in GB tweeted rarely and didn't respond at all to other users.

Figure 8 shows the breakdown of individual pages that were categorised as being official (organisational) or non-official (personal/individual) government pages. The graph shows that in GB, 86% (n=8) of FB and 100% (n=14) of TW pages are non-official government accounts. In DE the picture is slightly more mixed, for example, on FB just 50% (n=6) of accounts appear to be non-official. However, 75% (n=4) of TW accounts are non-official, similar to GB. In the two countries, out of a total sample of 32 individual pages, 26 have a social media page that is categorised as non-official. They are predominantly a mix of government (official) and personal communications (non-official).

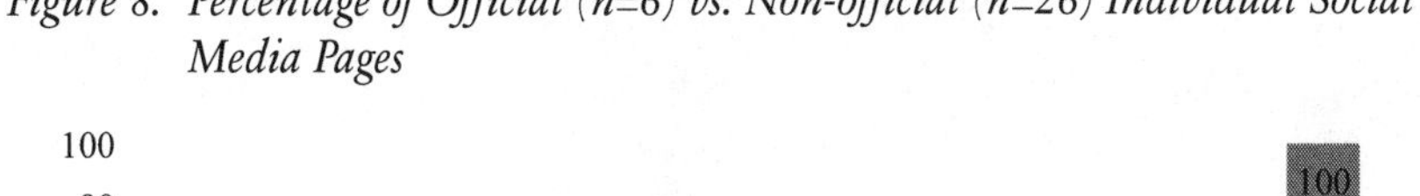

Figure 8. Percentage of Official (n=6) vs. Non-official (n=26) Individual Social Media Pages

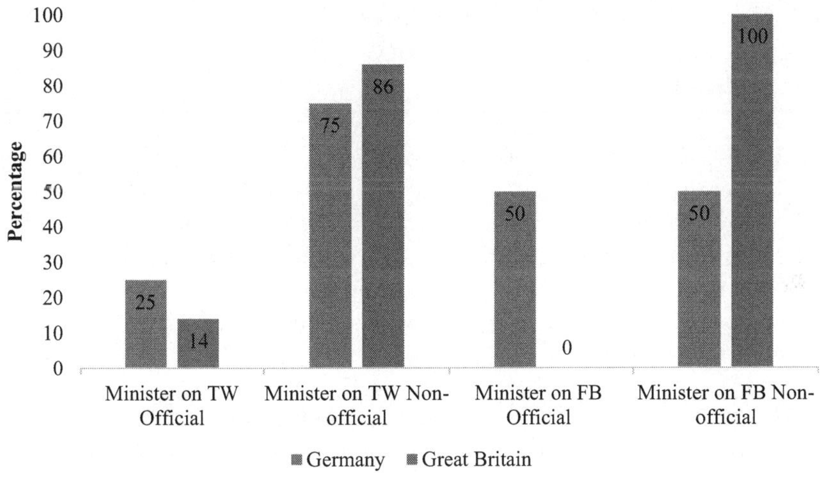

This means that the majority present a blurred identity on their individual pages. It is unclear whether the individual is speaking on behalf of the government and his or her ministry, or whether the individual is speaking in a personal or private capacity.

One of the questions in the codebook was, did these accounts include a link to a personal website, a government website or another website (see Appendix 3 for codebook). Out of a sample of 14 individuals with a TW account in GB, 9 (64%) of these featured a link to a personal website. In DE, 3 out of 4 (75%) individuals on TW featured a link to a personal website. All 8 (100%) individual FB pages in GB contained a link to a personal website, while 5 out of 6 (83%) individuals in DE had a link to a personal website. As Table 19 and 20 show, the majority of individual TW and FB pages in both countries link to the personal websites of individual government actors. These results suggest that these accounts are intended first and foremost to appear as personal accounts. They rarely featured a link to a government website.

Table 19. Personalisation on FB Pages (n=14) in DE and GB

Country	Great Britain (n=8)	Germany (n=6)
Link to personal website	100%	83%
Identify as political actor only	50%	0%
Identify as government actor only	0%	0%
Identify as both political and government actor	50%	100%

As Tables 19 and 20 demonstrate, the majority of individuals also presented or identified themselves (in the infobox on the top left-hand corner of each page) as being both a government minister (usually stating their ministerial title and the name of their ministry) and a politician (for example, in GB they often mentioned their constituency). In GB, 50% of government actors did not present themselves as being a government actor, but specifically a political actor.

Table 20. Personalisation on TW Pages (n=18) in DE and GB

Country	Great Britain (n=14)	Germany (n=4)
Link to personal website	64%	75%
Identify as political actor only	28,5%	0%
Identify as government actor only	0%	25%
Identify as both political and government actor	71%	75%

Although this study did not carry out a detailed qualitative analysis of the content of tweets and posts on these individual pages, it was clear that the tweets/posts were for the most part, a mix of political and government content. They tweeted and posted about their work as a member of parliament (MP) and in their constituency, but they also posted and tweeted about their work as a minister in government and often retweeted content by their own government ministry. The majority of individual pages in GB appeared to have no clear boundary between official government and political communications. Similar patterns were found in DE where government actors predominantly identified themselves as being both a politician and a government actor. The only government actor in DE whose account was explicitly presented as an official government account, was the Minister for Justice Heiko Maas. Both his FB and TW pages link to his Ministry's website rather than a personal website. In the profile section of this TW page, it states that staff at the ministry are responsible for tweeting most of the content. The only account that stated clearly that it was a personal account was Peter Altmaier in DE (the head of the Chancellor's Office). He stated clearly in the infobox that all tweets were his own personal opinions.

This study also compared the individual TW accounts of the heads of the centralised government communications offices in both countries, that is, Steffen Seibert Head of the BPA and Alex Aiken, Head of GCS. There were some interesting differences in how these actors presented themselves online. First, although Steffen Seibert's page appears in his name and is called @RegSprecher, the TW page is clearly an official government organisational page[57]. His TW profile clearly states it is a government account and that all his tweets are on behalf of the BPA/BR. The infobox also contains a link to the website of the federal government www.bundesregierung.de. This page is clearly official government organisational communications, although it is presented as the individual page of Steffen Seibert. In stark contrast, Alex Aiken's individual TW account is a strong mix of government and personal communications. In the infobox, he describes himself as a "Government Communicator, Chairman of Westminster Wanderers FC and Arsenal Fan". There is no link to any personal website or government organisational website. While this page appears to be more of a personal page, however, he describes himself first and foremost as a government communicator and much of the content in his tweets refers to the work of the GCS. The boundary between government and personalised communications is blurred in this case. This example of Steffen Seibert (along with the examples of Heiko Maas and Peter Altmaier) suggests a slight difference in approach to individualised social media

57 It is important to point out that the only TW page for the BPA was the TW page of Steffen Seibert. While it was in his name, this study categorised the individual page as an official government organisational page. The GCS in GB had its own organisational page, but Alex Aiken, Head of Communications at GCS, also had his own individual page.

pages in DE compared to GB. It suggests a slightly more formalised and transparent approach.

Nevertheless, the predominant representation of individual government actors on social media as a mix of personal, party political and government communications, calls into question the transparency of online government communications. It appears that on individual social media pages, there is for the most part no clear boundary between government, party political and personal interests both in how they present themselves and in the content on these pages. Individualised communications are being used in both countries in a way that blurs the boundary between government and party political communications and between organisational and individual communications. These findings suggest a lack of transparency in how government individuals communicate on social media. This raises possible concerns as to whether online government communications respects legal restrictions and codes of practice requiring governments to refrain from engaging or using government resources for election campaigning or more partisan communications, restrictions that are in place in both countries.

6.1.10. Transparency of government communication online

This category of analysis is closely connected to the previous category of analysis, analysing the blurring of identities on individual social media pages, as this could suggest a lack of transparency on social media pages. Therefore, one of the assumptions of this study is that individual social media pages will be less transparent than organisational social media pages. For example, the content analysis examined the extent to which organisational and individual social media pages made clear who was responsible for social media content and if there was information provided on TW or FB in relation to social media policies. This study examined profile descriptions on FB and TW, and also the "About" page on FB, to see if it was clear who was responsible for social media content, for example, their ministry's press office, parliamentary office or local constituency office, or themselves.

The results showed that government organisations in DE had a higher level of transparency on TW compared to in GB. In DE, 75% (n=16) of organisations stated who was responsible for content on TW, while only 32% (n=22) of British organisations stated who was responsible. Of the 14 individuals with a TW page in GB, not a single page stated who was responsible for the content, while two out of four individuals in DE (Heiko Maas and Peter Altmaier) stated who was responsible for content. Heiko Maas made it clear that staff at his ministry were responsible for tweeting and that any personal tweets by the minister were identified with the initials "HM" at the end of the tweet. Peter Altmaier stated clearly on his TW page that all tweets were his own.

In relation to organisations on FB only 17% (n=12) of organisations in GB stated who was responsible for content, while 100% (n=8) of organisations in DE stated who was responsible. There was a similar pattern in relation to individuals on FB with only 12,5% of individuals stating who was responsible for content in GB, while 100% of individuals in DE stated who was responsible. Table 21 lists the number and percentage of organisations and individuals that state who is responsible for content on their social media pages.

Table 21. Organisational vs. Individual Transparency on Social Media in DE & GB

	Organisations		Individuals	
	Twitter	Facebook	Twitter	Facebook
Germany	12/16 (75%)	8/8 (100%)	2/4 (50%)	6/6 (100%)
Great Britain	7/22 (32%)	2/12 (17%)	0/14 (0%)	1/8 (12,5%)

In relation to transparency on social media, there is a clear difference in approach between the countries. There was a notably higher level of transparency in DE across both platforms and at the organisational and individual level, that is, organisations on TW (75%), organisations on FB (100%), individuals on FB (100%), and to a lesser extent individuals on TW (50%). There doesn't seem to be a noticeable difference between individual and organisational pages. Transparency appears to be shaped by differences at the macro level rather than differences between the organisations.

In relation to those social media accounts that state who is responsible for content, a mix of different actors looked after the content. For example, in relation to individual FB pages in DE, Peter Altmaier's FB page is managed by the CDU party in his constituency of Saarland (suggesting it is more of a political page), Frank-Walter Steinmeier's by himself, Heiko Maas's page by the Internet editorial team at the BMJV, Andrea Nahles's by the Internet editorial team at the Federal Ministry for Work and Social Affairs (BMAS), Hermann Groehe by himself, and finally Barbara Hendrick's page is managed by the Federal Ministry for Environment (BMUB). This would suggest that in DE there is a coherent government policy of transparency around content on social media, but that each actor decides themselves who is responsible for the content.

Additionally, the results showed that 47% of German organisations provided information in relation to social media policy on their social media pages (e.g., so-called netiquette), while only 15% of British organisations provided the same information on social media pages. An analysis of government organisational websites in GB showed that 22% of these websites provided information on social media policy on their homepage. Overall, there seems to be a stronger policy of transparency with regard to social media in Germany, and little transparency on organisational and individual social media pages in GB.

In summary, there is a clear difference between the countries in relation to transparency and who is responsible for content on social media. The most important difference is a clear policy of transparency in DE in relation to organisational and individual social media pages. This pattern is found across all social media platforms in DE, and stands in stark contrast to GB where both individual and organisational pages lack any transparency. Overall, there doesn't seem to be any large difference between transparency on individual pages compared to organisational pages nor is there a noticeable difference between the platforms.

6.1.11. Changing press relations in an online sphere

The content analysis examined the extent to which media is a focus of organisational communications efforts on their websites. It was examined whether government websites contained a clear press section, for example, a link on the homepage to a section called “press” or “media” and whether this section contained specific resources for journalists, for example, press releases as well as other services like accreditation, information on upcoming press conferences and media events etc.

All government organisations in DE had a clear press section, while only 7% (2/24) of government organisations in GB had a press section with specific resources for journalists. Instead, there were a number of “media inquiries” sections on the British websites that simply provided contact details for media spokespersons, but they did not provide any services for journalists. There were also a number of additional TW pages specifically for the press offices (e.g., @Number10press). In DE, 94% of press sections contained contact information, whereas in Great Britain only 78% of press or media inquiries sections contained such information. Additionally, the German websites provided a larger variety of services for journalists, for example, important appointments/press calendars, special login areas, press photos, accreditation, contact details for spokespersons, special seminars and newsletters for journalists.

This section of the content analysis demonstrated how difficult it is to accurately assess government media relations simply by examining whether there are press sections and services for journalists on websites. The fact that there are clear press sections on the German websites and not on the British websites, does not necessarily reveal anything about the state of government media relations. It reveals more perhaps about the transparency of information available for the press in DE compared to GB. Mainly, it demonstrates how little one can interpret such results from an online content analysis and it is one of the reasons why a network perspective has been incorporated into this study. In order to gain a better insight into whether media is a focus of their online communications practices, Section 6.3 will present the results of the SNA of government retweet networks examining what type of actors feature in government organisational networks, and whether media actors feature prominently.

6.2 Interim Summary: Results of the Online Content Analysis

The findings of the structural analysis of websites and social media pages in Section 6.1.1 at the beginning of this chapter, revealed a number of similarities between the two countries in terms of the extent to which government actors are present online. The results show that websites and social media are omnipresent among government organisations in both countries. In particular, TW stands out as the social media platform of choice for government organisations in both countries. In GB, 81% of organisations have a TW page and in DE 94% have a TW page. Individual government actors in GB, however, have a much higher presence on TW than individual actors in DE (GB: 52%; DE: 23%). TW is used significantly more than FB in both countries. Government organisations in DE and GB have a similar percentage of FB pages (GB: 44%; DE: 47%) and also a similar percentage of individual FB pages (GB: 30%; DE: 35%).

While government organisations may be ubiquitous in terms of their presence online, this does not mean that they use these platforms actively, or for the purpose of interaction and networking. The findings of the online content analysis support the assumption of this thesis that government organisations in both countries use websites and social media predominantly for unidirectional communication. The findings found that government organisations almost never encouraged participation on social media, they rarely shared/retweeted content, actively followed others or rarely responded to other users on FB and TW. Even though they predominantly engaged in unidirectional communication, there were some examples of two-way asymmetrical communication and some limited examples of two-way symmetrical communication on websites and social media. But this two-way symmetrical communication was limited to just a few organisations (this will be discussed in greater detail below). One of the most important findings was that there were significant differences between the organisations in both countries in relation to their unidirectional communication.

These findings supported another assumption of this study, that is, that government organisations in DE and GB would use websites and social media differently. This study assumed that there would be differences between the organisations in the extent to which they use websites and social media for interaction and networking. The findings of the online content analysis suggest there are factors at the meso/organisational level that influence how government organisations use digital technologies. There was little consistency between the organisations in relation to how they use websites and social media for interaction. There were large deviations in relation to how many followers they had, how many actors they follow (following/follower ratio), how actively they post/tweet, how actively they share content, and how often they respond to comments or tweets on FB and TW. The largest differences in interaction levels between government organisations were found on TW.

This study also assumed that the centralised organisations for government communications – the BPA in DE and the GCS in GB – would be two of the most active organisations on social media in terms of interaction and networking. However, this was found to be only partly true. It was found that the most active and interactive organisation on FB in DE was the BPA, it posted and responded regularly. The BPA also tweeted actively and responded a number of times to other TW users, but it wasn't the most active organisation on TW in DE. In comparison, GCS in GB, wasn't a prominent actor on social media. However, a pattern emerged that the most active/interactive organisational actors on TW were lower profile government ministries and ministers. There were only a few government actors in both counties who stood out as being highly active in terms of tweeting and responding to other users on TW. This included the BMFSFJ and BMJV in DE and the DCMS and DfE in GB. The ministers (three out of four) of these ministries also behaved in a similar way on TW (Manuela Schwesig, Heiko Maas, and Nicky Morgan). While those actors who were found to be the most active and interactive on TW were lower-ranking government organisations and ministers, the opposite was the case on FB. There were only a handful of government organisations who were highly active/interactive on FB and these were three high-profile government organisations in DE. The three actors that stood out as being the most active in terms of posting and responding to posts on FB were the BR/BPA (same FB page), the AA, and the BMVg.

It was assumed that government actors in DE would engage exclusively in unidirectional communication on social media compared to those in GB. One of the reasons for this assumption was, that there is a stronger regulatory environment and more formalised structures for government communications in DE, compared to GB. However, the results show that these macro factors do not appear to influence the extent to which government actors interact with others on social media. Although there were just a few examples of organisations and individuals who use social media for interaction with others (i.e., two-way asymmetrical or symmetrical interaction), the few examples that existed were mostly found in DE. As mentioned above, these examples were limited to just a handful of government organisations (BMFSFJ and BMJV) and individuals (Heiko Maas and Manuela Schwesig) on TW, government organisations on FB (BPA, AA and BMVg) and two government organisations (BMVg and KA) on YT. Whereas the findings showed that it is British government organisations and individuals that engage almost exclusively in unidirectional communication and that this is the case across all social media platforms in GB.

In examining whether government actors predominantly engage in unidirectional communication online, the content analysis also considered a number of networking features of interaction on websites and social media. Networking was considered to be a form of two-way asymmetrical interaction. This author examined the extent to which government organisational websites linked to each other, the extent to which websites featured social media sharing icons, the extent to which government actors actively followed others on TW, and how often they retweeted others on TW. In this regard, the results suggest that online communications in GB is better networked, and therefore, more interactive. 100% of organisational webpages in GB linked to all ministries and agencies across government. In contrast, the majority of government organisations in DE only linked to those government agencies under the remit of each individual department. Additionally, it was found that government actors in GB more often connect with others on TW and follow other users (stronger follower/following ratio). British organisations also retweeted more often than their German counterparts. The findings of these networking features suggest that government actors in GB do not engage exclusively in unidirectional communication online, but there are signs that they engage in more networked forms of communication.

This study assumed that government organisations in both countries would engage in individualised communications on social media and they would take similar approaches to individualised communications, that is, individual government actors would present themselves in a way that blurs the boundary between official government (organisational) communications and more personalised communications. It was found to be true, that government organisations in both countries use social media to engage in more individualised communications. It was also found to be true, that the majority of individual actors in both countries blur the boundary between government, political and personal identities in their TW and FB profiles. The findings revealed that social media pages are predominantly presented as non-official government communications. Out of a total sample of 32 individual pages on FB and TW, 26 of these pages were categorised as non-official. However, there was one notable difference between the two countries, that is, the political identity was stronger in GB. Individuals in GB more often blurred the political and government identity. These findings raise a number of concerns around the transparency of government communications on social media and the separation of government communications from more partisan political communications.

Finally, it was assumed that individual social media pages would be less transparent than organisational social media pages. The content analysis examined and compared the extent to which organisational and individual pages stated who was responsible for content on these pages. In this regard, there was an important difference between the countries. The results showed that government actors in DE had a higher level of transparency on social media compared to in GB. In DE, 75% of organisational TW pages, 100% of organisational FB pages, 100% of individual FB pages, and 50% of individual TW pages clearly stated who was responsible for online content. Additionally, the results showed that 47% of German organisations provided information in relation to social media policy (e.g., so-called netiquette). In GB, both individual and organisational pages lacked any transparency. The content analysis showed that there was no difference in transparency between individual organisational pages, but there was a significant difference between the countries. This suggests that particular aspects of the macro environment influence approaches to transparency online. Table 22 presents an overview of the key findings of the online content analysis.

Table 22. Overview: Results of the Online Content Analysis

Content Analysis				
Categories of Analysis	Websites	Twitter	Facebook	YouTube
Interaction/ Participation	Unidirectional features dominate; large selection of two-way asymmetrical features; limited 2-way symmetrical options	– Predominantly unidirectional communication; large differences between organisations in terms of how actively they tweet/followers; extreme SDs in both countries; highest activity levels in GB – Didn't encourage any interaction & participation on TW – Organisations in GB and DE rarely responded to other TW users – Exception: two organisations in both countries actively tweeted and responded (BMFSFJ, BMJV, DCMS, DfE) – Ministers of BMFSFJ, BMJV and DfE also actively tweeted/ responded – Individual TW accounts tweeted & responded more than organisations in DE	– Predominantly unidirectional, but some examples of two-way symmetrical interaction – Organisations on FB in DE post more regularly and respond significantly more than GB (mean response rate: 69,25; compared to negative in GB) – Pattern of two-way symmetrical communication on FB in DE, but limited to 3 organisations: BR/BPA, AA and BMVg – Individual actors in DE post more often – Overall individuals show no efforts at interaction in DE or GB	– Almost exclusively unidirectional communication – Organisations in DE post more videos; very few posts in GB – Only one organisation actively posts and responds to user comments(BMVg in DE) – Government/ citizen interaction in videos on the website of the Chancellor's office (Kanzlerin Direkt)

Content Analysis				
Categories of Analysis	Websites	Twitter	Facebook	YouTube
Networking (form of interaction)	– Websites in GB better connected in terms of links and social media sharing options – 96% of webpages in GB connect with all government depts./ agencies – Websites in DE connect only with agencies under their remit	– Government actors in GB retweeted more often, but large differences between the organisations – Government actors in GB had a better followers/ following ratio; 7 actors had a ratio of 10 or less, compared to only 1 actor in DE	– Rarely shared content by other government actors	n/a
Individualisation on social media	n/a	– 18 individual TW pages in total – Individual TW pages almost exclusively presented as non-official government communications – Blur boundary between personal, government and political identities – Strong similarities across DE and GB – Stronger political identity in GB – Tweets are a mix of government and political content	– 14 individual FB pages in total – Individual FB pages almost exclusively presented as non-official government communications – Blur boundary between personal, government and political identities – Strong similarities across DE and GB – Stronger political identity in GB – Posts are a mix of government and political content	n/a

Content Analysis				
Categories of Analysis	Websites	Twitter	Facebook	YouTube
Press	Stronger press sections/ Media services in DE; 100% of websites in DE featured clear press sections compared to just 7% in GB; websites also provided more contact information for media	n/a	n/a	n/a
Transparency	Websites in GB appear to be more transparent – easily accessible information on British homepages on FOI (89%), transparency laws (81,5%), access to government publications – More info on German websites around organisational structure (82%)	Significantly higher level of transparency in DE on organisational and individual TW pages. 75% of organisations & 50% of individuals stated who was responsible for content – German social media pages featured more information on social media policies	Significantly higher level of transparency in DE on organisational and individual FB pages. 100% of FB pages stated who was responsible for content – German social media pages featured more information on social media policies	n/a

6.3 Social Network Analysis: Research Questions

This next section will present the results of a SNA of the retweet networks of government organisations and individuals in the two countries. The SNA seeks to answer the following overarching RQ:

RQ2. How are government organisations in Germany and Great Britain using Twitter to network with citizens and media in their day-to-day communications?

Related to this question are two sub-questions and listed underneath these sub-questions are the corresponding research guiding assumptions (RGAs) that were presented in Chapter 4:

RQ2 a. Who are government organisations networking with on TW? (e.g., political, media, citizens, or other government actors)

RGA5. Government organisations in both countries will predominantly network with other government actors on social media.

RQ2 b. Which actors occupy central positions in their TW networks?

RGA2. Both the BPA and GCS will be central actors within government social networks. They will occupy a central position in social media networks and they will be one of the most active actors on social media in terms of interaction and networking.

RGA3. The PM's Office will be a central actor within government social media networks in Great Britain. It will occupy a central position in social media networks and it will be one of the most active actors on social media in terms of interaction and networking.

This study was also interested in examining the possible macro factors that shape government networks. Therefore, there is another sub-question on the macro similarities and differences:

RQ2 c. Are there similarities or differences between the countries in how government organisations and individuals use Twitter to network with citizens and media in their day-to-day communications?

In Section 6.1.8, this chapter outlined how often government organisations retweeted information by other TW users within the two-week period of analysis. The results of the online content analysis revealed that government organisations in GB retweeted more often than their German counterparts. However, the online content analysis could only provide a limited analysis of the networking behaviour of government actors on social media. For this reason, this study carried out an additional SNA in order to examine their networking behaviour from a network perspective and focused on TW networks as TW is the most used social media platform by government organisations in the two countries.

This study chose to specifically examine the retweet networks of government actors as retweets represent a higher level of connectivity than simply linking to another website or following someone on TW[58]. It indicates a form of active, rather than passive, following and is therefore regarded as a form of interaction in this study (i.e., two-way asymmetrical). Using the retweet data collected and analysed for the online content analysis, this study carried out an additional analysis of retweets in order to identify who was retweeted[59]. With this information, the author was able to create the network matrices and visualise them using network visualisation software[60]. The purpose of applying this method was to examine, from a network perspective, to what extent they retweet other actors, which actors feature in their networks (i.e., who they retweet), which actors are central within these networks, to what extent do they network with other government organisations, and are there differences or similarities between the countries (e.g., does the macro level shape these networks).

There are a number of RGAs based on the network perspectives outlined in Chapter 4 and also based on differences in the political system outlined in Chapter 3. This study assumes that the macro-level environment will shape these networks. This author assumes that the centralised organisations for government communications – the BPA and GCS – will occupy central positions in both government networks. It is also assumed that due to the centralisation of government communications in the PM's office in GB (Dowding, 2013; Heffernan, 2006), the PM's Office will also play a central role in the British network. Similar to the assumption in the online content analysis, that government actors would engage predominantly in unidirectional communication, it is assumed that government actors in both countries will rarely network with others, but they will mainly network with other government actors. Despite this assumption, the SNA allows an exploratory analysis of other actors that may be present within their networks, such as, citizens, media actors and political actors. One of the assumptions of the network society perspective is that individual actors are becoming the central node within the network society and the boundary between the macro, meso and micro levels of analysis are dissolving (Kontopoulos, 1993; Reese & Shoemaker, 2016; Van Dijk, 2012; Van Dijk

58 This author recognises that this does not mean that a reciprocal relationship exists nor does it say anything about the strength of the ties.

59 See Appendix 5 for the SNA codebook.

60 See Section 5.10 in Chapter 5 for a more detailed explanation of the technological approach in creating and visualising the network.

& Winters-van Beek, 2009). Therefore, the retweet networks provide a possible insight into the different levels of analysis at play within government online networks and whether they are increasingly engaging with individual actors in this networked environment.

6.3.1. Retweet network Great Britain

Using the open-source network visualisation software Gephi (Version 0.92 Windows) (Bastian et al., 2009) this study was able to visualise the government retweet networks for GB and DE[61]. In Figure 9, the British network is first presented. The nodes (n=369) represent all those actors that were retweeted by government actors in GB and the ties (n=453) represent all retweets in GB within the two-week period of analysis. The nodes in Figure 9 are adjusted according to *indegree-based centrality*, that is, the bigger nodes represent those actors that were retweeted most often by government organisations and individuals in GB. The network is a directed network and it features both incoming and outgoing ties. The networks were visualised in Gephi using the layout algorithm *Force Atlas*. The network provides an insight into how often government organisations and individuals retweet other actors, which actors they retweeted most often and which actors are most central within the government TW network in GB.

The network in Figure 9 shows that government organisations are the most central actors within the British network. This means that government organisations in GB most often retweet each other. In the British network, the PM's Office (@Number10gov) is the most central and largest node in the network. It receives the highest number of incoming ties. This means that other government actors retweet the PM's Office more than any other actor. The second largest and most central node in the network is the Ministry of Defence (MoD). Overall, the network can be described as a dense network in which government organisations rather than individuals, dominate. They are well-connected with each other and are connected by many ties.

61 As explained in Chapter 5 (Section 5.10), these networks were originally designed as a two-mode network in Microsoft Excel. Using the two-mode network, the degree centrality values were calculated in UCINet. However, in order to visualise the network it was necessary to convert it from a two-mode network to a one-mode network using the open source statistical software *R*. The network was then visualised in Gephi.

Figure 9. One-mode Retweet Network of Organisations & Individuals (n=31) in GB [node size adjusted according to indegree-based centrality; incoming ties represent retweets by government actors; 369 nodes/453 ties; layout algorithm Force Atlas]

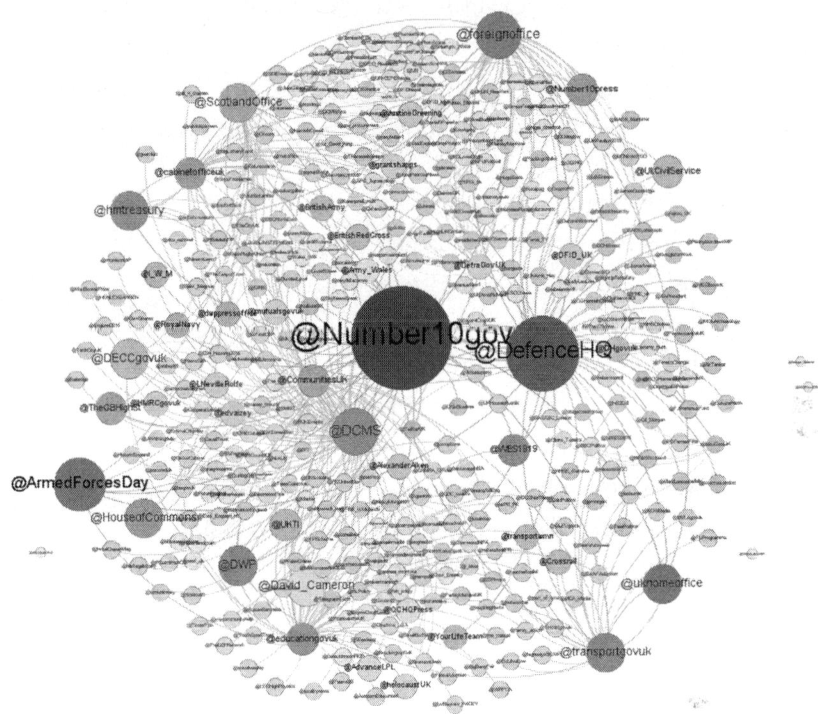

While Gephi was used to visualise the network, this study used the social network analysis software UCINet (Borgatti, Everett, & Freeman, 2002) to calculate the degree centrality values of the actors within both networks. Table 23 lists the degree centrality values of the most retweeted (i.e., best connected) actors within the British network. This table demonstrates that the most central actors are exclusively government organisations. It is also notable that these values are significantly higher than the degree centrality values for actors in the German network (see Table 24 in the next section). The British network is much more dense with actors connected by significantly more ties (see Figure 10 to compare with the German network).

Table 23. Actors with the Highest Degree Centrality Values in GB

	Twitter Account	Actor	Degree Centrality Value
1.	@Number10gov	Prime Minister's Office	0.361
2.	@DefenceHQ	Ministry of Defence	0.250
3.	@ArmedForcesDay	Ministry of Defence	0.167
4.	@DCMS	Department for Culture, Media & Sport	0.139
	@foreignoffice	The Foreign Office	
5.	@HouseofCommons	House of Commons	0.111
	@transportgovuk	Department of Transport	
	@hmtreasury	HM Treasury	
	@ukhomeoffice	UK Home Office	
	@dwp	Department Work & Pensions	
	@Scotlandoffice	Scotland Office	
	@David_Cameron	David Cameron	
	@DECCgovuk	Department Energy & Climate Change	

6.3.2. Retweet network Germany

Figure 10 shows a much sparser retweet network in DE (189 nodes and 217 ties compared to 369 nodes and 453 ties in GB). This is due to the fact that, first, there are simply less government organisations in DE compared to in GB (n=17 in DE; n=27 in GB), and second, those organisations that are on TW in DE retweet less often (as the results of the online content analysis outlined). Figure 10 shows that, similar to the British network, government actors are also the most central actors within this network. The network shows that the most central actors are the following: the international TW page of the AA (@germanydiplo), Minister Heiko Maas and the TW page of the BR/BPA/KA (as mentioned previously these three organisations share the TW page @RegSprecher).

Figure 10. One-mode Retweet Network of Organisations and Individuals in DE (n=15) [node size adjusted according to indegree-based centrality; incoming ties represent retweets by government actors; 189 nodes/217 ties; layout algorithm Force Atlas]

However, these central actors have only 3-4 incoming ties and very few outgoing ties. Overall government actors in DE do not network with others on TW to the same extent as government actors in GB. They do not seem to network with each other as there are very few ties connecting them. Each government actor is connected to only one or two other government actors. This is in stark contrast to the British network where government actors are connected to each other by many more ties. There are two government actors who are completely isolated from the network in DE, that is, Minister Peter Altmaier Head of the KA and also the Federal Ministry for Transport and Digital Infrastructure (BMVI). Nobody retweeted them during the period of analysis and they also didn't retweet any government actors within the network. Minister Manuela Schwesig connects with her own ministry, the BMFSFJ, and her cabinet and SPD colleague, Minister Heiko Maas, but she doesn't connect with any other government actor. Vice versa, Heiko Maas connects with his ministry BMJV, Manuala Schwesig and her ministry, the BMFSFJ.

As mentioned above the actors in this network are connected to each other by much fewer ties than in the British network. Table 24 lists the degree centrality values of the most central actors in the German network. Compared to the British network, the degree centrality values of the AA, Heiko Maas and the BR/BPA/KA are much lower than the most central actors in the British network. There is also less difference between those that are most central and those other actors that are within the network. Table 24 shows that the AA has a degree centrality value of 0.108, the next value is 0.081 (Heiko Maas and BPA), and the next value is 0.054. A large number of actors have a value of 0.054 (which is why more actors are featured in this table than the previous table). These values are so low it means that only one or two ties (retweets) connect most actors in this network.

Table 24. Actors with the Highest Degree Centrality Values in DE

	Twitter Account	Actor	Degree Centrality Value
1.2	@GermanyDiplo	Foreign Office (AA)	0.108
2.	@HeikoMaas @RegSprecher	Minister for Justice (BMJV) German Federal Government (BR) Bundespresseamt(BPA) Chancellor's Office (KA)	0.081
3.	@BMZ_Bund	Ministry for Economic Cooperation & Development (BMZ)	0.054
	@GermanyUN	Diplomatic actor	
	@SlmaYilkhan	Speaker Muslim Workers Group SPD	
	@DasGuteessen	Metro Group (economic actor)	
	@praesidentinDJB	President, German Legal Association	

Twitter Account	Actor	Degree Centrality Value
@BErfmann	Politician	
@BMJV_Bund	Ministry for Justice (BMJV)	
@baerbelbas	Politician	
@RenateKuenast	Politician	
@vonPlaten BPW	President, Businessplan Competition	
@jazmatab	Actress	
@morgenmagazin	ZDF news programme	
@anked	New media actor	
@ZaunerMargit	Citizen	
@feminismusheu-te	Citizen activists/political campaign	
@Nirthak	Journalist	
@sz	Suddeutsche newspaper	
@spdbt	SPD Parliamentary fraction	
@EvaHoegl	Politician	
@ardmoma	ARD media programme	
@tagesspiegel	Tagesspiegel newspaper	
@Gerdbillen	Politician/State Secretary BMJV	
@bankenverband	Industry Association	
@groehe	Government Minister for Health	
@KatriBertram	Head of NGO	
@BMBF_Bund	Ministry for Education and Research (BMBF)	

The degree centrality value of the PM's Office in GB was 0.361 and the next most central actors had values of 0.250, 0.167, 0.139 and so forth. Actors within the British network were connected by a much larger number of ties and the most central actor received significantly more incoming ties than all other actors in the network. Table 24 shows that German government organisations do not dominate the network like in GB. Although government actors in DE retweet less often, but when they do, government actors retweet a wide range of actors, including, government, political, media, and citizen actors. These actors are a mix of organisational actors (government, political and media) and individuals (political, government, media and citizen actors), whereas in the British network, it was government organisations rather than any individual actors, that were prominent in the network.

6.4 Interim Summary: Results of the Social Network Analysis

The two networks and the degree centrality values presented in the previous section provide a comparative perspective of the networking behaviour of government actors in the two countries. The RGAs for the SNA were as follows: 1) both the BPA and GCS will occupy a central position in social media networks, 2) the PM's Office will be a central actor within government social media networks in GB, and 3) government organisations in both countries will predominantly network with other government actors. The specific research questions included: who are government organisations networking with on TW? and which actors occupy central positions in their TW networks? This study also sought to examine the possible macro factors that shape government networks, and, therefore, also asked whether there are similarities or differences between the countries in how government organisations and individuals use TW to network with others? The results of the SNA revealed a number of interesting differences between the countries.

In relation to the first RGA, that the BPA and GCS would be central actors within the TW networks, this was found to be true in the case of the BPA. Similar to the results of the online content analysis which found the BPA to be the most active government organisation on FB, the BPA was also a central actor in the TW network in DE. However, it must be emphasised that although it appears to be a central actor, it was retweeted by other government actors only three to four times during the period of analysis. There was little difference between the position of the BPA, the AA and Heiko Maas at the centre of the network. The BPA may be central but it does not dominate the network. In GB, much like the results of the online content analysis, GCS doesn't appear to play a central role on TW. These results, once again, suggest that GCS does not play a central role in government communications in GB. GCS was not retweeted by any other government actor during the period of analysis. These results appear to confirm that GCS and BPA have very different functions as the centralised organisations for government communications. Another assumption of this thesis was that the PM's Office would be a central actor in social networks in GB. The results of the SNA support this assumption. The British network shows that, not only is the PM's Office the most central actor, it dominates the network. It has significantly more incoming ties than any other actor in the network. These results would suggest (as Chapter 3 outlined) that the PM's Office is the most important centralised organisation for government communications in GB, and this is reflected in its online government communications.

Similar to the assumption in the content analysis that government actors would predominantly engage in unidirectional communication on social media, this thesis assumed that government actors would also make little effort to network with others within social networks. It also assumed that government actors would mostly network with other government actors. There were, however, interesting differences between the countries in this regard. In GB, it was found to be true, that government organisations mostly networked with other government organisations. They retweeted regularly and almost exclusively with each other, whereas in DE, they retweeted less often but they networked with a wider selection of actors. They not only networked with a mix of government, political, media and citizen actors, they also networked with a mix of organisational and individual actors.

These results mirror the patterns found in the content analysis, that is, that British government actors appear to engage almost exclusively in unidirectional communication across all social media platforms. The few examples, of government actors who are highly active on social media in terms of posting and responding to others, were found in DE. These results suggest a more open approach to interaction and networking in DE (also more flexibility in terms of how ministries and ministers communicate online), while there appears to be a much more closed and controlled approach to interaction and networking in GB. On the other hand, it could also be argued that these results show government actors in GB are better networked online and reinforce the importance of considering interaction from a number of different perspectives. While government organisations in GB demonstrated very little interaction in the results of the content analysis, the networking results demonstrate that they engage in more networked communications (albeit among government actors only).

7. Discussion

One of the central theoretical arguments in this thesis is that both the macro level and the organisational environment of government organisations (Graber, 2003; Horsley et al., 2010; Liu & Horsley, 2007; Liu et al., 2010) strongly shape how government organisations use websites and social media. Previous studies have suggested that government and political organisations use digital technologies in a non-rational way due to a range of organisational factors and constraints (Donges & Jarren, 2014; Mergel & Bretschneider, 2013) and these must be considered. Very few studies have examined how different macro and meso-level environments are influencing the use of websites and social media by government organisations. In a similar vein, the network perspective argues that in today's networked media environment, an examination of the macro level alone cannot fully explain similar or different phenomena found at different levels in society (Reese & Shoemaker, 2016; Van Dijk, 2012), instead, a multi-level perspective of this communications environment is required (Monge & Contractor, 2003; Van Dijk, 2012). In a network society (Castells, 2000 a; Van Dijk, 2012), the clear distinction between different levels of society is dissolving, and one of the consequences for political communications, is that the boundary between organisational and individual communications is disappearing as the networked environment supports more personalised forms of interaction and political participation (Bennett, 2012; Van Dijk, 2012). This study attempted to incorporate these different theoretical considerations into the content and social network analysis of government communications in Germany and Great Britain. It incorporated an important multilevel perspective into the empirical analysis.

The overarching research question of this thesis was (RQ1) *How are government organisations and individuals in Germany and Great Britain using websites and social media to communicate with citizens and media in their day-to-day communications?* This chapter is divided according to the various research guiding assumptions of this study. In each section, the author will present a particular RGA(s) with the corresponding research question(s) and discuss and interpret the results. This chapter will discuss numerous similarities and differences found at the macro level and what these results reveal about which macro-level features are shaping government communications in the new media environment in Germany and Great Britain.

The author will also discuss some of the key differences found between organisations at the meso level and the possible influencing factors at the organisational level. The individualisation of government organisational communications on social media was also a central category of analysis in this thesis. This chapter will discuss and reflect on what these results reveal about the changing relationship between the meso and micro level and the consequences for government communications. Finally, this study will consider the most important results of the SNA and evaluate how these relate to the findings of the content analysis.

7.1 Government Organisations and Unidirectional Communications Online

One of the conclusions of a number of studies in the literature review in Chapter two was that government organisations use social media and websites predominantly for one-way information provision and they have not yet understood their potential for interaction and networking (Meijer et al., 2012; Mergel, 2012; Mossberger et al., 2013). According to Mergel (2012), social media triggers tensions within these organisations, that is, a tension between the demands for innovation, interaction and transparency, but also the requirement to use them responsibly. Based on the findings of these previous studies, one of the central research guiding assumptions in this thesis was, that (RGA4) government organisations would predominantly engage in unidirectional communication on their websites and social media. This thesis assumed that this would be a similarity across the two countries. In conducting the online content analysis, this thesis asked the following research questions: (RQ1 a) to what extent are government organisations and individuals using websites and social media to interact with media and citizens? (RQ1 b) To what extent are government organisations using websites and social media to connect/network with media and citizens? (this question will also be addressed in greater detail in Section 7.5) and finally (RQ1 f) are there similarities between Germany and Great Britain in how government organisations and individuals use websites and social media to communicate with citizens and media in their day-to-day communications? This study defined interaction as unidirectional, two-way asymmetrical and two-way symmetrical. Networking was considered to be a key aspect of interaction online and it was categorised as a form of two-way asymmetrical communication, for example, sharing information on social media and following others on TW.

The results of the structural analysis indicated that websites and social media are in prevalent use by government organisations in Germany and Great Britain. The structural analysis also indicated that TW is the dominant social media platform in both countries. In Germany, 94% of organisations have a TW profile and in Great Britain, 81% have a profile. Upon closer inspection on how they use websites and social media, it was found that the majority of organisations and individual government actors use these platforms predominantly for unidirectional communication. For example, on TW and FB the majority of organisations did not respond to any user comments online, they seldom encouraged active participation on these platforms (i.e., calls to action), made little effort to follow others online and there were low levels of sharing information (i.e., retweets/shared posts). It appears that while government organisations may have a large number of social media pages, these pages are rarely used to interact or network with others. Even with regards to their unidirectional communication, that is, posting content, there were large differences between the organisations in their activity levels, most notably, on TW.

Despite TW being the most popular social media platform among government organisations in both countries, and despite the fact that the majority of them have a presence on TW since 2009 in Great Britain and since 2011 in Germany, there were extreme deviations between the organisations in how often they tweeted information and their number of followers. The results in Chapter 6 showed that there was an uneven distribution between the organisations in relation to how often they tweeted information. Large deviations were found in both countries but the variation was larger in Great Britain. These findings seem to confirm previous findings by Mergel (2012), that government organisations do not yet use social media in a strategic way, but rather in a non-rational way. There appears to be no cross-government strategy or professionalised approach to the use of social media, whether it be unidirectional communication or higher levels of interaction. Each organisation uses social media in their own way, and most likely, according to their own organisational mission (Mergel, 2012). It appears that social media use is still very much in its infancy in terms of even the most basic forms of interaction and networking.

In relation to two-way asymmetrical communication, for example, the content analysis examined the extent to which government actors encouraged other users to participate on FB and TW, this included calling on users to take part in discussions and post comments on government policy topics. The results were negative for participation on both TW and FB in both countries. Social media is not used by government organisations in either country for the purposes of encouraging participation. This seems to correspond with previous studies examining the perceptions of government actors around the implementation of online initiatives. For example, in a study of local government motivations in Switzerland, Klinger et al. (2015) found that fostering participation is not a goal of government online initiatives and that government actors are sceptical of using social media for these purposes. These findings seem to confirm that this may also be the case in Germany and Great Britain.

Although the research assumption was correct, that they would predominantly engage in unidirectional communication, the results showed some examples of two-way asymmetrical communication and some more limited examples of two-way symmetrical communication on websites and social media. However, two-way symmetrical communication (i.e., direct interaction/dialogue) was limited to just a few actors and organisations. It was found that a few organisational and individual government actors in Great Britain and Germany used TW actively (i.e., they tweeted often) and for direct interaction with other users (i.e., they responded to user comments). In the case of Germany, this activity stemmed from Minister Heiko Maas and his ministry, the BMJV, and from Minister Manuela Schwesig and her ministry the BMFSFJ. It is noteworthy that they were both SPD ministers within the governing CDU/CSU/SPD coalition (2013-2017), with the SPD as the smaller coalition partner in the government. As SPD ministers within lower-profile ministries, this would suggest that these actors possibly use TW as a means to raise their profile within government. In Great Britain, there was a similar pattern, with just two ministries and one minister that stood out as being active and responsive on TW. This was the DCMS, the DfE and the Minister for Education, Nicky Morgan. Similar to Germany, these ministries and minister could also be described as lower-profile government actors compared to government ministries like the Home Office or the HM Treasury. This pattern across the two countries suggests that certain government actors use TW as a means to boost their profile within government. It suggests that the political context, in particular, the position of the minister within government, possibly influences which actors are more active on social media. It also indicates that there is a connection between those ministries that are most active and an equally active minister on social media. Although it is unclear who influences whom (i.e., whether the ministry is more active online and influences the behaviour of the minister, or the minister influences the ministry's communication), it seems to support the findings of Figenschou et al's (2017) study, that the personal ambitions and media competencies of individual ministers are factors influencing government communications. It must be emphasised that these are limited examples of government actors using TW for interaction. Overall, the assumption still remains true, that communication on TW is predominantly unidirectional.

A second research guiding assumption of this thesis, and which is connected to the assumption outlined at the beginning of this section, was (RGA6) that government organisations in Germany will use websites and social media exclusively for unidirectional communication. It was assumed that government organisations in both countries would predominantly engage in unidirectional communication, however, this author assumed that this would be stronger in Germany. This assumption is based on the macro-level analysis in Chapter 3 which concluded that a key difference between the two countries was the strong regulation of government communications in Germany through the federal constitutional court. In contrast, it was assumed that the non-statutory approach in Great Britain would facilitate a more open approach to interaction online and that differences in regulatory structures at the macro level would influence the extent to which they interact and network online. The results of the empirical analysis, however, did not support this assumption. In fact, the opposite was the case. There were only a limited number of organisations and individuals who actively used social media for interaction (two-way symmetrical communication) and these were mostly found in Germany (apart from the examples mentioned above). These examples included: Heiko Maas and Manuela Schwesig on TW; the BPA, BMVg and the AA on FB; BMVg and the KA on YouTube.

The strongest examples of two-way symmetrical interaction on social media were found on FB. There were eight organisations in Germany with a FB profile and three of these were highly active in terms of posting content and responding regularly to individual user comments, that is, the BPA, the AA and the BMVg. It is notable that these actors are high-profile government organisations in comparison to those low-profile government actors that are interactive on TW. The AA and BMVg are large and important ministries and the BPA is the centralised organisation for government communications. There were no similar examples found in Great Britain, which leads to the conclusion that British organisations engage exclusively in unidirectional communication across all channels. These findings reveal a tendency towards interaction in Germany, but only among a few organisations. It also confirms that the stricter regulatory environment (through the federal constitutional court) in Germany does not constrain interaction online. These findings could possibly be explained by the fact that Germany is a federal state with a decentralised political system, and as highlighted in Chapter 3, government ministries have significant freedom in how they conduct their government communications (Heinze, 2012). Communications is less centrally controlled in Germany. These macro-level differences between the two countries could help to explain why there are more examples of interaction by different government actors in DE, but almost none to be found in GB, where the political system and the structures of government communications are more centralised. However, these results also suggest that there are factors at the organisational level within Germany which determine why some particular organisations use social media more actively and in a more interactive manner than others.

Another possible explanation for the lack of interaction in Great Britain is Mergel and Bretschneider's (2013) theory of social media diffusion in government. They argue that the more institutionalised social media becomes, the more government organisations will try to constrain the use of these technologies through the implementation of regulations and codes of practices. In their view, institutionalisation leads to a formalisation of social media use within government organisations, and ultimately, more controlled and less interactive communications (Mergel & Bretschneider, 2013). In applying these theoretical arguments to the results of this study, it could be interpreted that social media has not yet been fully institutionalised in Germany and that this is one of the reasons why there appears to be more examples of direct interaction. In Great Britain, it could be argued that social media has been fully institutionalised and has become constrained through an increasing implementation of regulations and codes of practice governing government communications. Institutionalisation could also be referred to as professionalisation. Previous studies have highlighted the strong professionalisation of government communications in Great Britain compared to other countries (e.g., Gregory, 2012; Sanders et al., 2011; Sanders & Canel, 2013). Chapter 3 described the many steps taken to professionalise government communications in Great Britain, in particular, the establishment of GCS as a professional body and the introduction of numerous codes of practice and regulations governing government communications (see Table 2 in Chapter 3). It could be possible that this distinct process of professionalisation of government communications in Great Britain has resulted in a more formalised and controlled approach to social media use by government organisations in Great Britain.

In conclusion of this section, the results show that websites and social media are ubiquitous across government, but they are used predominantly for unidirectional communication in both countries. Examples of two-way asymmetrical and symmetrical interaction and networking are limited to just a few individuals and organisations and these are almost exclusively found in Germany rather than in Great Britain as was assumed. Despite a few isolated examples of interaction online, the majority of organisations in both countries appear to use websites and social media for top-down communication rather than to engage in any dialogue with users, connect and network with others, or encourage participation in government decision making.

7.2 Organisational Differences in Social Media Use

While there may be a less interactive and more formalised approach to social media use in Great Britain, this still does not explain the differences between organisations within both countries in terms of how they use social media for interaction and networking. Another central assumption of this thesis was that (RGA1) government organisations within Germany and Great Britain would use websites and social media differently and there would be differences between the organisations in the extent to which they use websites and social media for interaction and networking. The corresponding research question was: (RQ1 g) are there differences between government organisations within Germany and Great Britain in how they use websites and social media to communicate with citizens and media in their day-to-day communications? The results discussed in the previous section demonstrated that there are notable differences at the meso level between government organisations in how actively they use social media. A very small number of actors use social media actively (i.e., they post content regularly) and for interaction (i.e., they share content and respond to users), while the vast majority do not engage. Among the majority of these organisations, there are large differences in terms of their unidirectional communication.

As mentioned in the previous section, the large differences (i.e., standard deviations) between the organisations would indicate that there are internal organisational factors that determine how they use online platforms. There could be numerous meso-level factors that support more interaction by certain organisations than others. For example, those organisations that were highly active on FB – the BPA, BMVg and AA – are large important ministries and possibly have greater resources enabling them to respond actively on social media. There may also be particular policy reasons why certain organisations are more interactive than others. For example, the

BMVg has a campaign to recruit soldiers to the army and appears to actively use social media to reach and attract potential recruits. In this regard, social media supports its unique organisational mission and priorities. For other ministries such as the BMJV and BMFSFJ, who were found to interact on TW (as mentioned in Section 7.1), this could be due to the influence of the incumbent minister, for example, his or her personal ambitions, media competencies (Figenschou et al., 2017) and their position within the government.

According to Mergel and Bretschneider's (2013) social media diffusion theory, social media diffuses in three stages across government, and different government organisations are at different stages of diffusion (i.e., adoption). According to this theory, not only are different organisations at different stages, but not every organisation will go through each stage and institutionalise social media. They describe social media adoption as being non-rational. It is possible that some organisations may never use social media for anything other than top-down communication. The adoption of social media by government organisations depends on their own organisational goals and a number of internal organisational factors. Different organisations have different goals and will, therefore, integrate social media according to their own organisational priorities (Mergel, 2013, 2016).

One of the clear limitations of the empirical approach employed in this thesis is that it was not possible to identify the internal organisational factors that shape or delay the adoption of social media (e.g., a political decision, legal concerns or a lack of resources) (Graber, 2003; Horsley et al., 2010; Liu et al., 2010). Nor was it possible to identify their motivations behind the use of social media. For example, their motivations could be based solely on a duty to provide information, but they may not have any conception of what interaction should look like, nor do they believe it is their duty to engage in discussions online (Coleman & Firmstone, 2014; Klinger et al., 2015). This would have required an additional empirical method (e.g., qualitative interviews) in order to examine inside these organisations and identify the specific and unique constraints within each organisation.

While this study could not illuminate on specific meso-level constraints, nevertheless, the results of the online content analysis demonstrated that macro-level factors alone cannot explain why certain organisations use websites and social media for interaction and others don't. The results reinforce the necessity of explicitly examining the organisational level and considering it as a level of analysis distinct from other levels of analysis, something that political communications studies have failed to do (Donges,

2008; Donges & Jarren, 2014). Comparative studies have also lacked this organisational perspective. The results show that the assumption was true that government organisations would use online platforms differently and this should be considered in future comparative studies of government organisations.

7.3 Individualisation of Government Communications on Social Media

This thesis examined the changes taking place in the political communications environment from an organisational and network perspective. Both perspectives highlighted the role that individualised communications is playing in the new media environment and the changing relationship between meso and micro-level communications (Bennett & Segerberg, 2012; Bimber et al., 2005; Bimber et al., 2009; Monge & Contractor, 2003; Van Dijk, 2012). Chapter 4 examined how digital technologies are bringing about a transformation in how citizens engage with formal political organisations such as political parties (Bennett, 2012; Castells, 2008). Individuals are identifying and engaging less with political institutions as social media provides opportunities to affect change outside of formal political organisations (Bennett, 2012; Bimber et al., 2005; Bimber et al., 2009). This raises challenges for political institutions, such as political parties and governments, in trying to reach and engage with citizens. They must find ways of adapting and maintaining legitimacy (Borucki, 2014 b; Sarcinelli, 2011) in the new communications environment. One of the ways in which political parties are adapting is through a mix of formal and informal communications practices, practices that blur the boundary between organisational and individual communications (Bimber et al., 2005; Penney, 2017) presenting a hybrid identity (Chadwick, 2007).

This study assumed that government organisations, like political organisations, would also begin to adopt a similar approach to the use of social media and employ a mix of formal and informal communications practices, particularly in their use of individual social media pages. There were a number of research guiding assumptions and research questions related to this category of analysis. The first assumption (RGA7) was, that government organisations in both countries would engage in individualised communications on social media. The second assumption (RGA8) was, that they would take a similar approach to the individualisation of organisational communications blurring the boundary between organisational and individualised communications. Based on these assumptions, the following research questions were asked: (RQ1 c) to what extent do government organisations have an individual social media page and (RQ1 d) how do government organisations present themselves on individual social media pages? The second question investigated whether there was a clear boundary between individual and organisational communications in their TW and FB profiles or whether this boundary was dissolving. More specifically, it was examined whether individual social media pages were presented as formal government communications (i.e., organisational) or as informal government communications (i.e., personal communications).

While the previous section highlighted notable differences between government organisations within both countries in how actively they use social media, the analysis of individual social media pages revealed strong similarities across Germany and Great Britain. The first assumption, that government organisations would have individual profiles, was true. The findings show that a number of government actors have an individual profile on FB and TW (although there are more organisational pages in both countries). In Great Britain, 52% (n=14) of government ministers have an individual TW page, compared to just 23% (n=4) of ministers in Germany, while 35% (n=6) of ministers in Germany have a FB profile and 30% (n=8) in Great Britain. The second research assumption, that they would blur their identity online between official government communications and non-official communications, was also found to be true. Out of a total sample of 32 individual pages, 26 were categorised as non-official government communications. This means that it was unclear whether they were official government pages or non-official political/personal pages.

The majority of individual government actors on FB and TW presented a mixed identity in their social media profiles, that is, they presented the pages as a personal page (with a link to a personal website), but they also described themselves as being both a party political and government actor. Individual pages had no clear boundary between personal, government and political communications in their profile descriptions. This also appeared to be the case in relation to the content of tweets on these pages[62], which was often a mix of government and political content. Although this

62 The content on these pages was examined to assess whether it was a mix of personal, political and government content. However, this was not an official category within the online content analysis as the codebook contained only quantitative categories. This finding is based on an additional observation by the author of this thesis.

finding should be treated with caution (as explained in the footnote), this finding is similar to those in another study which qualitatively examined the content of politicians' tweets in Great Britain. The study by Adi, Erickson and Lilleker (2014) found that their content was a mix of the professional (in this case political) and personal, they said that "Twitter is a hybrid platform, blurring private, and professional messaging" (p. 12).

There were only two exceptions to this rule and these were found in Germany. For example, Heiko Maas and Peter Altmaier drew a clear line between personal and government communications in their TW profiles. Peter Altmaier made clear in his profile description that all tweets were his own, and Heiko Maas made clear his page was an official government page, but any tweets with his initials "hm" at the end were his own personal opinions. There were no similar examples found in Great Britain. Despite these two exceptions in Germany, the results still call into question the transparency of government communications on individual social media pages in both countries. It appears that individualised social media pages are facilitating a type of government communications that fluidly mixes political and government identities, and political and government communications content. As increasing numbers of government actors adopt an individual profile online, there is a risk that this could lead to more partisan government communications on social media. The strong regulatory environment in Germany and the strong professsionalisation of government communications in Great Britain (through codes of practice aimed at differentiating partisan from non-partisan communications) do not seem to prevent a blurring of the two on social media. This raises questions around the effectiveness of such codes of practice and regulations in drawing a clear line between political and impartial public communications. In a new media environment, social media obfuscates public sector and political interests.

The content analysis also examined whether there was a difference in transparency on individual pages compared to organisational pages. A third research guiding assumption, and which is relevant for this section, is the following: (RGA9) individual social media pages will be less transparent than organisational pages. Based on this assumption, this study asked the following question: (RQ1 e) to what extent are these individual pages transparent compared to organisational pages? The content analysis examined the extent to which organisational and individual social media pages made clear who was responsible for content on social media, and if there was information provided in relation to social media policies. In this regard, the results found a clear difference in approach between the countries with a much higher level of transparency in Germany. It was also found that there was no difference between transparency on individual and organisational pages. The majority of individual and organisational social media pages in Germany made clear who was responsible for content. In stark contrast, there is almost no transparency on organisational or individual pages in Great Britain. In conclusion, the assumption that individual pages are less transparent than organisational pages was not true, nor was there a noticeable difference between the platforms.

The findings suggest that, in Germany at least, there is a government policy of transparency around making clear who is responsible for the content on social media (even if the individual profile descriptions lack transparency). It appears that in this regard, transparency is possibly shaped by differences at the macro level. While Section 7.1 (on unidirectional communication) found that the stricter regulatory environment in Germany does not hinder interaction on social media, it appears to foster more transparency on social media, at least in relation to who is responsible for content and social media policies. However, macro-level factors do not explain why individual pages in both Germany and Great Britain present a blurred identity on individual TW and FB pages. It appears that these findings cannot be explained by the macro or meso level factors identified in this dissertation. Instead, it could be assumed that a mix of global trends and also the particular technological affordances of these social media pages (Ottovordemgentschenfelde, 2017), as well as an increasing mediatisation (Garland et al., 2017; Thorbjørnsrud et al., 2014) and personalisation of government communications (Figenschou et al., 2017) more generally, shape how individual government actors present and describe themselves in their individual profiles on these platforms.

The increasing individualisation of government communications raises a number of normative and legal concerns around the potential politicisation and transparency of government communications in the online sphere. These pages obscure what is personal, political and government/public sector communications. Although there are fewer individual pages than organisational pages and they appear to be used mostly for self-presentation purposes (i.e., these pages have low activity levels), it is presumed that the number of individual pages will increase in the years to come[63]. This continuing individualisation/personalisation of government communications

63 When the social media content for this dissertation was saved in March 2015, there were only 4 government ministers in Germany with an individual profile on TW. As of February 2019, 11 German government ministers have their own

could have negative consequences for the transparency of government communications, and consequently, implications for public trust in government. There are also potential legal consequences in how individual government ministers are using online government/public communication resources[64] (Drobinski, 2018). In the case of Germany, where there is a clear legal requirement that governments refrain from using government institutional resources for election advertising and that government communications remain neutral (Barczak, 2018), this kind of personalised communications makes it difficult to differentiate between what is government and what is political or electoral communications. Also, in the case of Great Britain, there were many efforts over the last fifteen years, since the publication of the 2004 Phillis Review, to de-politicise government communications following its politicisation during the Iraq War/Tony Blair era. It was an era in which government spin greatly damaged trust in politics and government in Great Britain (Gregory, 2012).

This section concludes that personalised communications on social media risks a politicisation (or re-politicisation in the case of Great Britain) of government/public sector communications in the new media environment. The fact that there is a total absence of transparency on individual social media pages in Great Britain (with regards to social media policies and stating who is responsible for content), this would suggest that the normative consequences of this individualised communications is greater in Great Britain. The consequences are also greater due to weaker regulatory structures in Great Britain. In contrast, in Germany, the mix of political and government content on these social media pages is counterbalanced, to some extent, by a higher level of transparency with regards to who is responsible for content and the availability of social media policies. However, the risks of a politicisation of government communications in both countries remain. From a network society perspective (Van Dijk, 2012),

---

TW profile (as calculated by this author). This demonstrates just how much online personalised communications among government actors has continued to grow since 2015.

64 For example, a judgement of the German federal constitutional court (Judgement from February 27, 2018 – 2 BvE 1/16) upheld the claim by the Alternative für Deutschland (AFD) that the former Federal Minister for Education Johanna Wanka wrongly used her position as a government minister in issuing a press statement on her Ministry's homepage criticising an AFD demonstration. The court found that she had misused the authority of her office (Drobinski, 2018). This case demonstrates how government online resources can be easily used for politicised communications.

these results show that there has been a clear dissolution of the boundary between what is organisational and what is individual communications in the online sphere. This is a phenomenon affecting government organisations as much as other political actors, but as outlined in this section, the consequences are greater for government organisations due to their public interest mandate.

7.4 Centralised Government Actors in Twitter Networks

One of the assumptions of this study was that particular macro-level structures would influence which organisational actors play a prominent role in government online communications. For example, one assumption (RGA2) was that the BPA and GCS would be central actors within government social networks. They would occupy a central position in social media networks and be one of the most active government actors on social media in terms of interaction and networking. This assumption was based on a number of previous studies which highlighted their centralised organisational structures as being a distinguishing macro-level feature of government communications in both countries (Gregory, 2012; Holtz-Bacha, 2013; Sanders et al., 2011; Sanders & Canel, 2013). It was assumed that the existence of strong and well-resourced centralised organisations would result in a centralisation of communications around these actors, the BPA and the GCS.

Another assumption (RGA3) was, that the PM's Office in Great Britain would also be a prominent actor online (alongside the GCS). This assumption was based on the background analysis of the political system and structures in Great Britain (see Chapter 3). Dowding (2013) has described a process of prime ministerialisation of politics in Great Britain and Müller (2011) refers to government in Great Britain as a prime ministerial government rather than cabinet government like in Germany. According to these scholars, political power and institutional resources (including media resources) are increasingly centralised in the PM's Office (Dowding, 2013; Heffernan, 2006; Korte, 2002; Vogel, 2010). Therefore, the assumption of this thesis was that the PM's Office would also be a central actor online. It would occupy a central position in social media networks and be one of the most active actors on social media in terms of interaction and networking. The research question related to these two assumptions was the following: (RQ2 b) which actors occupy central positions in their TW (retweet) networks? This research question and the two assumptions were answered as part of the SNA of government retweet networks. The content analysis also provided some additional insights into the prominence and centralisation of communications around these actors online.

The results of the SNA for Great Britain showed that the PM's Office (@Number10gov) was by far the most retweeted actor by other government organisations. It occupied the most central position within the retweet network and had a much higher indegree centrality than the next most central actor, which was the Ministry for Defence (@DefenceHQ). The GCS (@UKGovcomms) did not appear as a visible node within this network. The central position of the PM's Office would suggest that it plays a more centralised role in government communications than the GCS. While the GCS may be the main centralised organisation for government communications, the retweet network, however, suggests that power and resources are centralised within the PM's Office. In Germany, the BPA (@RegSprecher) played a central role within the German retweet network, however, it was not the most central actor and it did not dominate the network in the way that the PM's Office dominated the British network. The most central actor in Germany was the international TW account of the German Foreign Office (@GermanyDiplo) followed by Minister Heiko Maas (@HeikoMaas) and then the BPA.

The results of the online content analysis revealed that the BPA was also a prominent actor in terms of direct interaction with users on social media. In fact, the BPA was the most active and responsive government organisation on FB across the two countries. It was also active in terms of tweeting content on TW, but it was not the most responsive actor on TW (that was the BMFSFJ and BMJV). In Great Britain, the GCS did not play a prominent role on social media in terms of posting content or engaging in any form of interaction. The PM's Office did not use social media for direct interaction (British organisations engaged exclusively in unidirectional communication across all social media platforms), but it had the highest following and posted regularly on TW. The results suggest that the BPA plays a more centralised role in government communications in Germany compared to the GCS in Great Britain. These findings suggest that the PM's Office is in fact the main centralised organisation for government communications and that in examining and comparing centralised government communications structures in the two countries, more attention should be given to the role of the BPA and the PM's Office rather than to the GCS. These findings confirm that the GCS has a different function as a professional body for government communications and this is reflected in its low visibility online.

The findings showed that the research guiding assumptions were partly true. It was true that the BPA played a prominent role on social media in Germany, but it was not true for the GCS. The PM's Office was a highly centralised government actor in the TW networks, but it was not the most active actor across social media in GB. In this regard, DCMS and DfE were the most active organisations in Great Britain. The next section will answer in more detail who government actors are networking with online and what this reveals about approaches to networking in the two countries.

7.5 Government Networking on Twitter

A research assumption of the SNA (RGA5) was that government organisations in both countries would predominantly network with other government actors on social media. The corresponding research questions were the following: (RQ2) How are government organisations and individuals in Germany and Great Britain using TW to network with citizens and media in their day-to-day communications? (RQ2 a) Who are government organisations networking with on TW? (RQ2 b) Which actors occupy central positions in their retweet networks? (this question overlaps with the previous section examining the central role of the BPA, the GCS and the PM's Office within TW networks) And finally, (RQ2 c) are there similarities between the countries in how government organisations and individuals use TW to network with citizens and media in their day-to-day communications?

This study was interested in examining whether government actors mostly networked with each other or other actors, for example, political actors, media organisations, or citizens (for a similar empirical approach see Adi et al., 2014). The assumption that they would mostly network with each other was based on the findings of previous studies that governments are not yet taking full advantage of social media to interact or network with others (Meijer et al., 2012; Mergel, 2012; Mossberger et al., 2013) and are still using social media in a broadcasting mode (Chadwick, 2013). In addition, other studies have found the TW networks of politicians to be closed and elitist; they most often engage with other elite actors such as print and broadcast journalists (Adi et al., 2014; Nuernbergk & Conrad, 2016). Based on these different studies, it was assumed that government actors would use social media to engage predominantly in unidirectional communication and to network mostly with each other. In addition, the network perspective argues that individuals are increasingly becoming the central node within networks (Van Dijk, 2012) and for this reason the SNA examined whether they networked mostly with organisational actors or whether individual actors were more prominent within their TW networks. Finally, this study was also interested in analysing if there were possible macro factors that shape approaches to networking online.

The results of the SNA in Great Britain and Germany showed, that across both countries, the most central actors in each network were government actors. However, in Great Britain, the actor that was most central in the network – the PM's Office – dominated the network, whereas, in Germany, no one government actor dominated the network. Those government actors that were central in the German network (i.e., the BPA, AA and Heiko Maas), had an indegree centrality value that was only slightly higher than other actors in the network (they were only separated from other actors by one or two more incoming ties). There was an interesting difference between the two networks, for example, government actors in Great Britain predominantly retweeted other government organisational actors, whereas in Germany government actors retweeted a wider variety of actors including political actors (e.g., politicians and individuals from political associations), media actors (e.g., media organisations and individual journalists), citizens (e.g., citizen activists) and economic actors. Individual actors were also more prominent in the German network. For example, one of the central actors was a government minister (Heiko Maas) and government actors retweeted a variety of individuals and organisational actors from different spheres. In contrast, the most central actors in the British network were all government, and they were all organisational actors.

The assumption (RGA5) that government actors would predominantly network with other government actors was not true in Germany, but it was found to be true in Great Britain. As mentioned above, the British network differs to the German network in that it is dominated by one government actor. The PM's Office is retweeted more often than any other government actor. This suggests that government communications in GB is much more centralised around one government organisational actor. It is necessary to carry out a further analysis of government TW networks in Great Britain in order to see whether a similar finding emerges. However, based on the finding of this study, it could be concluded that government communications on social media in Great Britain is more centralised than in Germany and this is influenced by a highly centralised political system (Humphreys, 2012) and the centralisation of power in the PM's Office (Dowding, 2013; Heffernan, 2006).

In response to RQ2, how are government organisations and individuals in Germany and Great Britain using TW to network with citizens and media in their day-to-day communications?, the networks showed that government actors in Germany retweeted much less than government actors in Great Britain. While government actors in Great Britain mostly retweeted each other, the network was denser and government actors were connected to the network by significantly more ties. In Germany, a wider variety of actors appeared in the network, but there were very few ties connecting each actor in the network. The results of the content analysis suggested that government actors in Germany are using social media for direct interaction (albeit in a few limited cases), rather than for networking. The results of the content analysis could suggest that social media has not yet been fully institutionalised in Germany and it is this lack of institutionalisation that seems to be facilitating some examples of active and direct interaction to emerge (Mergel & Bretschneider, 2013). Similarly, the German TW network also suggests that networking has not yet been institutionalised and this could explain why their networking habits appear more open in terms of who they network with. For example, when they retweet, they retweet political, media and citizens, not just government actors. As mentioned previously in Section 7.1, these findings could also possibly be explained by a number of macro-level factors such as the fact that German government ministries communicate within a decentralised (less centrally controlled) political system (Humphreys, 2012), and as a result they have more freedom in how they conduct their government communications (Heinze, 2012). The results of the SNA and the content analysis seem to reinforce the conclusion that government communications in Germany is less institutionalised and less centrally controlled, and consequently, more open and interactive.

In the case of Great Britain, the SNA results, combined with the results of the content analysis, could be interpreted in two different ways, one is positive and the other negative. On the one hand, the results could indicate that government organisations in Great Britain understand and use social media explicitly for networking rather than for direct interaction. For example, there were few examples of direct interaction on social media (as highlighted in Section 7.1), but there were a number of examples of networking in Great Britain. Government actors, for example, not only reweeted more often, but followed more actors on TW (stronger follower/following ratio). Government websites were highly networked with each other and all British websites provided social media sharing options. Government communications in Germany was notably less networked. This could reflect a more professsionalised approach to networking in Great Britain. One could instead conclude that the results of the SNA simply demonstrate that government communications in Great Britain is highly centralised (around the PM's Office) and top-down. The results of the content analysis and SNA show that they engage exclusively in unidirectional communication and network only with other government actors. Therefore, these two results taken together, reflect a broader top-down centrally controlled approach to interaction and networking in the online sphere.

In summary, the SNA demonstrated the value in considering interaction from a network perspective and combining these two empirical methods, a content analysis and SNA. It enabled a broader analysis of interaction and engagement online rather than a narrow definition of interaction as dialogic only. However, it is arguable whether the same results would be found if the same SNA was carried out today. SNA provides only a small snapshot of a moment in time and this author is wary of over-interpreting the meaning of these networks. Future research needs to carry out a longitudinal SNA and also include more features that were not included in this study, such as, @mentions and @replies in order to acquire a fuller picture of their networking behaviour. Nevertheless, the results of the SNA display some patterns in behaviour that show similarities with those found in the content analysis. In this way, the SNA helped to strengthen and interpret the overall results of the content analysis. It revealed important differences between the countries and a number of macro-level factors shaping networking online.

7.6 Comparing the Use of Different Social Media Platforms

While the focus of this study was on comparing similarities and differences in how government organisations use websites and social media across (macro-level analysis) the two countries and also within (meso-level analysis) the countries, this section will discuss some important differences in how the platforms are used. This section will reflect on what these differences reveal about the overall approach to online government communications in Great Britain and Germany. The use of online technologies is not only shaped by macro-level influencing factors and internal organisational factors, but it can also be shaped by the technical affordances and architecture of these platforms (Ottovordemgentschenfelde, 2017; Papacharissi, 2009 a). According to Papacharissi (2009 a), the different architectural structures of different social media platforms influence, for example, the private\public balance, styles of self presentation and the types of interaction that take place. For example, the interface on TW has particular affordances and constraints which influences how actors can present themselves in their profile description (Ottovordemgentschenfelde, 2017). Equally, it is clear that the architecture of FB tends to support more discussion, while TW supports more networked forms of interaction. These factors should be considered when interpreting the final results. This section is not related to any particular research guiding assumption, but it helps to answer the overarching research question, that is, how are government organisations and individuals in Germany and Great Britain using websites and social media to communicate with citizens and media in their day-to-day communications?

The results of the content analysis demonstrated that there are a number of differences in how FB is used compared to TW. FB as a platform facilitates more dialogue and discussion among users than on TW and for this reason it is not surprising that the results reveal more examples of direct interaction (two-way symmetrical communication) on FB. According to the findings, a small number of German organisations used FB for actively posting content and responding directly and regularly to user comments, thereby supporting a genuine two-way dialogue between government organisations and citizens online. In the case of Great Britain, the results were very different. There was not a single organisation that used FB in an active and responsive manner. The difference between the two countries would suggest that the results are shaped by differences in approach to interaction online (at the macro and meso level), rather than by any technical affordances of FB.

TW was used predominantly for unidirectional communication in both countries, government actors rarely respond to other users and almost never encourage participation. However, an interesting finding was that there were just a handful of actors in both countries who actively tweeted and responded to users on TW. As mentioned earlier, these actors included lower-profile ministries and ministers in both countries. In contrast, the most active and responsive actors on FB were the BPA, AA and BMVg in Germany, government organisations that could be described as more important and higher profile. This finding corresponds with a similar finding in Nuernbergk and Conrad's (2016) study of the TW networks of German politicians in the Bundestag. In their study, they found that the most active actors on TW were the smaller parties such as the Green Party, the Left and the Free Democratic Party rather than the larger "catch-all-parties" like the CDU/CSU and SPD (Nuernbergk & Conrad, 2016, pp. 5-6). This finding suggests that a small group of actors, for example, those from smaller parties (or in the case of this dissertation, from the smaller coalition party in government) or lower-profile ministries, use TW in order to gain attention for themselves, most likely attention in offline media (Chadwick, 2013). In contrast, higher-profile actors do not need to worry about gaining media attention and are more likely to use FB for interaction.

Government actors in Great Britain seem to put most of their efforts into TW. It was the most used social media platform and had the highest activity levels. Previous studies have described a highly competitive hybrid media system in Great Britain and according to them social media is predominantly used for gaining attention in offline media or for engaging with traditional media actors (Adi et al., 2014; Chadwick, 2011 b, 2013; Davis, 2010 a, 2014). The focus on TW and the use of exclusively top-down communication suggests that social media use in Great Britain is also possibly shaped by a stronger media logic due to the mediatisation of government communications in Great Britain (Garland et al., 2017) and a competitive hybrid media system (Chadwick, 2013).

7.7 Summary

The findings of the empirical analysis revealed important similarities and differences both across the countries and among government organisations within both countries. These findings confirmed the importance of considering both the macro and meso-level factors that shape or constrain the use of digital technologies by government organisations. In terms of the macro-level influencing factors, the results suggest that the stronger regulatory environment in Germany supports a higher level of transparency on social media, but it does not hinder or constrain direct interaction on websites and social media. The results also indicate that Britain's centralised political system, in particular, the centralisation of power and organisational resources in the PM's Office, strongly shapes government communications online. Two centralised organisations play a prominent role online, that is, the PM's Office in Great Britain and the BPA in Germany. Until now, many studies examining government communications have theoretically considered the macro-level factors shaping government communications (Holtz-Bacha, 2013; Horsley et al., 2010; Kocks & Raupp, 2014; Sanders et al., 2011; Sanders & Canel, 2013), but there have been few studies empirically examining whether these assumptions hold true. In this way, these findings represent a significant advance for the field of government communications in trying to connect the different levels of analysis.

While government actors used websites and social media predominantly for unidirectional communication, there were large differences in activity levels between the organisations in both countries. The results seem to confirm that there is no strategic approach to social media use within government. These organisations use social media differently and adapt them according to their organisational goals and priorities (Mergel, 2012; 2013). The results confirm there are internal organisational factors that determine why certain government actors are more active and responsive online compared to others. Future comparative studies of government communications need to consider these meso-level differences and incorporate additional research methods such as qualitative interviews into the empirical design. This is necessary to examine the motivations behind the use of digital technologies within organisations and their perceptions of what interaction and networking means in an online sphere and to understand the specific organisational factors that facilitate or constrain interaction and networking online.

The analysis of individual government profiles on social media demonstrated that there has been a dissolution of the boundary between government organisational communications and individual communications in both Germany and Great Britain. The assumption was correct that government organisations would adopt individualised communications in this new media environment. This study assumes that the individualisation of government communications will increase in the years ahead and there is an urgent need for further analysis of the personalisation of government organisational communications and the consequences for the politicisation of public sector communications. In particular, comparative studies should qualitatively analyse the content on these pages and how they mix political, government and personal content. One of the conclusions of this discussion was that the individualisation of government organisational communications presents a possible threat to the transparency and legitimacy of government communications in the online sphere, as government communications becomes more persuasive and politicised. This study believes that the normative and legal risks could increase in the coming years as more government actors adopt individual profiles on social media, in particular, if government actors start to use these pages more actively (the results in this study showed that activity levels were for the most part lower on individual pages compared to organisational pages).

In Great Britain, unidirectional communication dominated across all social media platforms and government actors networked exclusively with each other. There was a marked difference in approach in Germany where there were a few prominent examples of interaction. A few actors in Germany were highly active and responsive across each social media platform. In addition, the retweet network indicated that German government actors tended to network with different actors rather than solely with other government actors. These findings seem to confirm that there is a more centralised and controlled approach to online government communications in Great Britain. In Germany, it appears to be less centralised and controlled, and consequently, it is more interactive and its network is more open. Based on Mergel and Bretschneider's (2013) theory of social media diffusion, this thesis concludes that Germany has not yet reached the stage of institutionalisation that has been reached in Great Britain. However, it is not possible to determine whether Germany will go in the same direction as Great Britain (i.e., more controlled communications as social media becomes more institutionalised), or whether government communications will continue to be interactive, but limited to just a few well-resourced ministries (on FB) or lower-profile actors (on TW).

The next chapter, Chapter 8, will provide an overview of the main contributions of this dissertation, discuss some of its limitations and how the study of government communications and comparative political communications should proceed in the years ahead.

8. Conclusion

The field of political communications has for too long overlooked government communications and how different governments are adapting to changes in the media environment (Canel & Sanders, 2012; Graber, 2003; Sanders et al., 2011) and the normative consequences of these changes. There has been a too narrow focus on political parties and politicians use of social media during election campaigns (Klinger et al., 2015; Sanders et al., 2011). However, it is not just government communications that has been overlooked. This thesis highlighted that comparative political communications has yet to catch up with the changes taking place in the media environment. As a result, there is little understanding of how different political systems and organisational environments are shaping the use of websites and social media by different political actors (De Vreese, 2017; Nitschke et al., 2014). As the literature review in this study demonstrated, there are still only a handful of comparative studies examining how political parties use websites for election campaigning (e.g., Foot et al, 2009; Gibson & Ward, 2000; Gibson et al., 2003; Russmann, 2011), and very little beyond this. It may seem like political communications has come a long way in understanding how digital technologies are changing government, politics and media, but many large gaps remain. This study filled a number of these gaps by focusing specifically on executive government organisations and comparing how these organisations, in two different countries, are using online technologies in their day-to-day communications.

One of the weaknesses of online political communications has been its failure to understand the social and political context of technology use (Gibson & Ward, 2009, p. 37). Hallin and Mancini (2004) have been to the forefront of the field in arguing for a theoretical analysis of the context of communications and in identifying how different political institutional structures shape communications. Comparative studies demand an in-depth analysis of the structural factors that shape political communications in each country. However, there has until now, been little theoretical reflection within the field around how these macro structures themselves are changing as a result of digital technologies, for example, changing media systems and changing media political relations and how these changing structures are shaping the use of digital technologies (Norris, 2011). This dissertation set out to make a valuable theoretical contribution to the field by identifying all those structural factors that are essential to understanding government communications in the new media environment in Germany and Great Britain. Chapter 3 outlined critical differences in their political systems, media systems, changing political media relations, the regulation of government communications and the development of centralised structures for government communications (see Table 3 in Chapter 3 for full overview). This dissertation assumed that differences in the centralised structures for government communications and different systems of regulation would strongly shape the way these governments communicate online. While numerous previous studies have examined particular aspects of these macro structures in Great Britain and Germany (e.g., Borucki, 2014 b; Gregory, 2012; Holtz-Bacha, 2013; Kocks & Raupp, 2014; Sanders et al., 2011; Sanders & Canel, 2013; Vogel, 2010), there have been few studies that have looked at all these macro factors together and empirically examined how these structures shape their actual online communications. In this regard, this study represents a significant contribution to the field of government communications and the wider field of online political communications.

As this thesis highlighted, the macro level alone cannot explain how government organisations use digital technologies and why some organisations use them differently than others. In Chapter 4, this thesis argued that the meso level has also been missing in the study of online political communications (Donges, 2008). It is necessary to understand how different organisational environments can influence the use of digital technologies by and within political and government organisations (Mergel, 2016; Nitschke et al., 2014). This thesis provided an organisational and network theoretical perspective of the transformations taking place in the new media environment and the consequences for organisational communications. These transformations pose enormous challenges for political and government organisations, as citizens increasingly engage in politics outside of traditional political institutions (Bennett, 2012; Bennett & Segerberg, 2012). Within the new communications environment, organisational communications has become increasingly personalised (Bennett, 2012). Organisations mix formal and informal communications practices (Bimber et al., 2005; Penney, 2017) and have taken on hybrid identities (Chadwick, 2007). However, this thesis assumed that government organisations would face far greater challenges than political organisations in adapting to these changes due to their bureaucratic and inflexible organisational structures along with a range of political and legal constraints (Graber, 2003; Liu et al., 2010; Olsen, 2006; Schillemans, 2012). Due to their unique organisational form and environment, it was assumed that their online communications would be top-down and controlled by their centralised organisational structures.

The network perspective provided the overarching perspective for understanding the complexity and changes in the new media environment. According to this perspective, digital technologies have transformed society and changes can be found at all levels of society and in how each level relates to each other (Castells, 2000; Reese & Shoemaker, 2016; Van Dijk, 2012). This thesis argued that a network perspective was the most suitable viewpoint for understanding the new media environment and the resulting challenges that organisations have to navigate. Just like the organisational perspective mentioned above, the central challenges include the changing relationship between levels of analysis, the increasing individualisation of communications, and how networking has become central to interaction in the online sphere. This thesis argued that this perspective could also address some of the weaknesses in comparative research designs to date. One of the shortcomings of comparative communications has been its hierarchical understanding of the communications environment which no longer reflects the complexity and changes of the new media environment. In contrast, the network perspective emphasises how the new media environment has changed and that the macro level is now just one of many levels shaping communications (Kontopoulos, 1993; Reese & Shoemaker, 2016; Van Dijk, 2012; Van Dijk & Winters-van Beek, 2009). Accordingly, research should focus on the changing relationship *between*, and *within* levels, of analysis. In this way, the network perspective strengthened the comparative research design of this study. Based on these theoretical conclusions from Chapter 4, and the macro-level analysis from Chapter 3, a number of research guiding assumptions were formulated.

The network perspective was incorporated into the comparative research design and methodological approach in a number of ways. First, the author sought to examine whether there has been an individualisation of government organisational communications and a dissolution of the boundary between meso and micro levels of analysis. Government communications was, therefore, defined as both the organisational and individual social media pages of all executive government actors that play an influential role in government communications in Germany and Great Britain. This definition was carefully formulated to also include the centralised organisations for government communications (e.g., the BPA and the GCS) and the head of government communications (e.g., Steffen Seibert in Germany). In fact, very few studies in political communications, or political science, have managed to define government communications (Vogel, 2010), and in this regard, this definition of online government communications can be considered an important contribution and progress in the field. It manages to provide an equivalent understanding of online government communications that can be applied to both countries.

Previous studies on government use of online technologies found that governments engage mostly in top-down communication and do not interact or network with others online (Chadwick, 2013; Gurevitch et al., 2009; Meijer et al., 2012). However, numerous political communications scholars have criticised previous understandings of interaction in an online age, an understanding that attached too much importance to rational deliberation and discussion (Chadwick, 2009; Dahlgren, 2005; Papacharissi, 2009; Wright, 2012). Prior research focused on hierarchical and linear flows of communication and two-way forms of interaction (Young & Pieterson, 2015). It is increasingly accepted that interaction online follows a network logic (Klinger & Svensson, 2015, 2016). In the methodological design, this study adopted a wider understanding of interaction and defined it as taking place at a number of different levels (Jenkins et al., 2013; Vaccari, Valeriani, et al., 2015; Van Dijk, 2012) and consisting of numerous network characteristics (Adi et al., 2014; Nuernbergk & Conrad, 2016). In order to answer the various research questions, relating to how government organisations interact and network online, this thesis combined a quantitative online content analysis of government websites and social media pages with a SNA of Twitter (retweet) networks in Germany and Great Britain. The empirical design of this study represents progress for the field of government communications and comparative communications, as it moves the field beyond a narrow examination of political party election websites and a constricted understanding of interaction online. It is the first comparative empirical study that combines these two methods to investigate the structural and organisational factors specifically shaping how government organisations interact and network online.

The findings of the empirical study confirmed a central assumption of this thesis that government organisations still predominantly engage in one-way push communications. However, the results also revealed a number of interesting patterns. They showed significant differences between government organisations within both countries in how actively they use social media. This confirmed another assumption that government organisations would use digital technologies differently. The results showed that there is no strategic or rational approach to social media use by government organisations (Mergel, 2012; Mergel & Bretschneider, 2013). These differences at the meso level could not be explained by any particular macro-level structure. Instead, the results confirm that government organisations have their own motivations and constraints that shape how they use (or don't use) social media.

There were also some positive developments suggesting that a limited number of government organisations are becoming more interactive online. One of the most interesting findings was that a small number of government organisations and individuals in Germany are highly actively and engage in direct interaction on social media. These examples confirmed that the stricter regulatory structures in Germany are not inhibiting interaction online, as had been assumed initially by this thesis. These macro structures may not be hindering interaction, however, they appear to facilitate a more transparent approach to communications on social media in Germany. In stark contrast, government actors in Great Britain engaged almost exclusively in top-down communications and there was almost no transparency on social media in Great Britain. When these findings are taken together with the findings of the SNA for Great Britain (which showed that government actors network predominantly with other government actors), it seems that particular aspects of Britain's macro-level structures are causing a more centralised and controlled approach to communications online. It appears that Great Britain's highly centralised political system (Humphreys, 2012) and the centralised role of the PM's Office (Dowding, 2013) are shaping a more top-down and controlled approach to interaction and networking online compared to a more open and interactive approach in Germany where the political system is decentralised and there is less central control of ministries.

This study drew attention to a particular feature of organisational communications in an online age that is also affecting government organisations, that is, the individualisation and personalisation of communications (Bennett, 2012; Bennett & Segerberg, 2012). A central finding of this study was that individuals are becoming more prominent within government organisational communications facilitated by social media. This individualisation was characterised by a mix of formal and informal communications practices. For example, individual social media pages were presented as a mix of formal government communications and informal personalised communications. These pages not only obscured what was official (organisational) and non-official (individual) government communications, but their profile descriptions and the content on these pages obscured what was personal, political and government communications. A kind of hybrid identity (Chadwick, 2007) was found on these pages in both countries.

However, there was one distinct difference. In relation to transparency on these pages, it was found that individual pages in Germany stated who was responsible for the content, whereas there was no transparency on these pages in Great Britain.

Despite some signs of greater transparency in Germany, these pages still raise a number of normative and legal concerns around the politicisation of government/public sector communications in the new media environment in both Germany and Great Britain. Recent studies examining, for example, the personalisation of ministerial communication (not specifically in the online sphere, but more generally) (Figenschou et al., 2017) and the mediatisation of public bureaucracies (Thorbjørnsrud et al., 2014) have already highlighted how the line is often blurred between public and political communications and how it is becoming increasingly difficult to separate these two in today's fast-paced media environment. The findings of this dissertation confirm these patterns can also be found in the online sphere. As increasing numbers of government actors adopt an individual profile and become more active on social media, there is a risk that the boundary between partisan and non-partisan government communications will disappear. That risk would appear to be quite high in Great Britain due to less transparency online and weaker regulatory structures. However, there is also a clear risk that this kind of personalised communications could infringe the neutrality of government communications in Germany (Neutralitätsgebot) (Barczak, 2018). The findings highlight the urgent need for further analysis of the personalisation of government organisational communications in a digital age. There is room for future comparative studies to qualitatively analyse the content on individual social media pages including how they mix political, government and personal content, including a textual and visual analysis. Future studies should widen this to include other highly personalised, but more visual, platforms such as Instagram[65]. While there are still many more aspects of personalisation that need to be investigated, this study acts as an important starting point in drawing attention to this emerging trend within government organisational communications in both countries. As individual social pages become more popular and active (possibly more popular than organisational pages), it could have normative and legal consequences, triggering fundamental questions about the transparency, neutrality and legitimacy of government communications in an online age. One only has to look to

65 The German Chancellor Angela Merkel has her own Instagram profile called "Bundeskanzlerin" since 2015.

U.S. President Donald Trump to see the negative consequences for politics and democracy when the boundary between the personal, political and government dissolves entirely.

In summary of the methodological approach, the SNA revealed important patterns of interaction and networking that could not have been identified through a quantitative online content analysis alone. While the SNA provided a small glimpse into one aspect of networking behaviour (retweets) at a particular point in time, it strengthened the empirical analysis and the interpretation of the results. There were clear patterns of interaction in the content analysis that were also mirrored in the SNA. For example, government organisations in Germany were more interactive on social media and had a more open Twitter network. On the other hand, British organisations engaged exclusively in unidirectional communications in the content analysis and the SNA revealed a closed and highly centralised Twitter network. Taken together, these results provided a fuller picture of how governments use digital technologies for interaction. The methodological approach demonstrated the value of taking a broader approach to interaction and combining these two methods. The SNA also provided an interesting insight into power dynamics within government and how macro level structures shape government networks and who is most central within the network. For example, the British network revealed that the main centralised government organisation for government communications in Great Britain is the PM's Office and not the GCS as previous literature, and this thesis, had assumed.

However, the empirical approach was not without its weaknesses. First, the SNA was limited to retweets only. Future studies should examine additional networking characteristics such as @replies and @mentions (e.g., see Nuernbergk, 2016; Nuernbergk & Conrad, 2016) and examine their networking behaviour over different time periods. It is possible that this would reveal different power dynamics within the networks than found in this thesis. Second, the other empirical weakness was the limited focus on the online communications output of government organisations only. This study was unable to identify the specific organisational factors and constraints that influence why some government organisations were more active and interactive than others. There is a need for future comparative studies of government communications to combine these approaches with qualitative interviews. This is necessary to examine the internal motivations behind social media use, how government actors within organisations understand interaction and networking in an online age and organisational constraints (e.g., specific political or policy decisions around social media use, budgetary constraints etc.) that prevent them using online technologies to their full potential. According to Klinger et al,

> The question that needs to be investigated is whether non-adaptation and one-way, non-participatory implementation are a result of misunderstanding the new medium (actors do not know what to do), a lack of resources (actors know what to do but cannot implement this), internal constraints (actors know what to do, but other actors or institutions prevent them from doing this), or strategic reasons (actors know what to do but choose to not do it). (2015, p. 1930)

It is essential that both approaches are combined, as interviews can also reveal gaps between perceptions of how they communicate online and their actual communication practices (Kocks, 2016; Nitschke & Murphy, 2016). While this thesis may not have identified the specific internal constraints or motivations that explain the differences found at the meso level in these two countries, it did demonstrate the need to consider interaction from different perspectives and to consider the different levels of analysis that shape government organisational communications in an online age.

This study was a first step in considering how different governments use online technologies and also how government organisations use online technologies differently. Some findings could be explained by differences at the macro level, while others could only be explained by looking inside those organisations, something that was beyond the bounds of this study. The findings showed that the relationship between meso and micro-level government communications is also changing. There is no longer a clear boundary between what is government organisational and individual political communications. The similarities found at the micro level could not be fully explained by factors at the macro or meso level and indicate that global factors may be influencing more individualised communications across countries (Ottovordemgentschenfelde, 2017). These findings demonstrate just how complex comparative government communications has become in an online age. Future comparative research needs to incorporate multi-level and multi-method research designs into the analysis of organisational communications in an online age.

The theoretical analysis and empirical findings also highlighted how much the wider field of comparative political communications needs to develop theoretically and empirically. Theoretical approaches in the field have almost entirely overlooked the role of digital technologies within media systems and how media systems have transformed (Norris, 2011). Comparative theoretical approaches (e.g., Blumler & Gurevitch, 1995; Hallin and Mancini, 2004; Pfetsch & Esser, 2012) assumed the predominant influence of the nation state and these models were based on traditional understandings of media systems, for example, the strong role of the press. Hallin and Mancini's (2004) model included a simplified understanding of political systems categorising them as being either presidential or multiparty parliamentary systems (Humphreys, 2012). In doing so, they overlooked other key aspects of political systems and institutions that shape government and political communications (Humphreys, 2012; Rice & Somerville, 2017). One such characteristic could be the increasing personalisation of political systems (Campus, 2010) and the effect that this is having on political communications at the meso and micro level. Previous models presumed distinguishable and hierarchical levels of analysis between individuals and the wider society (and the meso level was rarely considered). They were based on traditional presumptions around how citizens engage in politics. However, new organisational perspectives and the network society perspective challenge many of these old assumptions around how society is organised (Van Dijk, 2012). A further aspect of comparative research that appears to be no longer suitable to the new media environment is the *most different systems* and *most similar systems* approach to designing comparative studies (see Hallin & Mancini, 2004; Przeworski & Teune, 1970). This approach is outdated and restricts comparative studies to examining only similarities or differences. As this study demonstrated, there can be important similarities at one level of analysis, but critical differences at other levels which would be missed if this approach is strictly applied. In summary, there is a clear need for a new theoretical model for comparing government and political communications in a networked media environment, but unfortunately this was beyond the scope of this thesis. However, this author drew attention to numerous gaps and weaknesses in the field of comparative political communications that are rarely addressed. Future theoretical models need to incorporate more accurate variables at the macro level describing media and political systems, while also including the meso level and the changing relationship between the levels of analysis.

Finally, Wright (2012) warned that "revolutions can take time, and involve a variety of technologies and applications. Thus, we should not look to the latest technology in isolation." (p.252). In a similar vein, Chadwick (2013, 2017; Vaccari et al., 2015) argued that the most significant changes occurring are in how different actors within political communications use a mixture of traditional and new communications technologies. It is this combination of old and new media that is resulting in new forms of interaction and engagement. There is a need for government communications and comparative political communications to move beyond current approaches that examine how individual politicians use Twitter or websites in isolation from other platforms and offline communications practices. Research has shown that, for example, traditional media relations still continues to be a central aspect of government communications and that online technologies are used to simply gain attention or interact with traditional media rather than interaction with citizens (Adi et al., 2014; Chadwick, 2013; Davis, 2010; Kocks, 2016; Nuernbergk & Conrad, 2016). In order to fully understand government communications in an online age, research needs to consider the integration of online platforms with offline communications practices to fully capture government communications in an online age.

References

Adi, A., Erickson, K., & Lilleker, D. G. (2014). Elite tweets: Analyzing the Twitter communication patterns of Labour party peers in the House of Lords. *Policy & Internet, 6*(1), 1-27.

Ahrne, G., & Brunsson, N. (2011). Organization outside organizations: The significance of partial organization. *Organization, 18*(1), 83-104.

Andeweg, R. (1993). A model of the cabinet system: the dimensions of cabinet decision-making processes. In *Governing together: The extent and limits of joint decision-making in Western European cabinets* (pp. 23-42). London, UK: Palgrave MacMillan.

Andeweg, R. (2003). On studying governments. In J. Hayward & A. Menon (Eds.), *Governing Europe* (pp. 39-60). Oxford, UK: Oxford University Press.

Anstead, N., & Chadwick, A. (2009). Parties, election campaigning, and the internet: Toward a comparative institutional approach. In A. Chadwick & P. N. Howard (Eds.), *Routledge handbook of internet politics* (pp. 56–71). London, UK: Routledge.

Anstead, N., & Chadwick, A. (2017). A primary definer online: the construction and propagation of a think tank's authority on social media. *Media, Culture & Society*, 0163443717707341.

Applebaum, A. (2017). A transformed political landscape. *Journal of Democracy, 28*(1), 53-58.

Barczak, T. (2018). Staatliche Öffentlichkeitsarbeit aus rechtswissenschaftlicher Perspektive [Government public relations from a legal perspective]. In J. Raupp, J. N. Kocks, & K. Murphy (Eds.), *Regierungskommunikation und staatliche Öffentlichkeitsarbeit: Implikationen des technologisch induzierten Medienwandels* (pp. 47-72). Wiesbaden, Germany: Springer VS.

Bastian, M., Heymann, S., & Jacomy, M. (2009). Gephi: an open source software for exploring and manipulating networks (Version 0.92) [Computer software]. Retrieved from https://gephi.org/users/download/

BBC. (2015). Westminister lobby [Webpage]. Retrieved from http://www.bbc.co.uk /academy/journalism/article/art20130702112133781

Bennett, W. L. (2012). The personalization of politics: Political identity, social media, and changing patterns of participation. *The ANNALS of the American Academy of Political and Social Science, 644*(1), 20-39.

Bennett, W. L., & Segerberg, A. (2012). The logic of connective action: Digital media and the personalization of contentious politics. *Information, Communication & Society, 15*(5), 739-768.

Bimber, B., Flanagin, A. J., & Stohl, C. (2005). Reconceptualizing collective action in the contemporary media environment. *Communication Theory, 15*(4), 365-388.

Bimber, B., Stohl, C., & Flanagin, A. J. (2009). Technological change and the shifting nature of political organization. In A. Chadwick & P. N. Howard (Eds.), *Routledge handbook of internet politics* (pp. 72–85). London, UK: Routledge.

Block, A., & Feldgen, K. (2018). "Die Leute erwarten den Dialog und den liefern wir auch": Ein Gespräch über Regierungskommunikation in den Sozialen Medien ["The people expect dialogue and we deliver it": A conversation about government communications on social media]. In J. Raupp, J. N. Kocks, & K. Murphy (Eds.), *Regierungskommunikation und staatliche Öffentlichkeitsarbeit: Implikationen des technologisch induzierten Medienwandels* (pp. 251-258). Wiesbaden, Germany: Springer VS.

Blumler, J. G., & Gurevitch, M. (1995). *The crisis of public communication*. Psychology Press.

Blumler, J. G., & Kavanagh, D. (1999). The third age of political communication: Influences and features. *Political Communication, 16*, 209-230. doi:10.1080/105846099198596

Blumler, J. G., McLeod, J. M., & Rosengren, K. E. (1992). An introduction to comparative communication research. In J. G. Blumler, J. M. McLeod, & K. E. Rosengren (Eds.), *Comparatively speaking: Communication and culture across space and time* (pp. 3-18). Newbury Park, CA: Sage.

Borgatti, S.P., Everett, M.G. & Freeman, L.C. (2002). Ucinet for Windows: Software for Social Network Analysis (Version 6) [Computer software]. Harvard, MA: Analytic Technologies.

Borgatti, S.P., Everett, M.G. & Johnson, J.C. (2013). *Analyzing social networks*. Thousand Oaks, CA: Sage.

Borucki, I. (2014 a). Online-Regieren angesichts medialer Allgegenwart–Die Kanzlerin auf Youtube und ihr twitternder Regierungssprecher [Governing online in the face of media ubiquity – the Chancellor on YouTube and her twittering government spokesperson]. In H. Sievert & A. Nelke (Eds.), *Social Media-Kommunikation nationaler Regierungen in Europa* (pp. 34-50). Wiesbaden, Germany: Springer VS.

Borucki, I. (2014 b). *Regieren mit Medien. Auswirkungen der Medialisierung auf die Regierungskommunikation der Bundesregierung von 1982-2010 [Governing with media: the effects of mediatization on the government communications of the German federal government from 1982-2010]*. Berlin, Germany: Barbara Budrich.

Borucki, I., & Jun, U. (2018). Regierungskommunikation im Wandel – Politikwissenschaftliche Perspektiven [Changing government communications – political science perspectives]. In J. Raupp, J. N. Kocks, & K. Murphy (Eds.), *Regierungskommunikation und staatliche Öffentlichkeitsarbeit: Implikationen des technologisch induzierten Medienwandels* (pp. 25-46). Wiesbaden, Germany: Springer VS.

Brauck, M., & Schult, C. (2016, July). Regierungssprecher – Ein Job mit Rückfahrticket [Government spokesperson – A job with a return ticket]. *Der Spiegel, 31*. Retrieved from http://www.spiegel.de/spiegel/steffen-seibert-darf-zum-zdf-zu rueckkehren-a-1105441.html

Brüggemann, M., Engesser, S., Büchel, F., Humprecht, E., & Castro, L. (2014). Hallin and Mancini revisited: Four empirical types of Western media systems. *Journal of Communication, 64*(6), 1037-1065.

Bundespressekonferenz. (n.d.). Der Verein [Webpage]. Retrieved from www.bundespressekonferenz.de/verein/der-verein

Bundesregierung. (2014). *Digitale Agenda 2014-2017 [Digital agenda]*. Bundesministerium für Wirtschaft und Energie. Retrieved from https://www.digitale-agenda.de/Webs/DA/DE/Home/home_node.html

Bundesregierung. (2016). *Gut Leben in Deutschland was uns wichtig ist: Bericht der Bundesregierung zur Lebensqualität in Deutschland [Good life in Germany what is important to us: Report of the Federal Government on the quality of life in Germany]*. Presse und Informationsamt der Bundesregierung. Retrieved from https://www.gut-leben-in-deutschland.de/static/LB/index.html

Bundeszentrale für politische Bildung. (n.d.). Staatliche Öffentlichkeitsarbeit/Presse- und Informationsamt der Bundesregierung [Webpage]. Retrieved from http://www.bpb.de/nachschlagen/lexika/handwoerterbuch-politisches-system/202110/staatliche-oeffentlichkeitsarbeit-presse-und-informationsamt-der-bundesregierung

Burt, E., & Taylor, J. (2001). When 'virtual' meets values: Insights from the voluntary sector. *Information, Communication & Society, 4*(1), 54-73.

Cabinet Office. (2011). *Review of government direct communication and the role of COI: Matt Tee, Permanent Secretary for Government Communications*. Retrieved from https://assets.publishing.service.gov.uk/government/uploads/system/uploads/attachment_data/file/60819/coi-comms-review-march2011_0.pdf

Cabinet Office. (2013). *Cabinet Office annual report and accounts 2012-2013*. Retrieved from https://www.gov.uk/government/uploads/system/uploads/attachment_data/file/225980/HC_15.pdf

Campus, D. (2010). Mediatization and personalization of politics in Italy and France: The cases of Berlusconi and Sarkozy. *The International Journal of Press/Politics, 15*(2), 219-235.

Canel, M. J., & Sanders, K. (2014). Is it enough to be strategic? Comparing and defining professional government communication across disciplinary fields and between countries. In M.J. Canel & K. Voltmer (Eds.), *Comparing political communication across time and space* (pp. 98-116). London, UK: Palgrave MacMillan.

Canel, M. J., & Sanders, K. (2012). Government communication: An emerging field in political communication research. In H.A. Semetko & M. Scammell (Eds.), *The SAGE Handbook of Political Communication* (pp. 85-97). London, UK: SAGE Publications Ltd.

Castells, M. (2000 a). *The network society* (Second ed.). Oxford, UK: Blackwell Publishing.

Castells, M. (2000 b). Toward a sociology of the network society. *Contemporary sociology, 29*(5), 693-699.

Castells, M. (2007). Communication, power and counter-power in the network society. *International Journal of Communication, 1*, 238–266.

Castells, M. (2008). The new public sphere: Global civil society, communication networks, and global governance. *The Annals of the American Academy of Political and Social Science, 616*, 78–93.

Castells, M. (2010). *The rise of the network society: The information age: Economy, society, and culture* (Vol. 1). Oxford, UK: Blackwell Publishing.

Castells, M. (2011 a). A network theory of power. *International Journal of Communication, 5*, 773–787.

Castells, M. (2011 b). Democracy in the age of the Internet. *Journal of Contemporary Culture* (6), 96-103.

Chadwick, A. (2003). Bringing e-democracy back in: Why it matters for future research on e-governance. *Social Science Computer Review, 21*(4), 443-455.

Chadwick, A. (2007). Digital network repertoires and organizational hybridity. *Political Communication, 24*(3), 283-301.

Chadwick, A. (2009). Web 2.0: New challenges for the study of e-democracy in an era of informational exuberance. *I/S: A Journal of Law and Policy for the Information Society, 5*(1), 9-41.

Chadwick, A. (2011 a). Explaining the failure of an online citizen engagement initiative: the role of internal institutional variables. *Journal of Information Technology & Politics, 8*(1), 21-40.

Chadwick, A. (2011 b). The political information cycle in a hybrid news system: The British prime minister and the "bullygate" affair. *The International Journal of Press/Politics, 16*(1), 3-29.

Chadwick, A. (2013). *The hybrid media system: Politics and power*. New York, NY: Oxford University Press.

Chadwick, A. (2017). *The hybrid media system: Politics and power*. New York, NY: Oxford University Press.

Chadwick, A., & May, C. (2003). Interaction between states and citizens in the age of the Internet: "e-Government" in the United States, Britain, and the European Union. *Governance, 16*, 271–300. doi:10.1111/1468-0491.00216

Chadwick, A., & Stromer-Galley, J. (2016). Digital media, power, and democracy in parties and election campaigns: Party decline or party renewal? *International Journal of Press/Politics, 20*(3), 283-294.

Coleman, S., & Blumler, J. G. (2009). *The Internet and democratic citizenship: theory, practice and policy*. Cambridge, UK: Cambridge University Press.

Coleman, S., & Firmstone, J. (2014). Contested meanings of public engagement: exploring discourse and practice within a British city council. *Media, Culture & Society, 36*(6), 826-844.

Dahlgren, P. (2005). The Internet, public spheres, and political communication: Dispersion and deliberation. *Political Communication, 22*, 147–162. doi:10.1080/10584600590933160

Davis, A. (2009). Journalist-source relations, mediated reflexivity and the politics of politics. *Journalism Studies, 10*, 204–219. doi:10.1080/14616700802580540

Davis, A. (2010 a). New media and fat democracy: the paradox of online participation. *New Media & Society, 12*, 745–761.

Davis, A. (2010 b). *Political Communication and Social Theory*. London, UK: Routledge.

Davis, A. (2014). The impact of market forces, new technologies, and political PR on UK journalism. In R. Kuhn & R.K. Nielsen (Eds.), *Political journalism in transition. Western Europe in a comparative perspective* (pp. 111-128). London, UK: IB Tauris.

De Vreese, C.H. (2017). Comparative political communication research. In K. Kenski & K. Hall Jamieson (Eds.), *The oxford handbook of political communication*. New York, NY: Oxford University Press. doi: 10.1093/oxfordhb/9780199793471.001.0001

Deutscher Bundestag. (2015). *Antwort der Bundesregierung auf die Kleine Anfrage der Abgeordneten Dr. Konstantin von Notz, Tabea Rößner, Renate Künast, weiterer Abgeordnete und der Fraktion BÜNDNIS 90/DIE GRÜNEN: Öffentlichkeitsarbeit der Bundesregierung auf Social Media Kanälen [Answer of the federal government to the request of the parliamentarian Dr. Konstantin von Notz, Tabea Rößner, Renate Künast, and other parliamentarians and the Green Party faction: Public relations of the federal government on social media*]. Retrieved from http://dipbt.bundestag.de/dip21/btd/18/066/1806609.pdf

DiMaggio, P.J., & Powell, W.W. (1991). The iron cage revisited: Institutional isomorphism and collective rationality in organizational fields. In P.J. DiMaggio & W. W. Powell (Eds.), *The new institutionalism in organizational analysis* (pp. 63-82). Chicago and London: The University of Chicago Press.

Donges, P. (2008). *Medialisierung politischer Organisationen. Parteien in der Mediengesellschaft*. Wiesbaden, Germany: VS Verlag.

Donges, P., & Jarren, O. (2014). Mediatization of political organisations: Changing parties and interest groups? In F. Esser & J. Strömbäck (Eds.), *Mediatization of politics: Understanding the transformation of Western democracies* (pp. 181-200). Basingstoke, UK: Palgrave Macmillan.

Donges, P., & Nitschke, P. (2016). The new institutionalism revisited. In G. Vowe & P. Henn (Eds.), *Political Communication in the Online World: Theoretical Approaches and Research Designs* (pp. 118-132). New York, NY: Routledge.

Dowding, K. (2013). The prime ministerialisation of the British prime minister. *Parliamentary Affairs, 66*(3), 617-635.

Drobinski, M. (2018, February 27). Wanka gegen AFD – Warum das Urteil richtig ist [Wanka against the AFD – why the judgement is correct]. *Die Suddeutsche Zeitung*. Retrieved from http://www.sueddeutsche.de/politik/meinung-am-mittag-wanka-gegen-afd-karlsruhe-beschraenkt-zu-recht-die-meinungsmacht-der-regierung-1.3884651

Dunleavy, P., & Margetts, H. (2015). *Design principles for essentially digital governance*. Paper presented at the 111th Annual Meeting of the American Political Science Association, San Francisco, USA. Retrieved from http://eprints.lse.ac.uk/id/eprint/64125

Dunleavy, P., Margetts, H., Bastow, S., & Tinkler, J. (2006). New public management is dead — long live digital-era governance. *Journal of Public Administration Research and Theory, 16*(3), 467-494. doi:https://doi.org/10.1093/jopart/mui057

Dunleavy, P., & Rhodes, R.A.W. (1990). Core executive studies in Britain. *Public Administration, 68*(1), 3-28.

Döhler, M., Fleischer, J., & Hustedt, T. (2007). Government reform as institutional politics: Varieties and policy patterns from a comparative perspective. Research Paper *"Core Executives in Western Europe"*, (3). Potsdam, Germany: Universitätsverlag Potsdam.

Enli, G.S., & Skogerbø, E. (2013). Personalized campaigns in party-centred politics: Twitter and Facebook as arenas for political communication. *Information, Communication & Society, 16*(5), 757-774.

Esser, F. (2008). Dimensions of political news cultures: Sound bite and image bite news in France, Germany, Great Britain, and the United States. *The International Journal of Press/Politics, 13*(4), 401-428.

Esser, F. (2013). The emerging paradigm of comparative communication enquiry: Advancing cross-national research in times of globalization. *International Journal of Communication, 7*, 113-128.

Esser, F., & Hanitzsch, T. (2012). On the why and how of comparative inquiry in communication studies. In F. Esser & T. Hanitzsch (Eds.), *The handbook of comparative communication research* (pp. 3-22). New York, NY: Routledge.

Esser, F., & Pfetsch, B. (2017). Comparing political communication. In D. Caramani (Ed.), *Comparative politics* (Fourth ed.) (pp. 327-347). Oxford, UK: Oxford University Press.

Figenschou, T. U., Karlsen, R., Kolltveit, K., & Thorbjørnsrud, K. (2017). Serving the media ministers: A mixed methods study on the personalization of ministerial communication. *The International Journal of Press/Politics, 22*(4), 411-430.

Foot, K.A., Xenos, M., Schneider, S.M., Kluver, R., & Jankowski, N.W. (2009). Electoral web production practices in cross-national perspective: The relative influence of national development, political culture, and web genre. In A. Chadwick & P. Howard (Eds.), *Routledge handbook of Internet politics* (pp. 40-55). London, UK: Routledge.

Garland, R., Tambini, D., & Couldry, N. (2017). Has government been mediatized? A UK perspective. *Media, Culture & Society, 40*(4), 496-513.

Gibson, R., Margolis, M., Resnick, D., & Ward, S. J. (2003). Election campaigning on the WWW in the USA and UK. *Party Politics, 9*, 47–75.

Gibson, R., & Ward, S. (2000). A proposed methodology for studying the function and effectiveness of party and candidate web sites. *Social Science Computer Review, 18*(3), 301-319.

Gibson, R., & Ward, S. (2009). European political organizations and the internet: mobilization, participation and change. In A. Chadwick & P. N. Howard (Eds.), *Routledge handbook of internet politics* (pp. 25–39). London, UK: Routledge.

Giddens, A. (1984). *The constitution of society: Outline of the theory of structuration.* Polity Press.

Giddens, A. (1991). *Modernity and self-identity: Self and society in the late modern age*. Stanford, CA: Stanford university press.

Government Communication Service. (2015). *Government communication service (GCS) handbook*. Retrieved from https://gcs.civilservice.gov.uk/wp-content/uploads/2015/09/GCS-Handbook.pdf

Graber, D.A. (2003). *The power of communication: Managing information in public organizations*. Washington, D.C.: Congressional Quarterly.

Gregory, A. (2006). A development framework for government communicators. *Journal of Communication Management, 10*(2), 197-210.

Gregory, A. (2012). UK government communications: Full circle in the 21st century? *Public Relations Review, 38*(3), 367-375.

Grunig, J. E., & Hunt, T. (1984). *Managing public relations*. New York, NY: Holt, Rinehart and Winston.

Gurevitch, M., Coleman, S., & Blumler, J. G. (2009). Political communication—Old and new media relationships. *The ANNALS of the American Academy of Political and Social Science, 625*(1), 164-181.

Hallin, D.C., & Mancini, P. (2004). *Comparing media systems: Three models of media and politics*. Cambridge, UK: Cambridge University Press.

Hanitzsch, T. (2012). Comparing journalism cultures. In F. Esser & T. Hanitzsch (Eds.), *The handbook of comparative communication research* (pp. 262-275). New York, NY: Routledge.

Head, B. (2007). The public service and government communication: Pressures and dilemmas. In S. Young (Ed.), *Government communication in Australia*. New York: Cambridge University Press.

Heffernan, R. (2006). The prime minister and the news media: Political communication as a leadership resource. *Parliamentary Affairs, 59*(4), 582-598.

Heinze, J. (2012). *Regierungskommunikation in Deutschland: Eine Analyse von Produktion und Rezeption [Government communications in Germany: An analysis of production and reception]*. Wiesbaden, Germany: Springer VS.

Held, D., McGrew, A., Goldblatt, D., & Perraton, J. (1999). *Global transformations: Politics, economics, and culture*. Stanford, CA: Stanford University Press.

Holtz-Bacha, C. (2013). Government communication in Germany: Maintaining the fine line between information and advertising. In K. Sanders & M. J. Canel (Eds.), *Government communication* (pp. 45-58). New York, NY: Bloomsbury.

Holtz-Bacha, C., Langer, A.I., & Merkle, S. (2014). The personalization of politics in comparative perspective: Campaign coverage in Germany and the United Kingdom. *European Journal of Communication, 29*(2), 153-170.

Horsley, J.S., Liu, B. F., & Levenshus, A.B. (2010). Comparisons of U.S. government communication practices: Expanding the government communication decision wheel. *Communication Theory, 20*, 269–295.

House of Lords Select Committee on Communications. (2009). *First report of session 2008-09: Government communications report with evidence*. London: Authority of the House of Lords. Retrieved from https://publications.parliament.uk/pa/ld200809/ldselect/ldcomuni/7/7.pdf

Humphreys, P. (2012). A political scientist's contribution to the comparative study of media systems in Europe: A response to Hallin and Mancini. In N. Just & M. Puppis (Eds.), *Trends in communications policy research: New theories, methods and subjects* (pp. 157-177). Bristol, UK: Intellect.

Jackson, N., & Lilleker, D. (2011). Microblogging, constituency service and impression management: UK MPs and the use of Twitter. *The Journal of Legislative Studies, 17*(1), 86-105.

Jenkins, H., Ford, S., & Green, J. (2013). *Spreadable media: Creating value and meaning in a networked culture*. New York: NYU Press.

Keyling, T., & Jünger, J. (2013). Facepager (Version f.e. 3.3) [Computer software]. Retrieved from https://github.com/strohne/Facepager

Kleinnijenhuis, J., van den Hooff, B., Utz, S., Vermeulen, I., & Huysman, M. (2011). Social influence in networks of practice: An analysis of organizational communication content. *Communication Research, 38*(5), 587-612.

Klinger, U., Roesli, S., & Jarren, O. (2015). To implement or not to implement? Participatory online communication in Swiss cities. *International Journal of Communication, 9*, 1926-1946.

Klinger, U., & Svensson, J. (2015). The emergence of network media logic in political communication: A theoretical approach. *New Media & Society, 17*(8), 1241-1257.

Klinger, U., & Svensson, J. (2016). Network media logic: Some conceptual considerations. In A. Bruns, G. Enli, E. Skogerbo, A. O. Larsson, & C. Christensen (Eds.), *The routledge companion to social media and politics* (pp. 23-39). New York: Routledge.

Kocks, J. N. (2016). *Political media relations online as an elite phenomenon*. Wiesbaden, Germany: Springer VS.

Kocks, J. N., & Raupp, J. (2014). Rechtlich-normative Rahmenbedingungen der Regierungskommunikation – ein Thema für die Publizistik- und Kommunikationswissenschaft [Legal-normative conditions of government communications – a topic for journalism and communication studies]. *Publizistik, 59*(3), 269-284.

Kocks, J. N., & Raupp, J. (2015). Media relations online – zur Interaktion von politischer PR und Journalismus im digitalen Zeitalter [Media relations online – the interaction between political PR and journalism in a digital age]. *prmagazin, (2)*.

Kocks, J. N., Raupp, J., & Murphy, K. (2016). *Egos, elites & social capital: Analysing media government relations from a network perspective*. Paper presented at the European Consortium for Political Research General Conference 2016, Prague. Retrieved from https://ecpr.eu/Filestore/PaperProposal/e36b098e-b6d6-49ee-8081-0cb6a6c04fd4.pdf

Kocks, J.N., Raupp, J., & Schink, C. (2014). Staatliche Öffentlichkeitsarbeit zwischen Distribution und Dialog [Government public relations between distribution and dialogue]. In R. Fröhlich & T. Koch (Eds.), *Politik – PR – Persuasion*. Wiesbaden, Germany: Springer VS.

Kontopoulos, K.M. (1993). *The logics of social structure* (Vol. 6). Cambridge University Press.

Korte, K.-R. (2002). Regieren in Mediendemokratien [Governing in a media democracy]. In H. Schatz, P. Rössler, & J.U. Nieland (Eds.), *Politische Akteure in der Mediendemokratie* (pp. 21-40). Wiesbaden, Germany: Springer VS.

Lauf, E., & Peter, J. (2001). Die Codierung verschiedensprachiger Inhalte: Erhebungskonzepte und Gütemaße [The coding of multi-lingual content: Survey concepts and quality measures]. In W. Wirth & E. Lauf (Eds.), *Inhaltsanalyse: Perspektiven, Probleme, Potentiale* (pp. 199-217). Cologne: Herbert von Halem.

Leveson, B. (2012). *An inquiry into the culture, practices and ethics of the press*. London: The Stationery Office.

Liu, B. F., & Horsley, J. S. (2007). The government communication decision wheel: Toward a public relations model for the public sector. *Journal of Public Relations Research, 19*(4), 377-393.

Liu, B. F., Horsley, J. S., & Levenshus, A. B. (2010). Government and corporate communication practices: do the differences matter? *Journal of Applied Communication Research, 38*(2), 189-213.

Livingstone, S. (2003). On the challenges of cross-national comparative media research. *European Journal of Communication, 18*(4), 477-500.

Loader, B. D., Vromen, A., & Xenos, M. A. (2015). Performing for the young networked citizen? Celebrity politics, social networking and the political engagement of young people. *Media, Culture & Society, 38*(3), 400-419. doi:0163443715608261

Lombard, M., Snyder-Duch, J., & Bracken, C. C. (2002). Content analysis in mass communication: Assessment and reporting of intercoder reliability. *Human Communication Research, 28*(4), 587-604.

Maier, D., Waldherr, A., Miltner, P., Jähnichen, P., & Pfetsch, B. (2017). Exploring issues in a networked public sphere: Combining hyperlink network analysis and topic modeling. *Social Science Computer Review*, 0894439317690337.

Mancini, P. (2015). The Press. In E. Jones & G. Pasquino (Eds.), *The oxford handbook of italian politics*. Oxford, UK: Oxford University Press. doi: 10.1093/oxfordhb/9780199669745.001.0001

Margolis, M., & Resnick, D. (2000). *Politics as usual: The cyberspace "revolution"*. Thousand Oaks: Sage Publications.

Marx, S. (2008). *Die Legende vom Spin Doctor: Regierungskommunikation unter Schröder und Blair [The legends of spin doctors: government communications under Schröder and Blair]*. Wiesbaden, Germany: VS Verlag.

Mayntz, R., & Scharpf, F. W. (1975). *Policy-making in the German federal bureaucracy*. Amsterdam, Netherlands: Elsevier.

McNair, B. (2004). PR must die: spin, anti-spin and political public relations in the UK, 1997-2004. *Journalism Studies, 5*, 325–338.

Meijer, A. J., Koops, B.-J., Pieterson, W., Overman, S., & ten Tije, S. (2012). Government 2.0: Key challenges to its realization. *Electronic Journal of e-Government, 10*(1), 59-69.

Meijer, A. J., & Torenvlied, R. (2014). Social media and the new organization of government communications: An empirical analysis of Twitter usage by the Dutch police. *The American Review of Public Administration*, 0275074014551381.

Mergel, I. (2012). The social media innovation challenge in the public sector. *Information Polity, 17*(3,4), 281-292.

Mergel, I. (2013). Social media adoption and resulting tactics in the US federal government. *Government Information Quarterly, 30*(2), 123-130.

Mergel, I. (2016). Social media institutionalization in the US federal government. *Government Information Quarterly, 33*(1), 142-148.

Mergel, I., & Bretschneider, S. I. (2013). A three-stage adoption process for social media use in government. *Public Administration Review, 73*(3), 390-400.

Meyer, J. W., & Rowan, B. (1991). Institutionalized organizations: formal structure as myth and ceremony. In W. W. Powell & P. J. DiMaggio (Eds.), *The new institutionalism in organizational analysis* (pp. 41-62). Chicago: The University of Chicago Press.

Monge, P. R., & Contractor, N. S. (2003). *Theories of communication networks*. New York, NY: Oxford University Press.

Mossberger, K., Wu, Y., & Crawford, J. (2013). Connecting citizens and local governments? Social media and interactivity in major US cities. *Government Information Quarterly, 30*(4), 351-358.

Murphy, K. (2018). Lost in translation: the methodological challenges of comparative studies. In J. Raupp, J. N. Kocks, & K. Murphy (Eds.), *Regierungskommunikation und staatliche Öffentlichkeitsarbeit: Implikationen des technologisch induzierten Medienwandels* (pp. 203-215). Wiesbaden, Germany: Springer VS.

Murphy, K., Kocks, J. N., & Raupp, J. (2016). *Different governments, different approaches: political participation in the online sphere*. Paper presented at the European Consortium for Political Research General Conference 2016, Prague. Retrieved from https://ecpr.eu/Filestore/PaperProposal/569d6a29-04d5-4736-b546-91eba15e601 e.pdf

Müller, W. C. (2011). Governments and bureaucracies. In D. Caramani (Ed.), *Comparative politics* (Second ed.) (pp. 131-149). Oxford, UK: Oxford University Press.

Nitschke, P., Donges, P., & Schade, H. (2014). Political organizations' use of websites and Facebook. *New Media & Society, 18*(5), 744-764.

Nitschke, P., & Murphy, K. (2016). Organizations as an analytical category: conceptual and methodological challenges. In G. Vowe & P. Henn (Eds.), *Political communication in the online world: Theoretical approaches and research designs* (pp. 262-274). New York, NY: Routledge.

Norris, P. (2001). Political Communication. In N. J. Smelser & P. B. Baltes (Eds.), *International encyclopedia of the social and behavioral sciences* (pp. 11631-11640). Oxford, UK: Elsevier.

Norris, P. (2011). Political communication. In D. Caramani (Ed.), *Comparative politics* (Second ed.) (pp. 318-331). Oxford, UK: Oxford University Press.

Nuernbergk, C. (2016). Political journalists' interaction networks: the German federal press conference on Twitter. *Journalism Practice, 10*(7), 868-879.

Nuernbergk, C., & Conrad, J. (2016). Conversations and campaign dynamics in a hybrid media environment: use of Twitter by members of the German Bundestag. *Social Media+ Society, 2*(1), 2056305116628888.

Oltermann, P. (2018, January). Tough new German law puts tech firms and free speech in the spotlight. *The Guardian*. Retrieved from https://www.theguardian.com/world/2018/jan/05/tough-new-german-law-puts-tech-firms-and-free-speech-in-spotlight

Olsen, J. P. (2006). Maybe it is time to rediscover bureaucracy. *Journal of Public Administration Research and Theory, 16*(1), 1-24.

Olsen, J. P. (2009). Democratic government, institutional autonomy and the dynamics of change. *West European Politics, 32*(3), 439-465. doi:10.1080/01402380902779048

Ottovordemgentschenfelde, S. (2017). 'Organizational, professional, personal': An exploratory study of political journalists and their hybrid brand on Twitter. *Journalism, 18*(1), 64-80.

Papacharissi, Z. (2009 a). The virtual geographies of social networks: a comparative analysis of Facebook, LinkedIn and ASmallWorld. *New Media & Society, 11*(1-2), 199-220.

Papacharissi, Z. (2009 b). The virtual sphere 2.0: The internet, the public sphere, and beyond. In A. Chadwick & P. N. Howard (Eds.), *Routledge handbook of internet politics* (pp. 230–245). London, UK: Routledge.

Papacharissi, Z. (2010). *A private sphere: Democracy in a digital age*: Cambridge: Polity.

Penney, J. (2017). Social media and citizen participation in "official" and "unofficial" electoral promotion: a structural analysis of the 2016 Bernie Sanders digital campaign. *Journal of Communication, 67*(3), 402-423.

Perrow, C. (1986). *Complex organizations: A critical essay*. New York, NY: Random House.

Pfetsch, B. (2001). Political communication culture in the United States and Germany. *The Harvard International Journal of Press/Politics, 6*(1), 46-67.

Pfetsch, B. (2003). *Politische Kommunikationskultur: Politische Sprecher und Journalisten in der Bundesrepublik und den USA im Vergleich [Political communications culture: A comparison of political spokespersons and journalists in the German Federal Republic and the U.S.]*. Wiesbaden, Germany: Westdeutscher Verlag.

Pfetsch, B., & Esser, F. (2008). Conceptual challanges to the paradigms of comparative media systems in a globalized world. *Journal of Global Mass Communication*, 118-131.

Pfetsch, B., & Esser, F. (2012). Comparing political communication. In F. Esser & T. Hanitzsch (Eds.), *Handbook of comparative communication research* (pp. 25-47). New York: Routledge.

Phillis, B. (2004). *Final report of the independent review of government communications presented to the Minister for the Cabinet Office*. London: Cabinet Office.

Pötzsch, H. (2009). Deutsche Demokratien: Parteien [Web article]. Retrieved from http://www.bpb.de/politik/grundfragen/deutschedemokratie/39317/parteien?p=all

Press Gallery. (2015). The gallery today [Webpage]. Retrieved from https://pressgallery.org.uk/2015/03/06/the-gallery-today/

Prime Minister's Office. (2017). *Confidence and supply agreement between the Conservative and Unionist Party and the Democratic Unionist Party*. Retrieved from https://www.gov.uk/government/publications/conservative-and-dup-agreement-and-uk-government-financial-support-for-northern-ireland/agreement-between-the-conservative-and-unionist-party-and-the-democratic-unionist-party-on-support-for-the-government-in-parliament#confidence-and-supply-agreement-in-the-uk-parliament

Przeworski, A., & Teune, H. (1970). *The logic of comparative social inquiry*. New York: Wiley-Interscience.

Rainey, H. G., Backoff, R. W., & Levine, C. H. (1976). Comparing public and private organizations. *Public Administration Review, 36*(2), 233-244.

Raupp, J., & Kocks, J. N. (2018). Regierungskommunikation und staatliche Öffentlichkeitsarbeit aus kommunikationswissenschaftlicher Perspektive [Government communications and government public relations from a communications science perspective]. In J. Raupp, J. N. Kocks, & K. Murphy (Eds.), *Regierungskommunikation und staatliche Öffentlichkeitsarbeit: Implikationen des technologisch induzierten Medienwandels* (pp. 7-23). Wiesbaden, Germany: Springer VS.

Raupp, J., Kocks, J. N., & Murphy, K. (Eds.). (2018). *Regierungskommunikation und staatliche Öffentlichkeitsarbeit: Implikationen des technologisch induzierten Medienwandels [Government communications and government public relations: implications of the technologically induced media change]*. Wiesbaden, Germany: Springer VS.

R Core Team (2013). R: A language and environment for statistical computing (Version 3.4) [Computer software]. R Foundation for Statistical Computing, Vienna, Austria. Retrieved from http://www.R-project.org/

Reese, S. D., & Shoemaker, P. J. (2016). A media sociology for the networked public sphere: the hierarchy of influences model. *Mass Communication and Society, 19*(4), 389-410. doi:10.1080/15205436.2016.1174268

Reinemann, C., & Baugut, P. (2014). German political journalism between change and stability. In R. Kuhn & R. K. Nielsen (Eds.), *Political journalism in transition: Western Europe in a comparative perspective* (pp.73-91). London, UK: I.B. Tauris.

Rheingold, H. (1993). *The virtual communication: Homesteading on the electronic frontier*. Mass: Addison Wesley.

Rice, C., & Somerville, I. (2017). Political contest and oppositional voices in post-conflict democracy: the impact of institutional design on government–media relations. *The International Journal of Press/Politics, 22*(1), 92-110.

Russmann, U. (2011). Targeting voters via the Web: A comparative structural analysis of Austrian and German party websites. *Policy & Internet, 3*(3), 1-23.

Rössler, P. (2010). *Inhaltsanalyse* (Second ed.). Konstanz, Germany: UVK Verlag.

Rössler, P. (2012). Comparative content analysis. In F. Esser & T. Hanitzsch (Eds.), *Handbook of comparative communication research* (pp. 459-468). New York, NY: Routledge.

Sanders, K., Canel Crespo, M. J., & Holtz-Bacha, C. (2011). Communicating governments: a three-country comparison of how governments communicate with citizens. *The International Journal of Press/Politics, 16*, 523-547.

Sanders, K., & Canel, M. J. (2013). *Government communication*. New York, NY: Bloomsbury.

Sarcinelli, U. (2011). *Politische Kommunikation in Deutschland: Medien und Politikvermittlung im demokratischen System [political communication in Germany: media and policy communication in a democratic system]* (Third ed.). Wiesbaden, Germany: VS Verlag für Sozialwissenschaften.

Schillemans, T. (2012). *Mediatization of public services: How organizations adapt to news media*. Frankfurt am Main, Germany: Peter Lang.

Siebert, F. S., Peterson, T., & Schramm, W. (1956). *Four theories of the press: The authoritarian, libertarian, social responsibility, and Soviet communist concepts of what the press should be and do*. University of Illinois Press.

Sievert, H., & Nelke, A. (2014). *Social-Media-Kommunikation nationaler Regierungen in Europa: Theoretische Grundlagen und vergleichende Länderanalysen [Social media communication of national governments in Europe: theoretical foundations and comparative country analyses]*. Wiesbaden, Germany: Springer VS.

Svensson, J. (2015). Political participation on social media platforms in Sweden today: connective individualism, expressive issue-engagement and disciplined updating. *International Journal of Media & Cultural Politics, 10*(3).

Taylor, J. R., & Cooren, F. (1997). What makes communication 'organizational'?: How the many voices of a collectivity become the one voice of an organization. *Journal of Pragmatics, 27*(4), 409-438.

Thorbjornsrud, K., Figenschou, T. U., & Ihlen, Ø. (2014). Mediatisation in public bureaucracies: A typology. Retrieved from https://www.researchgate.net/publication/278165615_Mediatization_in_public_bureaucracies_A_typology

Vaccari, C. (2016). Online mobilization in comparative perspective: digital appeals and political engagement in Germany, Italy, and the United Kingdom. *Political Communication, 34*(1), 69-88.

Vaccari, C., Chadwick, A., & O'Loughlin, B. (2015). Dual screening the political: media events, social media, and citizen engagement. *Journal of Communication, 65*(6), 1041-1061.

Vaccari, C., Valeriani, A., Barberá, P., Bonneau, R., Jost, J. T., Nagler, J., & Tucker, J. A. (2015). Political expression and action on social media: exploring the relationship between lower-and higher-threshold political activities among Twitter users in Italy. *Journal of Computer-Mediated Communication, 20*(2), 221-239.

Van de Vijver, F., & Tanzer, N. K. (2004). Bias and equivalence in cross-cultural assessment: an overview. *Revue Européenne de Psychologie Appliquée/European Review of Applied Psychology, 54*(2), 119-135.

Van Dijk, J. (1999). The one-dimensional network society of Manuel Castells. *New Media & Society, 1*(1), 127-138.

Van Dijk, J. (2012). *The network society* (Third ed.). London, UK: Sage.

Van Dijk, J., & Winters-van Beek, A. (2009). The perspective of network government. The struggle between hierarchies, markets and networks as modes of governance in contemporary government. *ICTs, citizens & governance: After the hype*, 235-255.

Van Dijk, J. (2006). *The network society* (Third ed.). London, UK: Sage.

Vogel, M. (2010). *Regierungskommunikation im 21. Jahrhundert: ein Vergleich zwischen Großbritannien, Deutschland und der Schweiz [Government communications in the 21st century: a comparison between Great Britain, Germany and Switzerland].* Baden-Baden, Germany: Nomos.

Weber, M. (1968). *Economy and society: An outline of interpretive sociology*. New York, NY: Bedminister Press.

Wellman, B. (2001). Physical place and cyberplace: the rise of personalized networking. *International Journal of Urban and Regional Research, 25*(2), 227-252.

Wirth, W., & Kolb, S. (2004). Designs and methods of comparative political communication research. In F. Esser & B. Pfetsch (Eds.), *Comparing political communication: theories, cases, and challenges* (pp. 87-111). Cambridge, UK: Cambridge University Press.

Wright, S. (2012). Politics as usual? Revolution, normalization and a new agenda for online deliberation. *New Media & Society, 14.* doi:10.1177/1461444811410679

Yates, J. (1993). *Control through communication: the rise of system in American management* (Vol. 6). JHU Press.

Young, L., & Pieterson, W. (2015). Strategic communication in a networked world: integrating network and communication theories in the context of government to citizen communication. In D. Holtzhausen & A. Zerfass (Eds.), *The routledge handbook of strategic communication* (pp. 93-112). New York and London: Routledge.

Appendix

Appendix 1. Full Sample of Government Organisations in Great Britain

Number	Name of Government Organisation (individual government actor)
1	UK Government (David Cameron)
2	The Government Communication Service (Alex Aiken)
3	Prime Minister's Office (10 Downing Street) (David Cameron)
4	HM Treasury (George Osbourne)
5	Home Office (Theresa May)
6	Foreign & Commonwealth Office (Philip Hammond)
7	Ministry of Justice (Michael Gove)
8	Ministry of Defence (Michael Fallon)
9	Department for Business, Innovation and Skills (Sajid Javid)
10	Department for Work and Pensions (Iain Duncan Smith)
11	Office of the Leader of the House of Lords (Baroness Stowell)
12	Department of Health (Jeremy Hunt)
13	Department for Communities and Local Government (Greg Clark)
14	Department for Education (Nicky Morgan)
15	Department for International Development (Justine Greening)
16	Department of Energy and Climate Change (Amber Rudd)
17	Department for Transport (Patrick McLoughlin)
18	Department for Culture, Media and Sport (John Wittingdale)
19	Department for Environment, Food and Rural Affairs (Liz Truss)
20	Cabinet Office (Oliver Letwin)
21	Scotland Office (David Mundell)
22	Northern Ireland Office (Theresa Villies)

23	Wales Office (Stephen Crabb)
24	Attorney General's Office (Jeremy Wright)
25	Office of the Advocate General for Scotland (The Lord Keen of Elie QC)
26	UK Export Office (Sajid Javid)
27	Office of the Leader of the House of Commons (Chris Grayling)

Appendix 2. Full Sample of Government Organisations in Germany

Number	Name of Government Organisation (individual government actor)
1	Die Bundesregierung (Angela Merkel)
2	Das Bundespresseamt (Steffen Seibert)
3	Bundeskanzleramt (Peter Altmaier)
4	Bundesministerium für Wirtschaft und Energie (Sigmar Gabriel)
5	Auswärtiges Amt (Frank-Walter Steinmeier)
6	Bundesministerium des Innern (Thomas de Maizière)
7	Bundesministerium der Justiz und für Verbraucherschutz (Heiko Maas)
8	Bundesministerium der Finanzen (Wolfgang Schäuble)
9	Bundesministerium für Arbeit und Soziales (Andrea Nahles)
10	Bundesministerium für Ernährung und Landwirtschaft (Christian Schmidt)
11	Bundesministerium der Verteidigung (Ursula von der Leyen)
12	Bundesministerium für Familie, Senioren, Frauen und Jugend (Manuela Schwesig)
13	Bundesministerium für Gesundheit (Hermann Gröhe)
14	Bundesministerium für Verkehr und digital Infrastruktur (Alexander Dobrindt)
15	Bundesministerium für Umwelt, Naturschutz, Bau und Reaktorsicherheit (Barbara Hendricks)
16	Bundesministerium für Bildung und Forschung (Johanna Wanka)
17	Bundesministerium für wirtschaftliche Zusammenarbeit und Entwicklung (Gerd Müller)

Appendix 3. English Language Codebook

Technical Variables

T_01_Case number

The case number consists of the following, in the following order: the number of the Ministry as listed in the excel list, followed by the date that the coding is taking place (YYYYMMDD).
Example: The Prime Minister's Office is listed as number 3 among the list of government organisations in Great Britain in the Excel list and coding is taking place for example on 12.11.2015. Therefore the case number is:
0320151112

T_02_Coder

1 Kim Murphy
2 Tina Stalf
3 Jan Niklas Kocks

T_03_Gov_Org_name

Please write the name of the government organisation in full (as written in the excel list)
String variable

T_04_Website_date

Please write the date that the website was saved. See saved web content in the following folder Y:\Great_Britain_web_content. In this folder, please open the relevant folder in order to see what date the "Index.html" web link was saved.
YYYYMMDD

T_05_Website_Webpage

1 The organisation has its own website
2 The organisation has a webpage/or series of webpages as part of a larger website

Content Variables

Forms of Communication
Unidirectional
Unidirectional means the one-way flow of information, also known as, top-down communication.
Rule: You should not click more than 4-5 times in order to find a feature. If a feature cannot be found with 5 clicks, then please select "No" (i.e., that

the feature doesn't exist). However, if you find the feature later on while looking for another feature, then it is acceptable to go back to this question and change the answer to "Yes".
Is the following content available?

FC_01_News

Please note that this could appear under other terms such as "Headlines", or "Latest", or "Announcements", among others.
0 no
1 yes
-1 unclear
-2 not applicable

FC_02_Press_releases

0 no
1 yes
-1 unclear
-2 not applicable

FC_03_Gov_publications

For example, policy reports, consultations, performance reports, annual reports etc.
0 no
1 yes
-1 unclear
-2 not applicable

FC_04_Speeches

0 no
1 yes
-1 unclear
-2 not applicable

FC_05_Videos

Is it possible to view a selection of videos?
This includes videos that are embedded. However, if it is not possible to view the video directly without being directed to the organisation's YouTube page, then select "No".
If it is clear that a selection of videos exist, but they don't play due to technical problems with how the content was saved, then please still select "yes" below.
0 no

1 yes
-1 unclear
-2 not applicable

FC_06_Audio

Are there audio or podcasts available to listen to? Videos that can be specifically saved or downloaded as audio are also considered to be audio in this context
If it is clear that a selection of audio recordings/podcasts exist, but they don't play due to technical problems with how the content was saved, then please still select "yes" below.
0 no
1 yes
-1 unclear
-2 not applicable

FC_07_Photos

Are there a selection of photos available that can be downloaded? This includes photos that are available on platforms like Instagram and Flickr, as long as there is a direct link from the website.
0 no
1 yes
-1 unclear
-2 not applicable

FC_08_Events_calendar

I only consider it to be an events calendar if it lists, or features, three or more upcoming events or appointments. This feature is normally found in the press or media section.
0 no
1 yes
-1 unclear
-2 not applicable

FC_09_Livestreaming

Is there an option which allows viewers to view press conferences or government events as they happen?
0 no
1 yes
-1 unclear
-2 not applicable

FC_10_FAQs

Is an FAQ (most commonly asked questions and answers) available for download?
0 no
1 yes
-1 unclear
-2 not applicable

FC_11_Microsites

Is there a link, or a number of links, on the organisation's homepage ("Startseite") that directs the user to a microsite of the organisation/government? We will only consider those microsites that are linked directly from the homepage.
Definition Microsite: *a microsite is defined as an auxiliary website which functions as a supplement to a primary website. It has its own unique URL address; it usually has less content than the primary website, and typically focuses on a particular initiative\project\ campaign of a government department. Example:* http://www.freiheit-und-einheit.de/Webs/Einheit/DE/Startseite/startseite_node.html, *or* https://labuonascuola.gov.it/.
0 no
1 yes
-1 unclear
-2 not applicable

FC_12_Links_gov_depts

Are there any links to other government ministries/government departments?
0 no → select -2 in the next question and continue on to FC_14
1 yes
-1 unclear
-2 not applicable

FC_13_number_links

How many other ministries/government departments does the website link to?
Insert number
00
-2 not applicable

FC_14_Links_gov_agencies

Are there any links to other government agencies/public bodies?

Definition government agency/public body: it is an administrative branch of government that comes under the responsibility of a particular government department/ministry. Most government department websites feature links to important agencies or bodies funded by their department.
0 no
1 yes
-1 unclear
-2 not applicable

Participation (Interactivity)

Rule: You should not click more than 4-5 times in order to find each feature. If a feature cannot be found after 5 clicks, then please select "No" (i.e., that the feature doesn't exist). However, if you find the feature later on while looking for another feature, then it is acceptable to go back to this question and change the answer to "Yes".
If the features appear on a government microsite that is linked directly from the organisation/ministry's homepage ("Startseite"), we will include these features in our analysis.

Two-way asymmetrical & two-way symmetrical

P_01_sharing icons

Are there social media sharing icons available that allow users to share content on their own Facebook/Twitter accounts? For example, these icons typically appear at the end of a press release or a news story.
Definition social media sharing icon: these tabs/icons allow users to share or recommend the content of that page directly on their own personal social media pages. They usually feature the Facebook or Twitter symbol and clearly state "share this page", "share content", or "recommend this page".
In order to be sure that it is a social media icon, please click on it. If it leads you directly to the organisation's Facebook or Twitter page, then it isn't a sharing icon.
0 no
1 yes
-1 unclear
-2 not applicable

P_02_Apps

Is there an app(s) available for download?
This includes all apps that are offered on the website of a government organisation, or on an external website (e.g., a link to the "Itunes app store"), so long as it is directly linked from the website of the organisation.

If the app appears on a microsite linked from the homepage (“Startseite”) of the organisation, these will also be considered.
0 no
1 yes
-1 unclear
-2 not applicable

P_03_Epetition

Is there an option to sign an epetition or to start one’s own epetition?
Definition epetition: it is an online petition which citizens can sign (or create) calling on the government to, for example, introduce a new piece of legislation or regulation. We will only list those that are clearly marked as “e-petition”.
If the feature appears on a microsite linked from the homepage (“Startseite”) of the organisation, these will also be considered.
0 no
1 yes
-1 unclear
-2 not applicable

P_04_Survey

Definition: In a survey or questionnaire a group of citizens are asked to give their opinion on a particular matter of government. This could involve filling out an online questionnaire or a video/audio in which a group of citizens answer a particular question or series of questions.
If the feature appears on a microsite linked from the homepage (“Startseite”) of the organisation, these will also be considered.
0 no
1 yes
-1 unclear
-2 not applicable

P_05_General_contact

Is a general email contact provided, or is there an opportunity to submit general feedback\comments directly to the Ministry (e.g., an online form)?
0 no
1 yes
-1 unclear
-2 not applicable

P_06_Questions

Is there an opportunity to submit questions directly to the Ministry or the Minister that will be published on the website?
If the feature appears on a microsite linked from the homepage ("Startseite") of the organisation, these will also be considered.
0 no → select '-2' in P_07 and move to P_08
1 yes
-1 unclear
-2 not applicable

P_07_Response

Are there any government responses to these questions published?
If the feature appears on a microsite linked from the homepage ("Startseite") of the organisation, these will also be considered.
0 no
1 yes
-1 unclear
-2 not applicable

P_08_Public_Consultation

Is there an opportunity to provide a contribution to a consultation on a particular matter of government policy?
Definition public consultation: it is a process by which the government seeks input from the general public on a particular policy issue. It is an attempt to allow the public to contribute to the political decision-making process. For the purposes of this content analysis, a public consultation is understood to mean a feature on the website of a government organisation which specifically calls on\or allows users to submit a contribution on a policy matter.
If the feature appears on a microsite linked from the homepage ("Startseite") of the organisation, these will also be considered.
0 no → select '-2' in P_09 and move to P_10
1 yes
-1 unclear
-2 not applicable

P_09_Outcome_consultation

Are there any reports available on the outcome of public consultations?
If the feature appears on a microsite linked from the homepage ("Startseite") of the organisation, these will also be considered.
0 no

1 yes
-1 unclear
-2 not applicable

P_10_Subscriptions

Is it possible to subscribe to one or more of the following: RSS news feeds, newsletters, emagazine, videos blogs, or podcasts (or similar)?
0 no
1 yes
-1 unclear
-2 not applicable

P_11_Volunteering

Is there an option or information about how to volunteer in government campaigns/projccts?
Definition: Volunteering is any feature on the website of a government organisation which calls on citizens, or gives information to citizens, about how to become involved in a government project or campaign (this could also include at a more local level in their community). Terms such as "Get Involved" may be used on the websites in relation to volunteering.
If the feature appears on a microsite linked from the homepage ("Startseite") of the organisation, these will also be considered.
0 no
1 yes
-1 unclear
-2 not applicable
P_12_Citizens_Video
Are there any videos that feature citizens putting questions to the minister/ head of government or any official government representative? (This could take the form of an interview, a question and answer session, or a panel discussion. The important point is that citizens have the opportunity to ask questions and receive an answer).
Definition: it is considered a "citizen video" if there is an exchange (i.e., Q & A) between a minister/head of government, or a government representative, and a citizen, or citizens. It must be clear that citizens have the opportunity to pose questions and that these are genuine questions submitted by a citizen.
The coder must not view every video. Please look back at videos/embedded videos posted during the previous two months (i.e., two months prior to the date that the web content was saved).

If the feature appears on a microsite ("Startseite") linked from the homepage of the organisation, these will also be considered.
0 no
1 yes
-1 unclear
-2 not applicable
P_13_Hangout_videochat
Are there any videos available on the website using google hangout or another form of video chat which includes a minister or an official representing the minister answering questions with one or more persons?
The important point here is that a group of citizens have the opportunity to ask questions and receive answers, whether this is in the form of an interview or a group discussion.
Definition video-chat: it is a conversation held over the Internet by means of webcams and dedicated software. In the context of this study, this includes a conversation between a minister, head of government, or a government representative and one or more citizens.
The coder must not view every video. Please look back at videos/embedded videos posted on the website during the previous two months (i.e., two months prior to the date that the website was saved).
If the feature appears on a microsite linked from the homepage ("Startseite") of the organisation, these will also be considered.
0 no
1 yes
-1 unclear
-2 not applicable

P_14_Forum_chat_room

Definition: it is an online discussion site where people can hold conversations in the form of posted messages. I will include those that feature on the website of the government organisation, those that are linked from the website, or those that feature on a microsite linked from the homepage.
0 no
1 yes
-1 unclear
-2 not applicable

P_15_Other

Are there any other features that appeared on the website which should have been included in this section?
String variable
-2 not applicable

Transparency

Please note that there are clear guidelines in this section around how long a coder should search for a certain feature (1 click, 2-3 clicks or 4-5 clicks from the homepage).

T_01_Freedom_info_laws

How easy is it to find information related to laws on public access to information, such as, freedom of information or transparency legislation?
Definition freedom of information law: it is a law which allows citizens to apply for access to/disclosure of public information held by the government. In the context of this study, this will mean any feature that is clearly signaled “freedom of information” and that by clicking on this the user can find out information about the law, their rights around the law, or how to apply for information.
3 = There are clearly marked tabs on the homepage (“Startseite”) linking citizens to information on freedom of information and\or transparency legislation (1 click).
2 = There is information available, but only after 2-3 clicks
1 = There is information available but only after 4-5 clicks
0 = There is no information available
-1 unclear
-2 not applicable

T_02_Accountability

Is there any information available on efforts by the organisation to become more accountable or transparent?
3 = There is a specific link on the homepage (“Startseite”) referring to transparency, and when you click on this it provides information on government efforts and what they have achieved (1 click).
2 = There is information available, but only after 2-3 clicks
1 = There is information available but only after 4-5 clicks
0 = There is no information available specifically related to transparency
-1 unclear
-2 not applicable

T_03_Internal_structure

Is there information available on the structure of the organisation in the form of an organisation plan/chart? Here is an example:

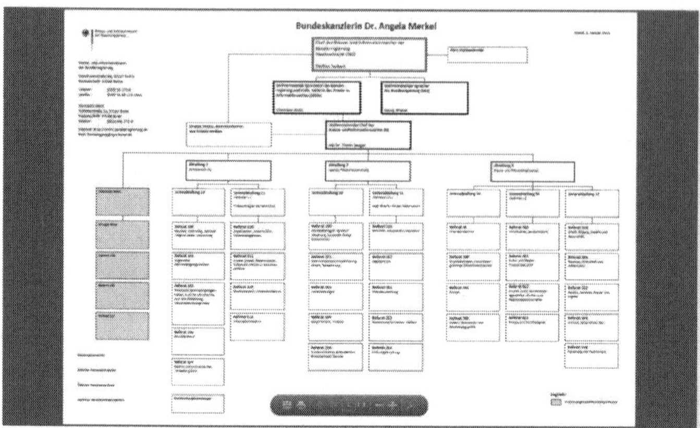

3 = An organisational chart is available with information on the different sections\divisions within the department and can be found after 1 click
2 = A chart is available and can be found after 2-3 clicks
1 = A chart is available and can be found after 4-5 clicks
0 = There is no information provided
-1 unclear
-2 not applicable

T_04_Social_media_policy

Is there any information provided on the organisation's social media policy/guidelines?
The coder is allowed to click on the live link to the organisation's social media pages in order to answer this question.
Definition social media policy: The social media policy will usually state, for example, who is responsible for updating content on the various social media pages, and\or the purpose of each social media page (e.g., to provide information or to foster dialogue), and\or any rules around what content is considered acceptable and unacceptable. This information may be provided on the website or on the individual social media pages. The social media policy may also be called other names such as "Netiquette".
3 = There is a specific link on the organisation's homepage ("Startseite") referring to social media policy (1 click)

2 = There is information available, but only after 2-3 clicks
1 = There is information available but only after searching through the various social media pages for information (4-5 clicks)
0 = There is no information available
-1 unclear
-2 not applicable

T_05_Openness_decision_making

How would you rate the availability of information related to government policies and decisions?
3 = There are clearly marked tabs\menus on the homepage ("Startseite") directing users to government publications where there is an archive of documents available going back a number of years, and there is a filter available to sort through them (1 click)
2 = There are a large amount of government publications available, but they are not easy to navigate because there is either no filter, or all publications are listed together making it difficult to differentiate between press statements and government reports (2-3 clicks)
1 = The availability of government reports are irregular and limited. It is only possible to find a desired report after 4-5 clicks
0 = There are no clearly marked sections on the homepage ("Startseite") directing users to government publications
-1 unclear
-2 not applicable

Press Section

PS_01_Press_section

Is there a section which contains a range of information specifically for journalists\press?
Definition press section: The press section is a specific section that contains information for journalists/media. It may be called different, but similar, names, but it is usually found under "Press". This section usually contains more than one of the following services specifically for journalists: info on press accreditation, press releases, speeches, articles, official photos, events calendar, audio, videos, and name and contact details for press spokespersons. If the section only contains for example press releases, this is not considered to be a press section. It must contain at least two of these services for journalists. Please note that a section called, for example "Digital" or "Media library", is something different. This may also contain videos and audio, but the target group is the wider public, not just the press.

0 no
1 yes
2 Other → please describe in PS_02_Other
-1 unclear
-2 not applicable

PS_02_Other

Please describe
String variable
-2 not applicable

PS_03_Spokesperson

Is there information provided on who is responsible for press?
0 no
1 yes there is information, and it features in the press section
2 yes there is information, but it appears in a different section
-1 unclear
-2 not applicable

PS_04_Contact_info

Is there contact information for press queries (email and/or telephone)?
0 no
1 yes
2 Other → please describe in PS_05_Other
-1 unclear
-2 not applicable

PS_ 05_Other

Please state
String variable
-2 not applicable

PS_06_Press_services

Are there one or more services on offer for journalists? (e.g., press accreditation, contact details for press spokespersons, press releases, information on press conferences, a special login section for journalists, press photos etc.)
0 no → select -2 in PS_07
1 yes → please list all the services in PS_07
-1 unclear
-2 not applicable

PS_07_Press_services

Please list all available services
String variable
-2 not applicable

External websites

Twitter

Before opening the saved social media content, please use the organisation's saved website link to answer this section (the "index.html" link). For all the sections that follow this section, you will use the saved social media content.

TW_01_Org_account

Is there an official twitter account for the organisation linked from the website?
0 no
1 yes

TW_02_Org_account_name

In whose name does this account appear?
1 It is in the name of the organisation
2 It is in the name of a spokesperson on behalf of the organisation (e.g., the twitter account for the Federal German Government appears in the name of the head of government communications "Regsprecher")
-2 not applicable

TW_03_Individual_account

Is there an official twitter account for the minister/head of government linked from the website?
0 no
1 yes

TW_04_Other_account

Are there any other twitter accounts linked from the website? (e.g., this could be the press office, an individual government spokesperson, or another actor within the organisation)
0 no → select -2 in TW_05
1 yes

TW_05_Other_detail

Please state what other twitter accounts are also linked from the organisation website
String variable
-2 not applicable

Twitter account – Organisation

Please refer to the saved social media content in order to answer all the following sections. Please answer all questions in this next section as "-2" if the organisation doesn't have a twitter account, and continue on to the next section.

TW_01_Org_date_saved_content

Please insert the date that the twitter content was saved
YYYYMMDD
-2 not applicable

TW_02_Org_joined_date

Please insert the date that the organisation joined twitter
This information is usually provided on the top left hand side of the twitter page. If for some reason, this doesn't appear, please select "-2".
YYYYMM
-2 not applicable

TW_03_Org_transparency

Does the account state who is responsible for the content of the page?
This will usually be outlined in the section to the left of the twitter page. This sometimes lists the head of communications or the press office, or includes a weblink with information on who is responsible for the online content. When a web link is given, then it is necessary to use the live twitter page to answer this particular question.
0 no → select „-2" in the next question
1 yes
-1 unclear
-2 not applicable

TW_04_Org_responsible

Please state who is responsible:
String variable
-2 not applicable

TW_05_Org_followers

Insert the number of followers that the account has:
Please write out the full number. For example, "26,8 Tsd" should be written as "26800" or "333 Tsd" should be written as "333000"
0000000
-2 not applicable

TW_06_Org_following

Insert the number of twitter accounts that the account is following
0000
-2 not applicable

TW_07_Org_total_tweets

Please insert the total number of tweets to date (this appears on the top left of each twitter account)
If the total tweets are "6.800", please write this as "6800"
00000
-2 not applicable

TW_08_Org_last_tweet

Please insert the date of the most recent tweet (according to the saved content). Please note that if the most recent tweet was just a few hours ago, then the date will be the same date as the saved content.
YYYYMMDD
-2 not applicable

TW_09_Org_fortnight_tweets

Please insert the total number of tweets (including retweets and answers etc.) posted by the organisation during the previous two weeks (counting back two weeks from the day the content was saved).
Please use the excel document (facepager data) saved alongside the fireshot image in order to count the total number of tweets in a two week period.
If there is no facepager data, then you will need to use the fireshot image to answer this question.
If there were no tweets during the two week period, please insert "0".
000
-2 not applicable

TW_10_Org_fortnight_retweets

Please insert the total number of retweets posted by the organisation in the last fortnight.

Again, please use the same excel document saved alongside the fireshot image in order to count the retweets in a two week period. Retweets can be identified as those that begin with "@RT" in the excel document.
If there were no retweets during the two week period, please insert "0".
000
-2 not applicable

TW_11_Org_connectivity

Please insert the number of times that the organisation retweeted something posted by a government minister (also called secretary of state), a government ministry, or a government press spokesperson/government press office during the previous two weeks.
Please use the same excel data in order to answer this question.
If there were no such retweets during the two week period, please insert "0".
00
-2 not applicable

TW_12_Org_gov_response

How many times does the organisation respond to comments posted during the previous two weeks?
Please use the excel data to answer this question. You will recognise answers to tweets as those that begin with "@", followed by the name of the person that is being responded to. Please see the guidebook for a more detailed description of how to recognise answers to tweets. It is also important to read the content of the tweet to ascertain if it as an answer or not.
If there were no answers during the two week period, please insert "0".
00
-2 not applicable

TW_13_Org_participation

Please insert the number of tweets during the previous fortnight that encouraged users to tweet comments, engage in dialogue or become active with a particular issue\topic. For example, does it use language like "get involved", or pose questions like "want to join?", or "tell us about".
Definition participation: it means content that encourages users to become active on the various online platforms (facebook, twitter, youtube) in the form of comments or contributions.
If there were no such tweets during the two week period, please insert "0".
00
-2 not applicable

Twitter account – Minister/Head of Government

Please mark all answers in the next section as -2 if no such account exists and continue on to the subsequent section "Facebook".

TW_01_Min_date_saved_content

Please insert the date that the twitter content was saved. Please see the folder with the saved social media content to see when the fireshot image was saved.
YYYYMMDD
-2 not applicable

TW_02_Min_Status

Please insert whether the individual twitter account is an official or non-official account.
Please see the coder guidebook (page.11) for a full definition of what is considered to be an official and non-official account
1 official
2 non-official
-2 not applicable

TW_03_Min_joined_date

Please insert the date that the minister or head of government joined twitter.
This information is usually provided in the information box on the top left-hand side of the twitter page. If this doesn't appear, please select "-2".
YYYYMM
-2 not applicable

TW_04_Min_transparency

Does the account state who is responsible for the content of the page?
This will usually be outlined in the section to the left of the twitter page. This sometimes lists the head of communications or the press office, or includes a weblink with information to who is responsible for the online content. When a weblink is given, then it is necessary to use the live twitter page to answer this particular question.
0 no → select „-2" in the next question
1 yes
-1 unclear
-2 not applicable

TW_05_Min_responsible

Please state who is responsible for the account
String variable
-2 not applicable

TW_06_Min_followers

Insert the number of followers that the account has
Please write out the full number. For example, "26,8 Tsd" should be written as "26800" or "333 Tsd" should be written as "333000"
0000000
-2 not applicable

TW_07_Min_following

Insert the number of twitter accounts that the account is following
0000
-2 not applicable

TW_08_Min_total_tweets

Please insert the total number of tweets to date (see top left of each twitter account)
00000
-2 not applicable

TW_09_Min_last_tweet

Please insert the date of the most recent tweet (according to the fireshot image). Please note that if the most recent tweet was just a few hours ago, then the date will be the same date as the saved content.
Please be aware of pinned tweets.
YYYYMMDD
-2 not applicable

TW_10_Min_fortnight_tweets

Please insert the total number of tweets (including retweets and answers) posted by the minister or head of government during the previous two weeks.
Please use the excel document saved along with the fireshot image in order to count the total number of tweets in a two-week period.
If there is no facepager data, then you will need to use the fireshot image to answer this question.

If there were no tweets during the two week period, please insert "0".
000
-2 not applicable

TW_11_Min_fortnight_retweets

Please insert the total number of retweets posted during the last two weeks.
Please use the same excel document in order to count the retweets in a two-week period. Retweets can be identified as those that begin with "@RT" in the excel document.
If there were no retweets during the two week period, please insert "0".
000
-2 not applicable

TW_12_Min_connectivity

Please insert the number of times that the minister retweeted something posted by a government minister (also called secretary of state), a government ministry, or a government press spokesperson/government press office during the previous two weeks.
Please use the same excel data in order to answer this question.
If there were no such retweets during the two-week period, please insert "0".
00
-2 not applicable

TW_13_Min_gov_response

How many times does the minister/head of government respond to comments posted during the previous two weeks?
Please use the same excel data to answer this question. You will recognise answers to tweets as those that begin with the following symbol "@". This symbol should be followed by the name of the person that is being responded to. It is also important to read the content of the tweet to ascertain if it as an answer or not.
If there were no answers during the two-week period, please insert "0".
00
-2 not applicable

TW_14_Min_participation

Please insert the number of tweets during the previous fortnight that encouraged users to tweet comments, engage in dialogue or become active

with a particular issue\topic. For example, does it use language like "get involved", or pose questions like "want to join?", or "tell us about".
Definition participation: it means content that encourages users to become active on the various online platforms (facebook, twitter, youtube) in the form of comments or contributions.
If there were no such tweets during the two-week period, please insert "0".
00
-2 not applicable

TW_15_Min_infobox

Which of the following features can be found in the information box on the top left-hand side of the twitter page (directly under the profile image)?
0 no weblink is given
1 there is a weblink to a personal website
2 there is a weblink to the website of his/her ministry
3 there is a weblink to both a personal website and also to his/her ministry
4 other → please describe in TW_16 under
-1 unclear
-2 not applicable
TW_16_Min_Other
Please describe
String variable
-2 not applicable

Facebook

Please refer back to the organisation's website (the saved "Index.html" link) to answer the following four questions in this section. For the rest of the codebook, please use the saved social media content (fireshot images and excel data).

FB_01_Org_account

Is there an official facebook page for the organisation linked from the organisation's website?
0 no
1 yes

FB_02_Actor_account

Is there an official facebook page for the minister/head of government linked from the organisations's website?
0 no
1 yes

FB_03_Other_account

Are there any other facebook accounts linked from the website? For example, this could be the press office, an individual government spokesperson, another actor within the organisation or a facebook account for a particular government campaign.
0 no
1 yes
FB_04_Other_detail
Please state what other facebook pages are also linked from the organisation website
String variable
-2 not applicable

Facebook account – Organisation

Please use the saved social media content to answer the rest of the codebook.
Please mark all answers in the next section as "-2" if no such account exists, and continue on to the next section.

FB_01_Org_date_saved_content

Please insert the date that the facebook content was saved
Please see the folder with the saved social media content to see when the fireshot image was saved.
YYYYMMDD
-2 not applicable

FB_02_Org_transparency

Does the account state who is responsible for the content of the page? In order to answer this question, you will need to refer to the "About" section and/or the Infobox. The "About" section is saved as a separate image in the same folder.
Or sometimes a weblink is provided in the infobox with further information on who is responsible for the content. In this case, it is necessary to refer to the live facebook page and click on the link to find out who is responsible.
0 no
1 yes
-1 unclear
-2 not applicable

FB_03_Org_responsible

Please insert who is responsible for the content
String variable
-2 not applicable

FB_04_Org_likes

Insert the number of likes that the account has
0 000 000
-2 not applicable

FB_05_Org_last_post

Please insert the date of the last (most recent) post.
Please note that if the most recent post was just a few hours ago, then the date is the same date as the saved content.
YYYYMMDD
-2 not applicable

FB_06_Org_fortnight_posts

Please insert the total number of posts posted by the organisation over the last two weeks (this includes all types of posts, e.g., updates, shared content, video posts etc.)
You will need to use the fireshot image to answer this question. If the content was saved for example on the 10.03.2015, then please count back to 25.02.15 (exactly 14 days).
000
-2 not applicable

FB_07_Org_commentary_option

Is it possible for users to leave comments under a post? You can see at the bottom of each post how many comments there are. This shows that it is possible to comment.
0 no
1 yes
-1 unclear
-2 not applicable

FB_08_Org_Response

How many times does the organisation respond to comments posted during the last two weeks?
If the content was saved, for example, on 10.03.15, then please count back to 25.02.15 (exactly 14 days).

In order to count the number of responses to comments, use the excel documents saved along with the facebook fireshot images. In these excel documents you will see all responses to comments. Simply count the number of responses that are saved. If an excel document is empty, that means that there were no responses. In this case insert "0" as the answer.
00
-2 not applicable

FB_09_Org_participation

How many posts during the last two weeks encourage users to post comments, engage in dialogue or become involved on a particular government topic? For example, do they use language like "get involved", or pose questions like "want to join?", or "tell us about".
Definition participation: it means content that encourages users to become active on the various online platforms (facebook, twitter, youtube) in the form of comments or contributions.
You will need to use the fireshot image to answer this question. If the content was saved for example on 10.03.15, then please count back to 25.02.15 (14 days).
If there were no such posts during the two-week period, please insert "0".
00
-2 not applicable

FB_10_Org_connectivity

Please insert the number of times that the organisation shared content posted by a government minister, a government ministry, or a government press spokesperson/government press office during the previous two weeks.
If the content was saved for example on 10.03.15, then please count back to 25.02.15 (14 days).
If there were no such posts during the two-week period, please insert "0".
00
-2 not applicable

Facebook account – Government minister/head of government

Please mark all questions in the next section as "-2" if no such account exists, and continue on to the next category.

FB_01_Min_status

Please insert whether the individual facebook account is an official or non-official account.

Please see the guidebook (page.11) for a full definition of what is considered an official and non-official account.
1 official
2 non-official
-2 not applicable

FB_02_Min_date_saved_content

Please insert the date that the facebook content was saved. Please see the folder with the saved social media content to see when the fireshot image for facebook was saved.
YYYYMMDD
-2 not applicable

FB_03_Min_transparency

Does the account state who is responsible for the content of the page? In order to answer this question, you will need to refer to the "About" section and/or the Infobox.
The "About" section is saved as a separate image in the same folder. Please open this to assess who is responsible.
Or sometimes a weblink is provided in the infobox with further information on who is responsible for the content. In this case, it is necessary to refer to the live facebook page and click on the link to find out who is responsible.
0 no
1 yes
-1 unclear
-2 not applicable

FB_04_Min_responsible

Please insert who is responsible
String variable
-2 not applicable

FB_05_Min_likes

Insert the number of likes that the account has
0 000 000
-2 not applicable

FB_06_Min_last_post

Please insert the date of the most recent post. Please note that if the most recent post was just a few hours ago, then the date will be the same date as the saved content.
YYYYMMDD
-2 not applicable

FB_07_Min_fortnight_posts

Please insert the total number of posts posted by the minister/head of government over the last two weeks (this includes all types of posts, e.g., updates, shared content, video posts etc.).
Please check the date that the fireshot image was saved. If the content was saved for example on 10.03.15, then please count back to 25.02.15 (14 days).
000
-2 not applicable

FB_08_Min_commentary

Is it possible for users to leave a comment under a post? You can see at the bottom of each post how many comments there are. This shows that it is possible to comment.
0 no
1 yes
-2 not applicable

FB_09_Min_response

How many times does the minister/head of government respond to comments posted in the last two weeks?
In order to count the number of responses to comments, please use the excel documents saved along with the facebook fireshot images. In these documents, you will see all responses to comments. Simply count the number of responses that are saved. If an excel document is empty, that means that there were no responses. In this case, insert "0" as the answer.
00
-2 not applicable

FB_10_Min_participation

How many posts during the last two weeks encourage users to post comments, engage in dialogue or become involved on a particular government topic? For example, do they use language like "get involved", "want to join?", or "tell us about".

Definition participation: it means content that encourages users to become active on the various online platforms (facebook, twitter, youtube) in the form of comments or contributions.
You will need to use the fireshot image to answer this question. If the content was saved for example on 10.03.15, then please count back to 25.02.15 (14 days).
If there were no such posts during the two-week period, please insert "0".
00
-2 not applicable

FB_11_Min_connectivity

Please insert the number of times that the minister shared content posted by a government minister, a government ministry, or a government press spokesperson/government press office during the previous two weeks.
You will need to use the fireshot image to answer this question. If the content was saved for example on 10.03.15, then please count back to 25.02.15 (14 days).
If there were no such posts during the two-week period, please insert "0".
00
-2 not applicable

FB_12_Min_infobox

In the infobox which of the following is included:
0 no weblinks included
1 a link to a personal website
2 a link to his\her ministry's website
3 both a personal website and a link to the ministry's website
4 other → please describe in FB_12
-1 unclear
-2 not applicable
FB_13_Min_Other
Please state if there are any other weblinks not listed
String variable
-2 not applicable

YouTube

Saved content is also used for coding youtube. The youtube content was saved as an "index.html" weblink. The links are saved in the relevant social media folder for each government department Y:\Great_Britain_Social_Media.

The homepage of each youtube channel has been saved, but when coders click on an individual video it will go to a live link. However, it is necessary to click on the live links in order to see what comments have been posted under each video, or to see the exact date that the video was posted. However, every time that you click on a link to a video, please return to the saved "index.html" link after you have answered the question.
Please mark all answers as "-2" (apart from "YT_01_Accounts"), if there is no youtube account.

YT_01_Accounts

0 no youtube account exists
1 the organisation has an official youtube page linked from the main website
2 the minister/head of government has an official youtube page linked from the main website
3 the minister/head of government and the organisation both have official youtube pages that are linked from the main website of the organisation
4 other → please describe in YT_02
-2 not applicable

YT_02_Other_account

Please state:
String variable
-2 not applicable

YT_03_Date_saved_content

Please insert the date that the youtube content was saved.
YYYYMMDD
-2 not applicable

YT_04_Channel_info

Please state when the account was established by clicking on the tab "About".
YYYYMMDD
-2 not applicable

YT_05_Views

Please insert the total views to date that the youtube channel has by clicking on the "About" section.
00000000
-2 not applicable

YT_06_Last_post

Please state when the most recent video was posted.
Please note that when a video says that it was published for example "5 days ago", this means that it was published five days prior to the date that the content was saved.
Please click on the video to get the full date. But please return to the saved content after you have answered this question.
YYYYMMDD
-2 not applicable

YT_07_Fortnight_posts

Please insert the total number of videos posted during the previous two weeks.
If the content was saved for example on 10.03.15, then please count back to 25.02.15 (14 days).
You will need to click on each video to see the exact dates that they were posted and whether they were within this 14 day time period. Some videos may say that they were posted "two weeks ago", but when you click on the video, you will see that it was posted more than two weeks ago but less than "three weeks ago".
If there were no videos posted in the last two weeks, then insert "0".
000
-2 not applicable

YT_08_Commentary

Is it possible to leave a comment under a video?
Please click on a video from the last two months to see if this is possible.
0 no → please select „-2" in YT_09
1 yes
-2 not applicable

YT_09_Response

Please insert the number of times that the organisation responds to comments posted under videos during the past two weeks?
In order to see all the answers to videos, please click on "show all comments".
If there are no answers to comments, please insert "0" as the answer.
If there were no videos in the past two weeks, please select "-2" for all the final questions in this section.
"-2" will also be selected if the comment function is deactivated.

"-2" will also be selected if there are no comments at all posted.
00
-2 not applicable

YT_10_Dialogic_content

Do any of the videos from the past two weeks feature dialogic elements?
Definition dialogic content: it means the direct communication or interaction between government and citizens. This does not include politicians in conversation with other politicians.
Select "-2" if there were no videos posted in the last two weeks.
0 no→ go to the final section "O_Observations" and select "-2" for all answers in between
1 yes→ YT_10 a
-1 unclear → go to the final section "O_Observations" and select "-2" for all answers in between
-2 not applicable → go to the final section "O_Observations" and select "-2" for all answers in between

YT_10a_Interview

Do any of the videos from the past two weeks feature the minister/head of government being interviewed by a citizen?
Select "-2" if there were no videos posted in the last two weeks.
0 no
1 yes
-1 unclear
-2 not applicable

YT_10b_Questions

Do any of the videos from the past two weeks feature the minister/head of government answering questions that appear to be submitted by members of the public?
Select "-2" if there were no videos posted in the last two weeks.
0 no
1 yes
-1 unclear
-2 not applicable

YT_10c_Hangout

Do any of the videos from the past two weeks feature the minister/head of government participating in a web conference or google hangout with other citizens (non-politicians)?

Select "-2" if there were no videos posted in the last two weeks.
0 no
1 yes
-1 unclear
-2 not applicable

YT_11_Other

Please state if there are other videos containing dialogic elements with citizens:
String variable
-2 not applicable

Appendix 4. Results Formal Reliability Tests DE & GB

German Results Formal Reliability Test

Federal Ministry for Health	Coder 1	Coder 2	Coder 3
Coder 1		14/119 (88%)	22/119 (82%)
Coder 2			9/119 (92%)

Total: 87% reliability

Federal Ministry for Finance	Coder 1	Coder 2	Coder 3
Coder 1			9/119 (92%)
Coder 2	3/119 (97,5%)		
Coders 3		8/119 (93%)	

Total: 94%

Overall reliability value: 90,5%

British Results Formal Reliability Test

Prime Minister's Office	Coder 1	Coder 2	Coder 3
Coder 1		5/119 (96%)	12/119 (90%)
Coder 2			16/119 (87%)

Total: 91%

Foreign & Commonwealth Office	Coder 1	Coder 2	Coder 3
Coder 1		9/119 (92%)	9/119 (92%)
Coder 2			14/119 (88%)

Total: 91%

Northern Ireland Office	Coder 1	Coder 2	Coder 3
Coder 1		2/119 (98%)	5/119 (96%)
Coder 2			7/119 (94%)

Total: 96%

Overall reliability value: 93%

Appendix 5. Social Network Analysis Codebook

FORMAL CATEGORIES
F01 Name of the government organisation
Write the name of the organisation in full
F02 Twitter name of the government organisation
hashtag followed by twitter name
@AuswaertigesAmt
F03 Full name of the source
Please write the full name of the actor that is being retweeted
F04 Twitter name of the source
Please write the twitter name of the actor that is being retweeted
e.g., @GermanyUN
CONTENT CATEGORY
C01 Type of actor
Please describe what type of actor they are, for example, here are a list of options:

1. A government ministry
2. A press office of a government ministry
3. Government agency/office/state body (Amt/Behörde)
4. An embassy/consul of Germany/ or a foreign embassy
5. A political party
6. A professional body/trade union/society (Verein/Stiftung)
7. NGO/Charity
8. Global/transnational organisation, e.g., European Commission, European Central Bank, UN, a global social movement
9. Political institution (e.g., Bundestag)
10. Corporation
11. Corporate individual
12. Head of government/head of state e.g., prime minister of Italy, president of…
13. Government minister
14. Press spokesperson for a minister
15. Politician
16. Staatssekretär
17. Lobbyist/political communications advisor
18. Media organisation
19. Journalists
20. New media actor (bloggers, online activists)
21. Citizen organisation (for example, community groups)

22. Individual citizen (any individual who doesn't fit into any of these categories)
23. Government campaigns/event/project (neither an organisation or an individual)
24. Political or non-political campaigns/event/project
25. Other